Communists
in Indonesia

LESLIE PALMIER, Senior Lecturer in Sociology at the University of Bath and Associate Fellow of St Antony's College, Oxford, has for several years specialised in the study of Indonesia, beginning with graduate work at the London School of Economics, followed by an appointment in 1956–7 as Research Fellow in Southeast Asia Studies at Yale University. His previous books on the country include *Social Status and Power in Java* (1960), *Indonesia and the Dutch* (1962), and *Indonesia* (1965). This interest has been set within the context of a wider concern with the developing countries, particularly those in Southern Asia. As Associate Professor of Asian Studies at the University of Wellington until 1962, he initiated the study of contemporary Asia in New Zealand. For the next five years he served the international community by organizing research on problems of development, first as Deputy Director of the Unesco Research Centre on Social and Economic Development in Southern Asia, Delhi, then as Programme Director at the U.N. Research Institute for Social Development at Geneva. He returned to academic work in 1967.

Communists
in Indonesia
POWER PURSUED IN VAIN

by **LESLIE PALMIER**

ANCHOR BOOKS
Anchor Press/Doubleday
Garden City, New York
1973

THE HISTORY OF COMMUNISM

Edited by F. W. Deakin and H. T. Willetts

The Anchor Books edition is
the first publication of *Communists in Indonesia.*

Anchor Books edition: 1973

To remember
GUY WINT

Contents

ABBREVIATIONS

AKSEF:	Unilateral Action Movement
BKSPH:	Youth-Military Cooperation Body
BPS:	Body Supporting Sukarnoism
BTI:	Barisan Tani Indonesia (Indonesian Peasant Front)
CPH:	Communist Party of Holland
CPR:	Chinese People's Republic
CSI:	Central Sarekat Islam
ECCI:	Executive Committee of the Communist International
FDR:	Front Demokrasi Rakyat (People's Democratic Front)
GRR:	Gerakan Revolusi Rakyat (People's Revolutionary Movement)
ISDP:	Indies Social Democratic Party
ISDV:	Indies Social Democratic Association
KAMI:	Indonesian Students' Organisation
KNIP:	Indonesian Central National Committee
NU:	Nahdatul Ulama (Muslim Scholars)
PARI:	Republican Party of Indonesia
PERBEPSI:	Ex-servicemen's Association
PFB:	Sugar Factory Worker's Union
PGRS:	Sarawak People's Guerrilla Movement
PKI:	Indonesian Communist Party
PNI:	Indonesian National Party
PPKB:	Labour Federation
PPKR:	Federation of Popular Movements
PRRI:	Revolutionary Government of the Republic of Indonesia
PSI:	Sarekat Islam Association
PVH:	Indies Labour Federation
RVC:	Revolutionary Federation of Trade Unions
SDAP:	Social Democratic Labour Party
SDP:	Social Democratic Party
SI:	Sarekat Islam (Islamic Association)
SOBSI:	Trade Union Congress
USI:	United States of Indonesia
VIPBOW:	Public Works Employees' Union
VSTP:	Rail and Tram Workers' Union

'. . . if the government really prohibits and penalises our freedom of action we shall not be able to nullify the government's decision. It is the government, after all, that possesses the power.'

Api (Indonesian Communist Party daily), 6 January 1925.

'It is necessary for each party that its members participate with full conviction in its activities, otherwise it is powerless, however many members it may have.'

From the report of a Netherlands Indies Government Committee of Investigation into the 1926–7 communist uprising.

'The Communist Party is not a grocery store where the more customers you attract, the more soap, rotten herring or other spoiled goods you sell, the more you gain.'

Mr Khruschev, the Russian prime minister, at the University of Gadjah Mada in Indonesia, in 1960.

Preface

Any merits this study may have it owes to those who have already ploughed the field of Indonesian communism. A selection of their work is given in the bibliography; here I should like to record my special debt to those who have made a particular study over many years of the *Partai Komunis Indonesia*, namely Arnold Brackman, Donald Hindley, Justus van der Kroef and Ruth McVey. They are of course not responsible for the shortcomings of this work.

LESLIE PALMIER

Communists
in Indonesia

1
The
New
Message

A Missionary

In 1913 the Indonesian islands suffered an event which was greatly to affect their political life for the next half century at least. There disembarked at Semarang on the north coast of Java a young Dutchman, Hendricus Sneevliet, an ardent propagandist for the new revelation known as Marxism. Though he was expelled from the country five years later, his work was of an enduring character; long after his bones had been interred, the conspiratorial missionary group he had formed, having survived two major reversals, had grown into the largest communist party in the world after the Chinese. Then disaster struck again; in 1966 the Partai Komunis Indonesia was proscribed and decimated. It is this sorry tale of fervour and failure which will engage our attention in the pages that follow.

Sneevliet had many of the marks of the missionary. He was of mystical bent, and having commenced his search for salvation in Roman Catholicism had ended it in Marxism, or, as he called it, social democracy. He considered this

'. . . rightly understood, more than a political teaching. It brings with it the heavy burden of bearing witness, of sowing the seed of propaganda at all times and in all places'.[1]

Too little importance has perhaps been given to the religious character of Marxism. For though it vehemently denies any supernatural entities, that it is eschatological seems beyond doubt. At bottom, it is a doctrine that the last shall be first and the first shall be last. The last are, as is well known, the proletariat, those who own nothing but their labour. The catapult of their propulsion will be the revolution. This is an apocalypse, an end of the world as conceived until then. It will be, said an acute student of Marxism,

> . . . the *great ordeal*, a sort of spontaneous last judgement, without a judge or a judgement seat; it will confirm and elect the good—the proletariat and its servants—by the same test which destroys the power of the wicked. Catastrophically conceived, the revolution is the day of wrath and the day of dread, the transition from the old order to the new, and not merely a change of political regime. Through the revolution we pass from this world to the 'world to come'; passing through the ordeal, we leave behind us the accustomed order of things (which is evolution, the slow accumulation of infinitely small quantitative changes). . . . The last become the first, and through the grace of the Proletariat, the elect of the Human Species, the entire Species is saved at last.[2]

Of course, Marxism is opposed to any other creed; it bases itself on what it asserts to be science, and, thereby, in the atmosphere of the nineteenth century, attracted to itself the faith previously given to religion. The 'science' is simply an analysis of nineteenth-century capitalism. This, evidently enough, was subject to 'crises', i.e. disjunctions between demand and supply. By simple extrapolation it was

[1] McVey, 1965: 13.
[2] Monnerot, 1953: 298.

deduced that one day, and not too far away at that, capitalism would be unable to recover from its crises, and collapse. Several generations of Marxists have been waiting for this event in much the same spirit, and with the same result, as early Christians awaited the Second Coming.

If this was alleged to be inevitable, why should Marxists bother to help it come? Their resources might have been better employed on enterprises of less certain outcome. The reason is again of an eschatological nature. It is part of the plan of History (which for Marxists, and some non-Marxist historians, plays God) 'that men must take pains, for although History will inevitably unfold in a certain manner, *this will not happen without pain;* and the trouble involved is part of the historical process'.[3]

Sneevliet went his own way to the promised land, moving from one organisation to another as he saw fit. (At the beginning of the century it was still possible for Marxists to do so. After the Russian revolutionary Lenin's design for a militaristic party had been accepted in 1903, and the consequences had ramified through the community of believers, such peripatetic allegiances became more difficult.) In Holland he had first joined the SDAP (*Social-Democratische Arbeiderspartij*) or Social-Democratic Labour Party, founded in 1894. Though a believer in violent revolution, Sneevliet did not accompany his like-minded friends when they left the party to form the Leninist SDP (Social Democratic Party) in 1909, a body which eventually became the Communist Party of Holland (CPH). He only did so three years later, when his own party refused to support a strike in Amsterdam. This was no light decision; he had been chairman of the railway workers' union controlled by the SDAP, and leaving the party meant losing his job. Having acquired a reputation as an agitator, he could find no work in private industry, there were no union posts vacant and so, like many other Europeans of all persuasions in similar circumstances, he decided to go east. Paradoxically, before leaving he rejoined the SDAP, as he disapproved of the

[3] *Ibid.*: 296–7.

SDP decision to oppose it in the elections and thus split the socialist vote; evidently Sneevliet was still idealistic or naive enough to believe that Leninist parties intended to achieve socialism, as distinct from power for themselves. Throughout most of his stay in the Indies Sneevliet remained formally a member of this more moderate Dutch Marxist sect. Even though his activities were more in accordance with Leninist precepts, there seems no ground for suspecting that he was an undercover communist. He was simply a socialist who believed in revolution as a means of achieving socialism; not a communist who wanted to increase his party's power by revolution or any other means.

Leninism

There was (and is) an all-important difference between the aims of communist and of socialist parties. The latter wish to abolish private property in the means of production, and seek power to do so. The communist parties, it is fair to say, then and now wished simply to increase their power, destroying any opposition in the way. Of course, private property would have to go, as it represented an obstacle, but so would all other independent institutions and groupings. Thus, for the socialists, power is a means to an end; for the communists power was an end in itself. It is regrettable that this distinction is still not sufficiently grasped.

The SDP was one of many social democratic parties throughout Europe which adopted the aims and organisation proposed by Lenin, as a means of saving Marxism from imminent bankruptcy. For since this faith claimed scientific status, and since it was believed that a characteristic of science was its ability to predict, Marxists at the end of the nineteenth century had been much disturbed by the fact that none of Marx's prophecies seemed to be coming true, in particular the one that with the further development of capitalism the workers would become more conscious, more revolutionary.

Lenin saved the faith by abandoning this inconvenient

tenet. Whereas Marx has asserted that class consciousness of the workers, that is their striving for socialism, was a *spontaneous* product of the economic conditions under which they lived, Lenin declared that

> Socialist consciousness cannot arise among the workers. This can be introduced only from without. The history of all countries shows that by its unaided efforts the working class can only develop a trade-union consciousness, that is to say, a conviction of the necessity to form trade unions, struggle with the employers, obtain from the government this or that law required by the workers, and so on. . . .[4]

Just as some parents insist that their children enjoy their holidays, whether they like them or not, so the workers were to be compelled to enjoy socialism. This had always been the product of middle-class intellectuals, such as Marx and Engels and the Russian intelligentsia who embraced their faith. Lenin pointed out, correctly, that the worker did not want socialism but higher pay, and that socialism had to be knocked into him by the outsiders, the intelligentsia.

Having thus stood Marxism on its head, Lenin declared that his was the true faith. This surprising position was taken in a pamphlet called *What is to be done?*, published in 1902. Its main concern was to design the structure of a party which would be able to effect revolution in the autocratic, dictatorial, secret-police-ridden Russia of the time. Lenin saw that it was essential to avoid alike the terrorism of the social revolutionaries, the gradualism of the Liberal Economists, and the discord of the various groups of socialists scattered round Russia. He therefore argued that the scientific doctrine of Marxism must be supplemented by a revolutionary faith, and that the Social Democratic Party must also resemble a military order. Accordingly, the new party was to be composed of professional revolutionaries, enlisting intellectuals and choosing its leaders from among

[4] Lenin, *Collected Works*, Vol. 5: 347.

them but avoiding their typical vices of discussion, indecision, humanitarian scruples and so on.

What was to be its relation to the workers about whom Marxism was supposedly concerned? It was to lead them to the promised land, making sure that on the way they were not led astray by their desires for a better livelihood and improved conditions of work. The party was to fight 'spontaneity' and 'opportunism'. The first is a modern equivalent of the mediaeval sin of sloth. The working classes tend all too easily to lose their class and militant drive. The party is to prod them, to explain their revolutionary tasks, and to endure until the victory is won. Opportunism is closely related to greed. Socialist leaders may be tempted to acquiesce in small victories and in concessions by their rulers, to be lured by governmental office, and so postpone revolutionary action. The party's job is never to lose sight of the promised land, to remind the workers that these oases and springs in the desert are not their final destination.

Who was to decide what was to be done in any specific instance? The party was to be a strictly hierarchic organisation, in fact Lenin likened it to an army sending out its detachments in all directions. Under the network of the local committees controlled by the central organs he envisaged a body of professional revolutionaries. He had no use for those who worked ten or eleven hours in a factory and then gave their 'spare time' to revolutionary activity. He wanted full-time specialists in revolution, living with forged papers.

In true military fashion, Lenin required unquestioned obedience to the leader, with all communication downwards, and neither from followers to leaders, nor among the led. It was the leader who was to decide the strategy and tactics of this political army. Where possible it was to work in public, but then it was to have in addition a parallel organisation which would work in secret. And just as Lenin had stood Marxism on its head and declared it to be still Marxism, so future leaders of independent communist parties, whether Russian or Chinese or Yugoslav, were to declare, and have accepted by their political armies, their own interpretation of the creed.

At the second congress of the Russian Social-Democratic Labour Party in 1903, where Lenin put forward the ideas in *What is to be done?*, he also prescribed the slogans that were to be used to attract a following. There was to be a 'maximum programme' and a 'minimum programme'. The former, namely revolution, was the real aim of the Communist Party. However, since neither the workers, as we have seen, nor the peasants, nor perhaps anybody apart from Lenin's adherents, could be expected to have much interest in this project, they were to be offered the 'minimum programme' in exchange for their support. This simply meant championing whatever grievances they had at the time, while disguising the party's real intentions; a confidence trick on the grand scale it may be called. This approach was, under certain circumstances, very successful. It enabled the party to enlist the peasant masses of Russia (and in due course to deprive them of their lands). It also enabled the party, with ideological backing, to form temporary alliances with any and all political groups (with the ultimate intention of destroying them). When, in addition, the definition of masses was widened from proletariat to peasantry, work could proceed in Asia, where there was virtually no industrial proletariat but a large number of peasants and a bureaucratic middle class.

The object of this form of organisation was, of course, to wage war on capitalism, which meant specifically tsarist Russia and, more generally, the western nations. But it was not long before any obstacle to the Russian party was regarded as an enemy, and not because of ideology. As the German-Russian Pact of 1939 showed convincingly, when it was in its interest that party could make common cause with totalitarians of completely opposed ideals.

To account for this endemic communist hostility to all other organisations one must look at its militaristic organisation. If, let us say, the party were to lack enemies, the credentials of the leader would immediately be open to challenge. In the nature of the case, he will have earned his spurs by valour in the war which the party is engaged; peace may condemn him to obsolescence. It will, of course, be not only the leader whose position is endangered but also all other functionaries, whose appointment or retention would in any case have been subject to his veto. Inevitably, therefore, the party to remain integrated must constantly seek new targets for attack, just as a competitive enterprise must constantly seek new opportunities for profit if it is to remain in business.

To this political mill all is grist, including Marxism, which is used primarily as recruiting propaganda. As such, it is superior to, say, nazism, which promised salvation only to the Aryan elect (though in its time that particular propaganda message persuaded quite a few to enlist); Marxism offers to rescue all who feel estranged and humiliated. It also promises them the satisfaction of bloody vengeance on the secure and established, as well as the catharsis of a great *götterdämmerung* which will usher in the new state of affairs when the mighty will be cast down from their seats and the humble exalted. This message, of course, appeals primarily to the proletarianised. Deprived of the security previously provided by their traditional social groups, politically ignorant, they are only too likely to be sympathetic to an ideology which not only unites them in some form of association with others in the same situation but which also promises to redeem them all. As is obvious, however, this faith is so general that it permits several interpretations, and the one in force at any time is that adopted by the leader, very often for the purposes of his own personal struggle against opponents within the party as much as for the party's war against other organisations.

Similarly with the various terms in the communist lexicon. The 'united front from above' (i.e. joining with non-communist parties in opposing the government) or the 'united front from below' (infiltrating the followers of non-communist parties and so compelling an alliance with the communists), though presented as doctrinal issues, were purely tactical discussions, concerned with the paramount question of how the party and its leader could best increase their power. The very phrases used are perhaps best understood as operational code-words indicating the action to be taken.

However useful the proletarianised may be as revolutionary fodder, no recruiting sergeant would regard them as a source of officer material, certainly not Lenin. They would make the revolution, but it would be led by the Communist Party of dedicated full-time conspiratorial workers. This officer class was to be devoted to the tasks of organisation and administration, functions particularly attractive to intellectuals who, especially but not only in Russia, were among the most uprooted of all.

The definition of an intellectual varies from society to society but it seems true that typically he wishes to impose his ideas on the world rather than adapt to it himself. He is predisposed to believe that he knows what is best for others and is unwilling to find out what they want or to believe their testimony if he does. Those particularly attracted to the party (and, it may be added, other totalitarian organisations) were often activists, concerned to put their ideas into effect and not really happy at discussing them; prepared more to accept orders from above provided their own orders are also accepted without question. Membership of the party gave many of them the feeling of power and significance available in no other way; in addition this could be portrayed as the pursuit of social justice.

However, while their motive in joining the party may have been to overthrow the established order in which they were poor relations, with the passage of time the normal human need of security and predictability in turn asserts itself. Instead of a party of zealots, there emerges in due course an organisation of bureaucrats, concerned principally with pleasing their superiors and assuring their own security and promotion rather than in encouraging revolutions which might bring to nothing all their prospects. Hence, of course, the Russian bureaucracy's support for

Stalin against Trotsky and the old bolsheviks, who still sought upheaval in the world, and on the other hand in China Mao Tse-tung's instigation of the 'cultural revolution' to destroy the bureaucracy which was making his revolutionary credentials irrelevant. As we shall see, the same tendency was to show itself in the Indonesian party.

2
Troubled
Society

Social Disintegration

Sneevliet's missionary field, the Netherlands Indies, was the Dutch crown's largest colony, a conglomeration of societies on several islands scattered across the equator between Asia and Australia, for a distance as great as that from the west coast of Ireland to the Black Sea. They had gradually been brought under Dutch control over a period stretching from the beginning of the sixteenth century to the end of the nineteenth, barely a decade or so before Sneevliet's arrival.

The most populous of the societies, and the specific locale of Sneevliet's work, was that of the Javanese, the people inhabiting the centre and east of Java. Though not the largest island in the archipelago, and not where the Dutch had first landed, it was the most fertile and had become the focus for their development efforts. This became especially so when, shortly after Java was returned to the Dutch at the end of the Napoleonic wars, their home finances were depleted by the secession of Belgium. They turned to develop the island as a large state plantation under what came to be known as the 'Cultivation System' (*Cultuurstelsel*). It succeeded in its object of saving Holland, but only at the price of misery for the Javanese peasantry, well depicted in the famous nineteenth-century Dutch novel *Max Havelaar*. That the sufferings were never intended but arose from abuses of the system did not make them any less painful.

The success of the Cultivation System ensured its own demise; it gave rise to a new middle class in Holland who demanded a cut of the cake for themselves. They had their way, and from about 1870 onwards the system was dismantled and the country opened up to private plantations. The era of liberalism had begun, so ending the exactions of forced labour and crop deliveries which had been the system's essential constituents.

Paradoxically, however, it was not when the peasants were being oppressed that they protested but in the liberal era. In 1890, when a generation had come of age which had not known the Cultivation System, a movement, led by one Samin, declared itself in Central Java. By 1907 he had enrolled some three thousand family heads; the government then arrested him and eight other peasant leaders and sent them into exile. The movement, however, is said to have continued in being until the 1920s.

What appears to have happened is that the termination of the Cultivation System had released many from their traditional duties and primary groups. Their consequent rootlessness naturally made them opposed to the existing dispensation. Hence they refused to pay taxes in kind or labour, which under the Cultivation System they had done without protest, simply as part of their traditional obligations. The core of their demands was that they 'be left free to lead their own lives'. One may be permitted to deduce that they did not consider the liberal system was worth its social costs; in much the same way as an increasing number in western society doubt whether technological progress is truly beneficial. Otherwise put, they wished to regress to traditional society, pursuing their life in their own ways,

with only the sketchiest of contact with outsiders and the
supreme authority. In contemporary jargon, they were turning their backs on modernisation. It was an attempt to resist
the collapse of their society caused by the new dispensation.

An insight into the cycle from pacification to disintegration is to be gained from a book published in 1929 at
Batavia, the capital of the Netherlands Indies, and called
*The Effect of Western Influence on Native Civilisation in
the Malay Archipelago*. As an example of the effects of
pacification, look, for instance, at Borneo, which was
brought under Dutch control only in the last decade of the
nineteenth century:

> Just the presence of a 'controleur' and about fifty
> armed policemen in a district twice as large as Holland
> was sufficient to awaken a feeling of peace, hitherto
> unknown, in the heart of every family; they were all
> able to work peacefully at their agricultural pursuits
> and clothes and important items of their daily food
> have become much cheaper.[1]

The writer was Dr A. W. Nieuwenhuis, at the time of the
book's publication professor of ethnography at Leyden University, who in 1894 had taken part as a physician in a
scientific expedition which made virtually the first contact
with the people of East Borneo, preceding the establishment
of Dutch rule over the area. One may perhaps see in his
account a microcosm of the initial stages of the establishment of European rule over large stretches of Asia, when
the perennial wars were stopped and people could live and
produce in safety.

The price of peace, however, may be estimated from
another contribution to the same volume:

> Practically speaking, the chiefs . . . previously
> acquired their authority by recognition of the people,
> from the lowest classes to the highest . . . this

[1] Schrieke, 1929: 33.

authority was extended by favour of the people and by
preventive and repressive action by force of arms. Now
that force of arms is abolished the people have to
bring their complaints regarding their chiefs to the
higher authority . . . [traditional] institutions are
losing their power. Although we tried as much as
possible to apply ourselves to existing conditions, we
brought and had to bring a totally different
administrative system. *The old one collapsed* [my
italics].[2]

Nor was it only the institution of a new system of administration that destroyed the old society; the unintended
consequences of the European presence were equally important. For hand in hand with the western peace just
mentioned, there came western medicine. Between them,
they increased the population by geometric progression.
Especially was this so in Java, which the Dutch had controlled for a century and a half. In 1814, when Raffles was
briefly holding the colony for the British crown, he made
the first estimate of the population and arrived at a
figure of four and a half million. A century later, in 1920,
it had risen to thirty-four million. With high density and
the absence of primogeniture went fragmentation of land-
holdings, gradual impoverishment of the peasantry and
their increasing dependence on work for the sugar plantations (who leased land in rotation from the villages) or in
the towns.

Matters were not helped by Dutch policy, which generally attempted to maintain traditional society, even when its
economic component was obviously attenuated. Rather than
contemplating any radical changes, liberal sentiments produced a set of welfare measures collectively known as the
Ethical Policy. Its object was declared to be the improvement of the social and economic lot of Indonesians and
their preparation for association with Europeans. The principal protagonists of these views had been colonial officials; and a consequence of the adoption of the policy

[2] *Ibid.*: 53–6.

was much more intervention by government, even in areas previously left to the native heads, thus requiring many more such officials. Traditional society was fatally shaken; the recognised authorities were discredited in the eyes of the people by the increasingly evident foreign presence. Nor was it only the traditional rulers who were undermined. Rather, as a senior official, Meyer Ranneft, noted, everything old was being overthrown by the improvement in means of communication (railways, motor cars, money). But though economic activity had consequently increased, primarily as a result of the government's conservative agrarian policy 'the masses have remained farmers and only the subsidiary work has increased'.[3] It would have been surprising if they had looked upon the liberal dispensation with favour. At the time, however, this sowing of the wind was regarded with complacency, if not indeed with self-congratulation, by the European officials principally responsible.

But if official intervention and economic liberalism had fatally weakened traditional society, they offered no new basis of association; in accordance with liberal doctrines these were to emerge spontaneously. The theory was not proved false; though the associations that did emerge were perhaps not altogether to the liking of the colonial power. As Ranneft also observed: 'For the last twenty-five years over this densely populated country has swept a wave of colonisation such as it has never experienced before, but at the same time all kind of nationalist waves are rolling in higher and faster. Thus are breakers formed'.[4]

Saminism was a rejection of the western world; the new movements were attempts to come to terms with it by providing new bases of association for individuals uprooted from the old social order. They too were an outgrowth of the Ethical Policy, which for the first time permitted political activity. Elections were held to local councils with representative functions (responsibility continued to reside

[3] *Ibid.*: 80.
[4] *Ibid.*: 84.

in the Civil Service). Press censorship was lifted and Indonesians were thus able to express their opinions both in print and in voluntary assemblies.

The first of the political movements to answer this obvious invitation was the *Budi Utomo* (High Endeavour), with members coming from the Javanese nobility. It advocated the development of traditional and western education among Indonesians (choosing Malay or Javanese as its medium), and the advancement of agriculture, industry and commerce. Founded in 1908, within a year it had attracted ten thousand members, nobility, intellectuals and officials. By then, too, the number of Indonesian students in Holland reached twenty-three; they then formed the Indies Society. It was to play a leading role in the nationalist movement. Nationalism proper, however, began in 1912 with the *Indisch Partij* (Indies Party) founded by two Indonesians and a Eurasian, and based on cooperation between their communities. It attracted about six thousand Eurasian and thirteen hundred Indonesian members, and was sympathetic to the Marxist faith. With the motto 'the Indies for those who make their home there', it represented the interests of Eurasians against the increasing numbers of Europeans who came out to the Indies with the intention of retiring to Holland as soon as they had made enough money. Too radical for the government, it was suppressed within a year, most of its members joining a purely Eurasian party called *Insulinde*.

Islam and Politics

Also in 1912 an Islamic reformist organisation, called the *Muhammadiyah*, was founded. This was the Indonesian expression of the Modernist movement in Islam, launched in the late nineteenth century by Muhammad al Afghani in Persia and Muhammad Ábduh in Egypt, whose aim was to strengthen Islam so that it could face the onslaught of the west by assimilating its knowledge. To do so, it rejected the various schools of Islamic interpretation which had accumulated over the centuries and based itself directly on the two holy books, the Koran and the Hadith or Tradition.

The significance of the Muhammadiyah, and of Islamic Modernism in general, is not to be underestimated. Snouck Hurgronje, the eminent Dutch Islamicist and Indies Government adviser, had rejected Islam as a viable re-integrator of Indonesian society, on the grounds that this would be to condemn the country to mediaeval sterility. He evidently failed to recognise the possibility of Islam modernising itself from within, even though at the time he was writing (late nineteenth century) the Modernist movement was well established. And it is to the Muhammadiyah that the Islamic community in Indonesia owes many of its most prominent leaders, though the movement itself kept clear of politics.

The Muhammadiyah was part of the process of re-adjustment of the Muslims of Indonesia to the changes brought about by European liberalism. And this in turn was an echo of the acceptance of Islam into the archipelago in the sixteenth century. Wherever the Portuguese went, they found that Islam had just preceded them. It would seem that, threatened with the disruption of their society by these aggressive westerners, Indonesians turned for help to another social order which, though also new, nevertheless was more hospitable to their own (in permitting many of their traditional beliefs and practices) and which, being opposed to their enemy, was their friend.

This reliance on Islam as a symbol of opposition to the west, and even a source of support against it, remained a constant theme in Indonesian history. As late as the closing years of last century, when the Atjehnese of North Sumatra were resisting Dutch control, they turned for help to the sultan of Turkey as caliph of Islam. They learnt what everyone else already knew, that the Muslim states were now impotent against the west.

Those who bore Islam to South-East Asia were traders from Gujarat in North-West India, who were naturally sympathetic to the mysticism they found in Java. The re-

ligion was embraced, initially, by the coastal states who saw
their commerce threatened by first the Portuguese and then
the Dutch. They found in their new faith a basis for alliance with the Muslim traders and so a means of withstand-
ing Christian depredations. The strength thus acquired
made them dangerous to the inland kingdoms, so that these
too eventually amalgamated Islam with their Hindu-Buddhism. But their concerns were not in trade and so, fundamentally, not in the Islam of South-East Asia.

These divisions of interest persisted under Dutch rule
and survive in our own day. Broadly speaking, the people
on the northern coast of Java and the trading communities
of the other islands are more devoted to Islam than are the
inland Javanese, and those whose living lies in trade are
more likely to identify themselves with Islam than those
who work the fields or serve the state. The reasons for this
situation are of interest. Acceptance of Islam had been
largely an act of state, as far as can now be determined,
on the principle of *cuius regio, ejus religio*. The ruling
houses remained devoted to their Javanese way of life and
its considerable infusion of Hindu-Buddhism. So the followers of Islam had often been adherents rather than converts, and the religion became simply another layer of belief
laid on the previous skins of animism and Hindu-Buddhism.

Javanese culture and social structure have no room for
the merchant; at official ceremonies even in the early part
of this century a rich trader would take precedence after
the lowliest clerk in the local administration. But whilst
discouraging commerce, Javanese social structure offered no
means of social ascent for poor but able young men—their
promotion depended on the strength of their right arm, or
the favour of the ruler. With the imposition of Dutch
control, both of these alternatives were closed. Dutch
superiority in organisation made short shrift of any revolt,
while the nobility, particularly after the Java war of 1830,
became loyal members of the establishment. The Dutch
on their side reserved the responsibilities of subordinate

government almost exclusively for the nobility. *La carrière ouverte aux talents* could not be the colonial dispensation.

Commerce, therefore, increasingly became the one means of social mobility, but since it was outside the pale of Javanese values they offered the trader neither a guide to life nor a necessary esteem. For this he was compelled to turn to Islam. This may seem paradoxical, considering that some 95 per cent of Indonesians profess the religion. But for most this is simply the compliment that apathy pays to fervour. And just as nominal Catholics in France may be violently anti-clerical, so many 'Muslims' in Java fulminate against their religion.

However, if in France Catholicism has been identified with the establishment, in Indonesia the reverse is the case for Islam. In the first place, it emphasises the equality of all believers. Unlike the hierarchies of many Christian sects, for example, in Islam there is no official priesthood, and any believer can lead prayers in the mosque. The practice of equality may—and indeed often does—not extend beyond the confines of the mosque and the time of devotions but it serves as an ever-present counterpoise to the inequalities which naturally proliferate in any society. Thus Islam was always available to support the poor and oppressed, and it is perhaps significant that the more fervent adherents were to be found not among the Javanese nobility but among the commoners.

Another characteristic of Islam of relevance here is its opposition to rule of the faithful by unbelievers. When the nobility (and the mosque officials who were often their relatives) turned to serve the Dutch, they seemed to the faithful to be denying their religion. The Dutch were able to subdue the Atjehnese rebellion after thirty years only by following Snouck Hurgronje's advice to bear down heavily on the religious leaders but favour the traditional elite, and not to impede in any way the practice of religion, while firmly suppressing all attempts at revolt. This implied a western division between politics and religion, which Islam may accept when it has no alternative but which it does not in principle know.

In brief, the social organisation of Islam in Indonesia rested on two structures. One, the official, consisted of the mosque functionaries, headed by the *penghulu* in each regency. He was often, in Java, a relative of the regent or local native head and, perhaps partly for that reason, was usually loyal to the Dutch. This structure was quasi-bureaucratic, in that the holders of offices had relatively clearly defined areas of responsibility, ranks, grades and emoluments.

Parallel with this structure was the looser, more informal one of the *kyayi* and the *ulama*. Here there were no recognised norms of recruitment; essentially there was no body into which they were recruited. Kyayi were simply men who acquired a reputation for holiness, which often meant miraculous powers, while ulama were those who had a reputation for being learned in Islamic law. In neither case were their interests linked to the establishment; the one looked out of this world, the other out of Indonesia for his inspiration. Together, they provided latent spores of resistance throughout colonial rule.

It was only to be expected, therefore, that the first mass political party should adopt Islam as its banner. Originally, an association called *Sarekat Dagang Islam* (Society of Muslim Merchants) was formed in 1911 as a means of mutual protection by Javanese and Arab traders in Central Java against the encroachments of the Chinese, which the new liberalism was permitting to leave the coastal towns to which they had been previously confined. Within a year, however, its original aim had been overwhelmed by wider ambitions. In 1912 it re-emerged as the *Sarekat Islam* (Muslim Association), with as its leader a nobleman called *Raden*[1] Umar Sayed Tjokroaminoto. It was to become one of the most important Indonesian associations of the early twentieth century, due in considerable part to his great determination to keep it as the all-embracing Indonesian

[1] Titles italicised.

association, united whatever the cost. As its object the Sarekat took the commercial, social and religious advancement of Indonesians. This was of course an echo of the aim of the Ethical Policy, and the leaders of the Sarekat, while they were Javanese, without doubt looked on the world through western eyes. For the most prominent of them, though coming from families of lesser nobility and with middling incomes, and not among the most highly educated Javanese, had had sufficient contact with western culture to conceive their desires in its terms. But it is doubtful if the masses who followed them saw things in the same light.

The Sarekat grew rapidly and, despite the western orientation of its leaders, its members mainly came from not the cities and towns but the rural areas. The magnet that drew them was of course religion. As news of the Sarekat spread through the villages, preparations for forming a branch were usually laid by the local religious teacher or official. The actual inauguration of the branch was accompanied by secret oaths, pledges and rituals of a religious nature, and by semi-religious mystical practices such as the selling of charms promising invulnerability or a special favour. Of course those who joined were afforded the sense of belonging to the elect and, most important, they once again felt part of a group which cared for them. The social vacuum created in their lives by progressive colonial policies was at last filled. The structure of the Sarekat, with its topmost branches in western culture but its roots in Islam and animism, is worthy of note. For it has been one to which perhaps most associations in Indonesia have had to conform in order to survive.

Given its aim of improving the lot of the Indonesian masses, the Sarekat conceived it its duty to voice their grievances. But, like political associations elsewhere, it was not content with simply acting as a postbox but actively bestirred itself to discover discontents and even, perhaps, to suggest them where they were not obvious. One way or another its major activity became the collection of complaints and putting the blame for them on superficially likely sources. This activity of course encouraged its growth, since the people soon recognised that their complaints were more likely to be heard by Sarekat officials than by the local administrator who was hemmed in by official regulations. That the Sarekat grew to be the largest Indonesian association is not surprising; but size did not mean strength. First, its membership was uncertain. For one joined by paying a small fee; no further contributions were required, though of course appreciated. The nominal rolls therefore could not distinguish the active members from the lapsed.

This uncertainty of membership was an obvious source of weakness; so was the Sarekat organisational structure. In 1913, the year of Sneevliet's arrival, the then governor general, Idenburg, had refused to give it a national charter, on the grounds that it had not yet demonstrated sufficient organisational and financial strength. However, he allowed the local associations to exist autonomously and the central leadership at Surabaya, East Java, to act as an information centre, until his requirements were met. The association accordingly took this form, and when three years later the governor general decided to recognise the movement nationally, it was too late to change. In consequence, the Central Sarekat Islam had no power to discipline the branches and any of these could propagate its views through the association without let or hindrance. As we shall see, Sneevliet and his friends were not slow to take advantage of this situation.

3
Before
the
Comintern

Social Democrats

In the Indies of just before the first world war educated
Europeans were in such demand that Sneevliet had no
difficulty in finding employment first on the most important
newspaper in East Java, which was also the organ of the
powerful sugar cartel, and then, through the good offices
of a fellow-socialist, as secretary of the *Semarangsche Han-
delsvereniging* (Semarang Commercial Association). Ironically, it was from this base in the world of private enterprise
that he set out to urge its destruction.

Sneevliet exerted himself to acquire Indonesian and Javanese, so as the more easily to reach the natives of the
island. His method of propaganda was not so much to
preach his gospel but rather to insinuate himself into the
good graces of the Javanese by offering assistance in their
immediate problems. In addition, he took an interest in the
railway workers' union, the VSTP, and edited its newspaper;
he had after all been secretary of its Dutch counterpart.
He was successful in his efforts: within a year of his ar-

rival the organisation concerned itself with demanding improvements in the lot of the unskilled and impoverished Indonesian workers. In acting in this way, no doubt from the best motives, Sneevliet was following the method which has become the hall-mark of communist parties. He made no attempt to create his own labour organisation but instead placed himself in a position to influence an already existing one, in particular by his control over its newspaper. In Indonesia, as elsewhere, the trade unions at an early stage of industrialisation were typically composed of the estranged, the uprooted, the disoriented, seeking both intellectual guidance in the new world and association on a basis of esteem. Sneevliet's dramatic script, with the 'workers' as its central actors, provided them with precisely what they sought, and which at the time was offered by no other organisation.

However, this was not enough to satisfy Sneevliet, and he sought to form a proselytising group from the socialist faithful already in the Indies. They met in Surabaya, East Java, in May 1914. Nearly all present were Dutch, who in the Netherlands had become members of the SDAP, not its radical rival, and were fairly recent immigrants. Once in the Indies, their socialist faith had suffered a sea change. Either it had ebbed, and they concluded that Marxism was inapplicable to Indonesia; or it had surged forward, and they insisted on advocating revolution, irrespective of circumstances. Needless to say, Sneevliet was of the latter persuasion.

The object of the meeting was to found the *Indische Sociaal-Democratische Vereniging* (ISDV), or Indies Social Democratic Association. But the moderate group wanted only a discussion club and fact-finding centre for socialists in the Dutch parliament. They felt they could not participate in Indonesian politics, being foreign themselves and not knowing the local languages well. And, more important from the point of view of the tenets of their faith, they thought that socialism was only meaningful in countries with a well developed industrial proletariat. Sneevliet's enthusiasts, on the other hand, conceived it their mission to propagate socialism in the Indies, and particularly to organise revolution. In the event, as not infrequently happens, the fanatical tail wagged the moderate dog. All agreed that the party's function was to unite the Indies socialists, to inform social democrats in Holland of conditions in the colony, but also to spread socialist propaganda in it.

At the time, there was hardly any industrial proletariat of the type predicated by Marxism for successful revolution. Industrialisation began only during the first world war (which broke out three months after the meeting) under government stimulus to overcome shortages of manufactured goods. Even a quarter of a century later, in 1939, there were only some three-million-odd people engaged in manufacturing, or about 10 per cent of the labour force, and the great majority of these were in small industries. Thus the doctrinaire Marxists were right in asserting that conditions were not ripe for socialism. They overlooked the fact, however, that the gradual disintegration of society was offering the prophets of revolution a fertile field for their labours. The absence of an industrial working class meant only that the revolution could not be of the type postulated by Marx: this did not diminish the attraction of Marxism as the only faith which championed the newly uprooted and gave them a basis for association.

In considering the development in the Indies of dissident movements in general, and of the ISDV in particular, the political context in which they operated is of obvious importance. Not only was the Indies government controlled by a democratically elected assembly in the Netherlands, but also many of its subjects were resident Dutch. Indeed, at the time of which we are writing they were the largest component of the effective political public. The government could not therefore proceed with any severity against Sneevliet without impugning the democratic rights of other Dutchmen. Matters were to change later, when the majority of resident Dutchmen felt their position threatened by the

Indonesians' use of the same rights to demand a change in the existing order.

The newly-formed ISDV, it must be remembered, was almost entirely Dutch and very small in numbers. In 1915 it had 85 members, in 1916 only 134. Its policies were based in European thought, not Indonesian. They were officially moderate but this did not prevent the party being led by its extremists. Just as they had won the day at the foundation meeting, so they continued to impose their point of view. When the party founded a newspaper, called *Het Vrije Woord* (The Free Word), it was captured by this faction. The editor was a protégé of Sneevliet's, by name Adolf Baars. A graduate of the Delft engineering school, known for the fanaticism of its students, he was employed as a teacher in the state technical school at Surabaya. Leninist at heart, he appears to have been more attached to revolution for its own sake than to socialist principles, though he had a considerable knowledge of Marxism, and *Het Vrije Woord* became his voice. With Baars as editor, and Sneevliet on the editorial board, the newspaper championed causes which agitated the Indonesian political public, minuscule though this was.

And with the best of intentions, the Indies government now provided a forum which would magnify the agitation. A growing sympathy in Holland with nationalism in the Indies resulted in the approval in 1916 of a representative, but not responsible, assembly called the *Volksraad*. This body had no legislative powers, but the government was required to consult it in matters of finance, including the budget, and might take its advice in other matters. Half the members were to be elected and more than half were to be Indonesians. But in the nature of the case even those elected were mostly government employees, and so the franchise was in fact very restricted. On the other hand, officials in the Indies were permitted to criticise government at will and took full advantage of this right in the Volksraad. Furthermore, the provision that government should seek the advice of the Chamber implied that it would usually take it. In brief, the assembly had far greater powers than was implicit in its charter.

However, the Volksraad was irresponsible; whatever advice it might choose to give, it would be the Indies government which suffered the consequences. Consequently the deliberations took a predictable form. Since the members of the assembly could never envisage a time when they would have to bear responsibility, they indulged themselves in unbridled criticism of every aspect of the administration; and concessions simply encouraged further acerbity.

The year 1916 was important for all Marxists but especially for those in the colonies. It saw the publication of Lenin's *Imperialism: The Highest Stage of Capitalism*. His immediate object was to explain why the capitalist system still persisted in spite of its contradictions, and why the conditions of the European workers, or at least of a section of them, had greatly improved, contrary to Marx's predictions. Lenin's explanation was that a new devil, in the shape of imperialism, had entered the scene about 1898–1900. Its essential characteristics were the concentration of capital, the merging of industrial and banking capital into 'finance capital', and the division of the world between national and international monopolies. In his view this was the last state of the capitalist system, which would precede its final collapse and the victory of the proletariat. As a noted authority on Marxism has pointed out: 'It should be observed that imperialism thus denotes the predominance of a certain form of capital. It does not signify the direct domination over foreign lands, though such domination usually takes place'.[1] Because the developed countries were producing more goods than their home markets could absorb, they were driven to find markets in backward areas, which they then annexed and to whom they sold surplus products in exchange for cheap raw materials. Thus colonies were essential for capitalist countries, and since there were no more of them available imperialism must lead to war. Furthermore, investment abroad at higher rates of interest

[1] Hunt, 1957: 83.

than were obtainable at home increased the number of parasitic rentiers and thus sharpened the class struggle; yet, contradictorily, Lenin also argued that these super-profits dampened revolutionary ardour by enabling the capitalists to bribe the workers, particularly the more skilled, with higher wages and better conditions. Instead of accepting the one true Marxist faith, these had formed trade unions, cooperatives, sporting clubs, religious sects, etc. For Lenin this was evidence of their corruption (what he would have said about trade unions investing in Unit Trusts or Mutual Funds is no doubt unprintable). In consequence, though 'capitalism' would inevitably give way to 'socialism', since the Founder of the Faith had so decreed, the collapse was not quite imminent.

Lenin thus managed to show that the purposes of History had been postponed by the entry of the new demon on the scene (though History, being inevitable, would of course eventually be fulfilled). The failure of Marx's Law of Increasing Misery was satisfactorily worded away, and wars could now be explained in the terms of the sacred doctrine (i.e. economic causes). A further conclusion is more important for our present purposes. Marxist analysis assumed that the proletarian revolution would take place only in the most highly industrialised countries, because it would be there that the contradictions inherent in capitalism would be most fully developed. Lenin's identification of the new devil made it possible to evade this assumption, as industrially backward countries could now be brought into the demonology as appendages of capitalism and so be eligible for revolution. Thus was the uprising in Russia legitimised; had the country not been conceptually linked with capitalism in this way, a communist party would have had no business engaging itself there. But if revolution in Russia was in line with the faith as now interpreted, so also would it be in any other backward area (the immense differences between a semi-industrialised Russia and the European colonies were conveniently glossed over, as facts usually are when they run contrary to beliefs essential to one's position).

So for Sneevliet, Baars and friends, the new interpretation simply bestowed the grace of received truth on their predisposition; to propagate revolution in the backward Indies was now entirely in line with the commands of History.

Tentative Approaches

The Dutch Marxists who made up the ISDV soon realised that, given its European character, it could not hope to attract much support, and attempts had to be made to reach the Indonesian people on their own ground. In addition to championing their grievances in *Het Vrije Woord,* Baars founded two Indonesian-language newspapers in rapid succession. But the written word alone was not enough; it needed organisational backing, and Baars, as ever the principal protagonist, established in Surabaya the first Indonesian socialist group. In 1917, the year of its foundation, it had some 120 members. Though this figure was comparable with the ISDV's, by Indonesian standards it was minute. The Dutch organisation wondered for some time whether to merge with its Indonesian offshoot, but evidently concluded, what other and later communist parties were to learn, that the Marxist message, or 'maximum programme' as Lenin had dubbed it, was of very limited appeal. It therefore sought to batten on to other existing social organisations, i.e. to offer a 'minimum programme' which would offer a basis for cooperation and, no doubt, eventual control by the ISDV.

Its first approaches were to Insulinde, which we remember as largely composed of Eurasians and agitating for an 'Indies nationalism'. But though Insulinde was disaffected, it did not have the same aims as the ISDV. It was not planning revolution, or even trying to aggrandise its own power as such; it merely wanted to replace the ruling European elite with one of Eurasians and educated Javanese. Not surprisingly, this incompatible alliance lasted barely a year.

Sneevliet and Baars, however, had already begun to court

the Sarekat Islam. By 1916 it had become by far the largest Indonesian political organisation and claimed 360,000 nominal members. As will have been noted from the above, its aims were unclear and its discipline weak, and for Marxists it was 'bourgeois' (i.e. non-revolutionary) in character. All these features rendered it very tempting, and Sneevliet and Baars made their overtures. They do not seem to have realised that the Sarekat's message was in direct competition with theirs. For, as we have noted, not only did Islam preach equality, it had also been opposing Dutch 'imperialism' before Marx was even thought of. Then, both faiths looked ultimately outside the archipelago for salvation; Islam to Mecca and the caliph in Turkey; Marxism to Europe, at this time to the Second International, later to Moscow. Experience was to show, in the one case as in the other, that the external support was unreliable. Lastly, if the Marxist political organisations offered, as we shall see, opportunities for social mobility otherwise denied, so also did the Islamic community, as we have observed above.

Since the individual branches of the Sarekat went their own way, and multiple memberships were usual, Sneevliet and Baars had no difficulty in inducting its younger members into the ISDV. Among the most important converts was a sixteen-year-old named Semaun who worked for the state railways in Surabaya and was secretary of the local branch of the Sarekat Islam.

The attraction of Leninist organisations to young men like Semaun should not be underrated; it is a cardinal principle of Leninism that leadership talent should be sought and, when found, nurtured. Semaun himself came from the lesser nobility, a class which usually filled the less responsible offices in the state administration. His chances of advancement in this rigidly hierarchic structure were slight. Nor were they much greater in the Sarekat Islam, an organisation, as we have noted, rooted in the Muslim merchant group and inimical to the bureaucratic classes from which Semaun sprang. Not surprisingly, in the ISDV he found his road to esteem.

Semaun was transferred by his employers to Semarang, which gave him his opportunity. The town was then the centre of what little industrialisation there was in the Indies, and naturally the repository of the new proletariat. It was also the headquarters of the railway union and of Sneevliet's ISDV. Accordingly, the Sarekat branch there was far more radical than the Surabaya central organisation from which, as we remember, it was independent. Semaun's arrival gave the town a new demagogue and in turn it provided him with a springboard to prominence.

At the time the Indies, after a decade of prosperity, were suffering the effects of the first world war (in which the Netherlands remained neutral) in the shape of higher prices and consequent privation and social instability for those in the money sector of the society, like the new industrial workers. Hence revolutionary gospels such as Semaun propounded found no lack of listeners. Within a year the membership of the Semarang SI had grown from seventeen hundred members to twenty thousand (though membership did not always imply a commitment to Marxism; often it meant no more than a desire to join an association where apparently one was esteemed). Now, however, there began to unfold the strategy credited to Sneevliet of the 'bloc within', that is of a group of Leninist zealots within an established organisation who would direct it, whether or not the members were sympathetic to Marxism or Leninism. The Semarang Sarekat began to challenge the Surabaya Central Sarekat Islam, directing its appeals through its own newspaper to urban SI branches. Betraying the Leninist animosity to any independent social organisation, it attacked the nominal leadership only a little less vehemently than it did the colonial government.

The Central Sarekat Islam did indeed gradually begin adopting more radical policies, but pressure from the ISDV was only one cause. The Sarekat had become aware that its rural members were only summer soldiers. They had flocked to its standard seeking new leadership but had found that its officials were even less regarded by the

Dutch and Indonesian Civil Service than the traditional heads. Rapid desertions had ensued (though, having paid their subscription, the lapsed remained on the books as active).

In consequence, it was the disoriented of the urban branches who provided the Sarekat with backbone. Their increasing radicalism was supported by the ISDV's propaganda, and the CSI resolved to demand that the movement break off all relations with it. But when at the October 1917 congress other branches, too, supported the Semarang line, Tjokroaminoto, determined to retain the Sarekat entire at all costs, gave way, and the congress adopted a programme that accepted revolt if parliamentary action failed, condemned capitalism of the foreign variety (only this was sinful), demanded freedom of political organisation, much improved labour and agrarian legislation and free public education.

Mirage

Meanwhile, in March 1917 revolution had broken out in Russia. Sneevliet, intoxicated by the event, advocated a similar prescription for the Indies. He was put on trial, but acquitted. His attitude, however, made the moderates in the ISDV resign in a body and form a branch of the Dutch SDAP, the ISDP. The ISDV then became in fact what its actions had betokened for some time, an association of Leninists. It received a further shot in the arm from Lenin's November revolution, which seemed to confirm the wisdom of agitating in a capitalist but non-industrial society. Invigorated, the party began organising soviets among sailors and soldiers. Within three months three thousand had been enrolled as 'Red Guards'. But these were principally Europeans, for the ISDV's eyes were on Europe, not the Indies. They saw efforts to overthrow the Indies government as a means not of liberating Indonesians but of contributing to revolution in Europe. They were simply accepting Lenin's description of the backward areas of the world as being mere appendages of capitalism, and revolution there only of relevance as a means of weakening the principal devil. Indeed, until the 1920s even the Russian Communist Party expected the 'true' revolution to occur in the industrialised states of Europe; in a sense they accepted the revolution in Russia only *faute de mieux*. In the case of the ISDV this bias was further reinforced by the fact that most of its members were Europeans who, apart from Sneevliet and Baars, were concerned to proselytise other Europeans, not Indonesians. In order better to accomplish their purpose, they moved the party headquarters to Surabaya, which held the largest European branch.

Consistently enough, the ISDV congress of May 1918 discussed how to encourage 'revolutionary defeatism' in the Netherlands Indies forces. Perhaps more important, however, it debated the problem of the place of nationalism in the Marxist gospel. It concluded that the revolution against capitalism was more important than national liberation. This decision was hardly surprising.

Blinkered by their European experience, which blamed the failure of the prewar socialist movements on to nationalism, the ISDV leaders failed to see any constructive role for it in the Asian colonies. And, indeed, at the time the only party of an overtly nationalist character was Insulinde, which in composition was predominantly Eurasian, not indigenous. It was therefore argued that nationalism was a European importation which had no indigenous roots in the Indies. (History was to show, perhaps, that the cult of nationalism was necessary if control by European nations was to be successfully opposed. But that was for the future.)

What about the Sarekat Islam? The ISDV argued that it was simply a cross-cultural movement which paid no regard to the concept of nation, and they denied it was 'bourgeois'. Indeed, they regarded the Indies as singularly blessed in that the revolution there would combine national liberation and the proletarian stages of struggle, unlike other Asian countries were a rising native bourgeoisie existed and where the independence movement was in nationalist hands. They thought, in brief, that the Indies would emerge independent under their dictatorship, with no doubt the Sarekat Islam as ancillary. However genuine this analysis may have been, the cynic may be forgiven for thinking that had the ISDV opposed the SI, they would have condemned themselves to impotence. There were therefore important reasons for finding the Sarekat among the blessed.

The ISDV's policy was at bottom a very simple one: to have no truck with any established institutions nor with any nationalist initiatives. Thereby, if anything, they sacrificed a possible influence over Indonesian popular movements. Perhaps the truth of the matter is that they were Marxists who took the gospel too seriously; not for them the cunning of a Lenin, who was prepared to use every means, work with any institution, and collaborate with all parties, if it increased his party's power.

In 1918 elections to the Volksraad were held. The ISDV thought of participating, but its radicals opposed the idea on the grounds that the Volksraad was doomed to failure. Neither for the first nor for the last time their prophecies proved wrong. Matters so turned out that the majority in the Volksraad were solidly in favour of Indonesian-Dutch association in governing the Indies, and provided support for those who opposed revolutionary courses; hardly to the ISDV's advantage.

When rumours (ill-founded, it eventually proved) reached the Indies in November that the home government was about to fall to a revolt organised by the SDAP, the ISDV organised Red Guard demonstrations among soldiers and sailors and advocated revolution. The other Marxist organisation, the ISDP, was not minded to rebel, but formed a 'Radical Grouping' from other reformist groups (Sarekat Islam, Budi Utomo and Insulinde) which agreed to demand that the Volksraad become a popularly elected parliament within three years. The ISDV was invited to join provided it ceased opposing participation in the Volksraad.

It refused, and also tried to keep the si from joining. In this it failed, and thus yielded the field to its rivals, who became the Sarekat's chief advisers in the assembly.

The governor general, van Limburg Stirum, soon learnt that the home government was still holding its balance. He then made far-reaching but indefinite promises of reform, among them a Revisional Commission on the Constitution, which effectively defused the discontent felt by Indonesians. For its part, the isdv was completely demoralised by the failure of revolution in Europe, where lay its members' hearts and minds.

4
Enlisting Under the Russian Flag

Going Native

The failure of revolution in Europe compelled the ISDV
to turn its attention away from the Europeans in the Indies and towards the Indonesians (much as a few years
later the Russian Communist Party, having concluded that
revolution in Europe was not on the cards, adopted the
policy of revolution in one country). Though the cardinal
principle of Leninism is that the party of the faithful
should attempt to expand its power at all costs, the ISDV
by concentrating its attention on Europeans had hobbled
its own efforts to fulfil this imperative. The failure of
revolution in Europe may be said to have put it on the
Leninist track, for thereafter it turned to seek support in
the vastly more numerous Indonesian population, and
achieved some success in infiltrating their organisations and
subjugating them to its purposes.

At its May 1918 conference the ISDV decided to establish
itself as an Indonesian movement, not as an offshoot of its
Dutch parent. This resulted in a rapid expansion of mem-

bership (without much insistence on ideology) which brought in its train the possibility of conflict between the Europeans in control at the party headquarters and the Indonesian members in the branches. Happily for the party, this risk was avoided as a consequence of official policy.

With the recovery of its nerve, the government had disciplined the European missionaries of revolution. Baars had been dismissed from his teaching post in October 1917; his fanaticism was too much even for the wide freedom of expression the government permitted its servants. A year later, in November 1918, it expelled Sneevliet. He left as the ISDV's international spokesman, to achieve a certain notoriety as the Comintern's representative in China under the name of Maring. In 1919 Baars left for Europe, still convinced that his Holy Grail, the Revolution, lay there. By this time most of the European members of the ISDV had also been removed. Their places had been taken by new Indonesian recruits, among whom Darsono was prominent; he became the PKI's first full-time propagandist.

The Indonesian ISDV leaders had an advantage denied to the Europeans; nominally Muslims, there was no bar to their belonging to the Sarekat Islam (as already mentioned, Indonesian organisations at the time permitted multiple memberships). This opportunity Semaun and Darsono put to good use. They were helped by the deteriorating economic situation, giving rise to social discontent, expressed at the 1918 congress of the Sarekat.

The next year, 1919, was to show how effectively the Sarekat Islam had been infiltrated. Inflation and poor harvests gave rise to trouble in many parts of the Indies. In the Celebes a European official was killed; his death was laid at the door of the Sarekat Islam. In West Java a secret Sarekat Islam association, known as 'section B', was discovered, having nebulous links with the official organisation. Apparently it had gained support by urging the richer peasants there to resist the government's forced collections of rice; an interesting application of the 'minimum-programme' approach. Two members of the ISDV, Alimin and

Musso, both to become leaders of the Indonesian Communist Party, and the latter to lead the 1948 uprising, were implicated. The ISDV itself officially disapproved, but it is fair to suspect that these two may well have been engaged in the 'parallel activity' enjoined by Lenin.

However, it was the Sarekat, not the ISDV, which bore the brunt of the consequences. Several hundred of its members were arrested, others left in droves either because they disapproved of section B or feared that it might be held against them, and important SI branches in West Java were dissuaded only with difficulty from dissolving themselves.

Some benefit, nevertheless, did accrue to the Sareket. Fearing further outbreaks, the government went into an unnatural alliance with it. Official efforts to improve the miserable conditions of the workers had met obduracy on the part of the employers. The government therefore sought to apply pressure on them by encouraging the growth of labour unions. (President Roosevelt was to act similarly many years later in the United States.) It also hoped that in this way the workers would follow more moderate political paths. The Sarekat itself was quite happy to avoid any possibilities of further violence and thought that labour unions would act as a lightning conductor.

This development represented a new opportunity for the ISDV. Its popular bases were only among the new urban workers, especially in the Rail and Tram Workers' Union, the VSTP. It had tried to increase its influence by organising rural labourers, both in the villages and on the estates. But whatever their economic situation may have been, and it was often worse than obtained in the towns, they evidently required no new ideological basis of association and remained faithful to the more traditional type of leadership offered by members of the Central Sarekat Islam. There was no foothold here for the ISDV. It might have hoped to control the rural white-collar workers. But these petty officials were dominated by the Pawnship Employees' Union, which distributed its favours among the ISDV, Insulinde and the Sarekat, in fairly even measure.

In brief, the countryside was apparently impenetrable to the ISDV. It drew the appropriate Leninist lesson, and sought to achieve control over the SI organisations. It calculated that the new government backing for the Sarekat's organisation of the workers would be to its advantage. The influence of the Semarang branch, virtually a pocket borough of the ISDV, could only increase, while the pressure from the disaffected workers would make the Central Sarekat Islam leaders themselves less able to resist control by the ISDV.

Its strategy to acquire control over the Sarekat organisations was to establish a Federation of Labour Unions, and it had started working towards this end in 1915 but with little success. Its luck now turned. For not only government support, but also a business boom, favoured the unions. A wave of strikes which had begun the previous year developed strongly in 1919, achieving considerable success. This brought in new members, and most organised workers came under the leadership of the Sarekat. Radicalism having been successful, the ISDV's position was strengthened. Leaders of both ISDV and SI unions came together and outlined a plan to unite in a common front, a tactic which invariably works to the advantage of the Leninists. So also in this case: it was Semaun who was given the task of drafting the declaration of purpose and constitution of the new federation.

Not surprisingly, the Sarekat Islam congress that year gave great support to the ISDV, and urged that the new labour grouping be called the Revolutionary Socialist Federation. The organisation came into being at the end of the year, embodying twenty-two unions with seventy-two thousand workers. Most of the unions were loyal to the Semarang (i.e. ISDV) branch of the Sarekat, but the majority of members, though they were grouped into a smaller number of unions, followed the CSI. Semaun scored a

further success when he manoeuvred himself into the
leadership of the interim executive and placed its first
headquarters in Semarang. The revolutionary title had represented an unnecessary declaration of a 'maximum programme', it was abandoned for fear of alienating the white-
collar unions such as the Pawnshop Employees', and the
name 'Labour Federation' (*Persatuan-Persatuan Kaum
Buruh* or PPKB) was adopted.

The ISDV's guile in labour matters was not matched in
the political field, where its own prejudices stood in the
way. As a counterpart to the PPKB, a 'Federation of Popular
Movements' (PPKR) was formed as a 'true Volksraad'; the
PPKB was to be its upper house. The policy of this new
grouping was very similar to the ISDV's, but as it put the
liberation of Java from foreign control as its first priority, the
ISDV refused to take part and thereby deprived itself of a
promising opportunity to influence and lead it.

This same dogmatic opposition to nationalism put the
ISDV at a disadvantage against a rival suitor for the favours
of the Sarekat. In June 1919 one of the leaders of Insulinde,
Douwes Dekker, took his followers out of it on the grounds
that it had become a mere platform for Eurasian ambitions,
and formed the Sarekat Hindia. But he had wider intentions; his eyes, like the ISDV's, coveted the SI. He urged
it to abandon its religious orientation and to adopt a programme of national liberation and social justice. This was,
of course, completely opposed to the policy of the ISDV, but
to its chagrin it found that Dekker's propaganda was gaining converts not only within the Sarekat, but also within
its own ranks. However, fortune was on its side. Not only
were the Sarekat Hindia's leaders Eurasians, and therefore
set apart from the main body of Indonesians, but also they
were too enthusiastic for their own good and the public
disorders which they fomented led to their imprisonment.
By 1920 they offered no competition to the ISDV.

Joining the Comintern

At this time (1919) the ISDV was following a policy which emphasised ideological training and organisational work rather than mass revolutionary agitation. It was the ISDV's Surabaya branch, largely European, which supported this line; its Semarang branch, with many Indonesian members, was all for revolutionary action. But this was also the last year in which the party was to be entirely autonomous in policy.

For in 1919 the Third or Communist International, or Comintern, was founded at the first world communist congress, held in Moscow in March, marking the end of the independence of national communist parties. Though its final constitution was only to be promulgated at the second world congress in Smolny in July and August of 1920, immediately after its foundation the term 'social democracy', which we remember Sneevliet had used to identify his faith only a few years previously, came to designate those who continued to support the Second International and refused to follow Lenin. Marxists everywhere made haste to indicate where they stood. The Dutch SDP renamed itself the Communist Party of Holland (CPH); and the Indies' SDAP adopted the name ISDP (Indies Social Democratic Party). In May 1920 the ISDV met at their seventh congress to decide what they should call themselves. Their conclusions are of great interest. First, the European Surabaya group, while approving of the Comintern, still did not wish to call themselves communists, as indicating too close a link with what they considered a small sect of the world movement. They lost the day to Semarang, and it is worth noting that one of the latter's leaders, Baars, emphasised that the dictatorship of the proletariat (read communist party) and the soviet system were both essential to the communist programme. Simultaneously, a new executive was elected and for the first time Indonesians were given leading positions. They were in any case of a revolutionary persuasion, as were the Dutch in the new executive. In brief, the new party was committed to revolutionary agitation, party dictatorship, and a soviet system. Both the party's new policy, and its greater Indonesian membership, were aptly symbolised by its new name: *Perserikatan Komunis di- India* (PKI) or Communist Association of the Indies, the first such association in Asia outside Russia.

The PKI therefore anticipated the conclusions of the second world communist congress, whose task was conceived to be the organisation of the all-out struggle for the communist revolution. The deliberations of the congress were dominated by the ideas expressed by Lenin in his paper *Left-Wing Communism, an Infantile Disorder*, published in June 1920 (a document which, like *What is to be done?*, remains a basic instructional text for communists the world over). He had been concerned to urge his followers to infiltrate and seize control of trade unions by every means possible, to combine illegal activity with legal, and to set up an International which would be a genuinely controlling central authority. The second world congress accepted all these arguments in the two documents which it approved: the Twenty-one Conditions (for admission to the Communist International), and the Statutes of the International. The latter gave the Comintern's executive committee effective control over the member parties, and in turn gave the central committee of the Russian Communist Party and the Russian State Security Service mastery of the Comintern. Until the dissolution of the International in 1943, these rules remained in force.

There was no ambiguity about the nature of the Comintern or of its component parties. The Twenty-one Conditions were principally a means of excluding from the latter any who might be disposed to argue for reform instead of revolt. On the other hand, the new International was emphatically not an association of independent parties but a single world communist party, and the parties working in the individual countries would attend merely as separate sections of the Comintern. The target of this organisation was the destruction of the liberal state and its replacement by a communist government.

Since only the Russian communists had been successful, the second world congress declared that their revolution was the model to be followed. But Lenin himself argued in *Left-Wing Communism* that if the revolution should prevail in even one of the advanced countries, then Russia would soon no longer be the model but would once more become a backward country. However, his country remained the only one, until the second world war, where communist revolution had in fact been achieved; its prestige therefore remained unimpaired. Moreover, as the Russian party was the only one to rule a state, and all world congresses were held on its territory, the main weight of work of the executive committee of the Communist International (ECCI) was assumed to fall on to it. In compensation, it was awarded five of the twenty-five votes on that committee. As a result, virtually right from the start the Russian party was exercising direct control over Comintern affairs, not even bothering to go through its representatives on the committee.

Thus, in the Comintern as in the individual sections (i.e. parties), Lenin's scheme or organisation expounded in *What is to be done?* was followed. Extreme centralisation, unquestioning obedience, the increase of communist power by any means, were the hall-marks of this system. As the individual communist was subject to the leader of his party, so the individual parties were subordinate to the Comintern executive committee. And this, in turn, owed unquestioning obedience to the Russian Communist Party.

The second congress also set up a Commission on National and Colonial Questions, which discussed the situation in the colonies. Its importance was indicated by placing Lenin, no less, as chairman. The secretary was Sneevliet, who under his Comintern name of Maring was attending

the congress as representative of the ısdv and the Semarang
Sarekat Islam.

Lenin, applying his minimum/maximum programme
strategy, argued that communists should support the 'bourgeois-democratic' liberation movements (i.e. nationalism).
He was too devious for his followers, some of whom felt
that any movement not advocating revolution should be
attacked. Prominent among these was the Indian delegate
M. N. Roy, who argued that purely communist movements
should be developed in the colonial and semi-colonial ter-
ritories, based on the increasing landlessness he foresaw.
He also rejected the idea that the Asian communists should
wait for revolution in Europe, asserting that the latter
would be successful only if European capitalists were deprived of the profits they drew from semi-colonial countries. In the event, however, Lenin's views were accepted,
with the minor amendment that support was to be given
to the 'national-revolutionary' rather than the 'bourgeois-
democratic' liberation movements. Despite the insistence on
discipline, however, of the various sections of the Comintern, only that in China, under Mao Tse-tung, applied
Lenin's teaching and collaborated with the 'national bourgeoisie', with disastrous consequences to itself.

This policy, which came to be known as 'the united
front from above', was to be followed from 1920 to 1927,
and instructed communists the world over to conclude
alliances with parties to the non-communist Left where
possible, to participate in elections, and to use their parliamentary position to strengthen the leftist alliance. Needless
to say, this in no way involved abandonment of 'parallel
activity', nor of minimum/maximum programme strategy.
It was a policy to use existing popular movements for
communist purposes.

As we have seen, the ısdv/pkı's guiding policy had been
to influence and if possible control the Sarekat Islam. The
Comintern's attitude to pan-Islam is therefore of interest.
In brief, it faithfully reflected Russian interests. The Russian communists had flirted with pan-Islam when they

were concerned to encourage revolt against tsarist authority among Russia's Muslim peoples in Asia. But once they
were in power they saw Islam as an obstacle to the Russian
centralisation beloved of Lenin. Accordingly, the second
world congress agreed with him to oppose not only priests,
Christian missions, and similar obstacles, but also pan-Islam and pan-Asiatic movements.

Since the Sarekat was both against colonial government,
i.e. 'national revolutionary', and also 'pan-Islamic' (and,
given its origins in the Muslim traders, as near as was
possible in Indonesian society to a bourgeois movement),
the advice of the congress, however valuable for the Russian party, was no guidance to its Indies subordinate. The
'final theses' embodying this muddled counsel were drafted
by Sneevliet himself; in the Comintern he was regarded as
an Asian 'expert'.

The confused nature of the intellectual leadership that
the Comintern had to offer its Asian sections makes it
unlikely that the attraction of communism lay in its anal-
yses of the political situation in the Asian colonies. A
better explanation perhaps lies simply in the fact of the
Third International's concern with Asians. This had not
been its primary intention; at first its emphasis had been
on Europe. But just as the Dutch, centuries before, had
gone east only when Philip II of Spain and Portugal had
closed the port of Lisbon to them, so now the Comintern,
Europe denied, turned its attention to the Asian colonies.
That it did so in order to promote revolution and thereby,
as it hoped, weaken the European powers was perhaps less
important than the fact that to achieve its aims it took an
interest in those who had been uprooted from their customary social soil. The Second International, in contrast,
had had no serious concern with the colonies.

The ISDV policies of non-cooperation could not have been
called overwhelmingly successful. In any case, they were
now abruptly reversed by orders from on high. In December 1920 the PKI held a special congress to discuss affiliation with the Comintern. There, it was learnt that the

Comintern had decreed a 'united front from above', which of course tipped the balance in favour of participating in the Volksraad. Elections for its second session were due to be held in early 1921. It is interesting to record that one of the Dutch communist leaders, Bergsma, obviously insufficiently imbued with Leninism, argued against blind acceptance of Comintern decisions. The other members of the PKI, however, decided otherwise.

The congress then went on to its main business. The major problem, of course, was the Comintern's denunciation of pan-Islam and its application to the PKI's relationships with the Sarekat. The delegates also observed that the Comintern call for land redistribution had no relevance in Indonesia, where there were very few holdings and where the land was generally communally owned by villages. They saved their faces by saying that clearly the Comintern programme was not intended for them and that there was therefore no reason to consider changing their basic policy. On which note they agreed to affiliate.

Their decision to take part in the Volksraad was more a sign of obeisance to their new masters than realistic appreciation of possibilities. Bergsma pointed out that they could not hope to win a seat by election, and would therefore have to rely on appointment by the governor general. But though the latter, after the 1918 elections, had turned the other cheek and appointed many Indonesians opposed to the colonial regime, predictably his face had been slapped; resistance had grown more violent. He was therefore somewhat less enthusiastic about this policy, but in any case he was certainly not going to appoint the representative of a party which was committed to disrupt the Volksraad. He went further; having ignored him (it happened to be Baars, returned from Europe), he then ordered his expulsion.

5
Loss
of
Grip

Party Discipline

The attenuation of the SI after the section B affair worked
to the advantage of the PKI, for those who remained were
among the more militant and better organised, and loyal
to the Semarang branch. The party also benefited by the
Sarekat's involvement with labour, for it was able to influence many of the trade union branches. In consequence,
the CSI turned to emphasise the religious aspect of the
Sarekat as a counterpoise to the communist gospel preached
by Semarang. And since the leaders identified with Islam
were to be found in the Jogjakarta branch, leadership of
the movement gravitated there from Surabaya. Thus were
drawn the lines for the battle over the body of the Sarekat
between Semarang and Jogjakarta; the only question was
which group would oust the other from the organisation.

The struggle became focused on the question of organisational discipline. As mentioned already, it had been the
custom to permit members of one political association to

belong also to others. But in August 1920 the PKI issued
instructions to its new branches outside Java demanding
that communists work only with proletarian groups and
not with those higher in the income and status scale;
even skilled workers were excluded. In this way, of course,
the PKI showed their awareness that they could hope to
influence only the rootless and ignorant; it was not that
they were concerned to lead only those committed to their
ideology. On the contrary, as has been emphasised previously, their definition of proletariat was adjustable, and in
the Sarekat, as we can see, they wished to control the
whole organisation.

Shortly afterwards, the other political associations followed the PKI's example, demanding that their members
recognise no association but theirs, with one exception.
That was the Sarekat Islam, the only mass grouping, which
was regarded as the 'Indonesian' association, and with
which therefore every other wished to be linked.

Within the Sarekat itself the struggle between Jogja
and the PKI had an element of personal animosity in addition to its ideological fervour. Both Semaun of the PKI,
and Suryopranoto of the Jogjakarta Sarekat, sought to seize
the leadership of the Sarekat for themselves. The latter was
head of the Sugar Factory Workers' Union, known as the
PFB, and was acquiring the reputation of the 'strike king';
he was, as a matter of fact, a member of one of the Javanese royal houses. The man they individually hoped to
dispossess was, of course, Tjokroaminoto, whose great
weakness was his desire to maintain the SI undivided.

The first rounds in the struggle went to Jogjakarta.
Suryopranoto called a strike of his union and thereby caused
a division within the PKI itself, for Semaun, expecting failure, opposed the strike on behalf of his party but only
against the opposition of the other members of his executive. The strike was naturally supported by the Sarekat,
but when the authorities threatened dire measures, it withdrew gracefully though not without accusing the PKI of
cowardice.

The failure of the strike, however, eliminated the PFB. At its peak, it had thirty-one thousand members, while associated unions accounted for thirty-three thousand. By 1922 its own membership had fallen to four hundred, while the other unions had ceased to exist altogether. It never revived during the colonial period.

The PKI's next move was equally unsuccessful. Its chief propagandist, Darsono, attacked the integrity of Tjokroaminoto, the very man who in 1917 had prevented the expulsion of the ISDV from the Sarekat. Though much of the thrown mud stuck, it had the effect of moving control of the Sarekat into the hands of the militantly anti-communist Jogjakarta branch, and not unnaturally the PKI lost Tjokroaminoto's sympathy.

The struggle between the two branches now gathered intensity, mutual accusations being liberally dispensed. Both expressed their opposition to 'capitalism', but the Jogja group blamed the PKI for their divisive tactics and further accused them of being opposed to Islam and of being cowardly in facing government repression. However, a truce was observed for the occasion of the Sarekat Islam congress of March 1921. Semaun, hoping to take over the organisation, immediately before the meeting agreed on a policy based on both Muslim and communist principles. The congress agreed to end the dispute between Jogjakarta and Semarang but also resolved to carry out a survey among the branches on the question whether party discipline was to be introduced.

The PKI took the inclusion of a censure of capitalism to mean that the congress had been a victory for them. They were soon undeceived. For Tjokroaminoto and Hadji Agus Salim, a leader of the Jogjakarta group, immediately toured the non-communist branches of the Sarekat, urging that communism be extirpated.

In the meantime, a meeting of the PPKB, or Labour Federation, was held, in which the representatives of the Jogjakarta Sarekat outwitted the communists on the executive into resigning. These then attempted to recoup their losses by forming a grouping called the RVC, or the Revolutionary Federation of Trade Unions, and followed the classic tactic of the united front from below by issuing a manifesto which claimed the loyalty of their opponents' followers. They succeeded in drawing away some twenty-seven thousand of the sixty thousand PPKB members! This was a signal for battle, the end of the surface unity of the March SI congress, and the beginning of a rapid decline in union membership.

Fate then placed victory in the grasp of the Jogjakarta anti-communists. Tjokroaminoto was arrested on a charge of perjury at the time of the investigations into the 'section B' affair. With him out of the way, the Jogjakarta group was able to control the SI's special congress, in October, to discuss party discipline. The outcome was not in doubt; the meeting voted in favour, thus ending the 'bloc within' which the PKI had considered its contribution to Leninist tactics of disruption. However, this applied only to the central organisation of the Sarekat; it will be remembered that the branches were virtually autonomous. Furthermore, the ending of the 'bloc within' did not preclude cooperation between PKI and the Sarekat.

Revolutionary Failure

Political changes in both the Indies and the Netherlands had now produced a less liberal regime. In April 1921 van Limburg Stirum was succeeded as governor general by Dirk Fock, a *laissez-faire* liberal. The Indies were at the time in the grip of a depression, and in accordance with ideas then generally held his remedy was to reduce government expenditure and increase taxes. The sufferers from both these measures were mostly the Indonesians. Fock would listen to no protests, and while maintaining the civil rights in which he believed, greatly limited the freedom of action of the political groups. He brought home to them, and to Indonesians in general, that they were powerless.

From this situation arose an obvious slogan for the PKI's eighth congress, held in December 1921 at Semarang: unity of all political groups against the Dutch. There was to be no 'bloc within', but the PKI wished to set up a national committee or federation to oppose 'modern organised capital', or 'sinful capitalism', both terms referring to the Dutch. The meeting, attended by representatives of the Jogjakarta Sarekat, was marked by recriminations and only saved by, of all people, the representative of the Modernist Muslim Movement, the Muhammadiyah, who argued for unity. This led to an agreement that both Islamic and communist groups would cooperate and set up a central organ.

The desire for unity did not, of course, preclude recourse by the PKI to the 'united front from below'. To group the SI units that had left the main body when the communists were expelled from the CSI, the congress approved of the formation of the *Persatuan Sarekat Islam* (PSI), or Sarekat Islam Association, which would group the dissident Sarekat branches, to be known as the 'Red SI'. It was really a means of competing with Jogjakarta for SI members, and all branches of the Sarekat were invited to join. This gambit met with complete failure; only ten branches, all from the Semarang area, and therefore under the influence of the PKI itself, transferred their allegiance.

This congress is significant for its election of a new chairman to replace Semaun, who had departed in October on a visit to Moscow. Tan Malaka by name, he had been very successful in establishing self-financing PKI-influenced schools and was to be of some importance in later years. He agreed with the need for a united revolutionary movement but his way was not Semaun's. The latter had emphasised prudence and organisation. Malaka was for a campaign that would force the government to relinquish its 'extraordinary rights' and other restrictions on civil liberties. His revolutionary enthusiasm was put to the test the very next month when the Indies suffered its first really large union-supported strike. Nominally the

cause was the refusal by employees of government pawn-
shops to perform the manual labour of carrying goods
themselves, the general factotum previously employed having been sacrificed to the government's economy measures.
The strike began with one employee walking out of his
pawnshop in a small central Javanese town but within
two weeks 79 of 360 such establishments had been affected,
and between one and two thousand of the total five thousand employees were involved. Whatever the declared
reason for the strike, both the Indonesian organisations and
the government saw it as a trial of strength.

Though the Pawnshop Workers' Union was under the
control of the Jogjakarta Sarekat Islam, the PKI expressed
its support. But neither of the rivals gained much from
the strike. The government imposed strict disciplinary
measures. In Jogjakarta the right of assembly was suspended, and the city was invested by the police and a
civilian guard. One-fifth of all pawnshop employees were
dismissed, and their union collapsed, its membership drop-
ping from two thousand to two hundred. With it went
Jogjakarta's hopes of controlling the Indonesian labour
movement, but this was in any case now paralysed by the
aftermath of the strike. The leader of the Pawnshop Union, Abdul Muis, one of the strongest anti-communist Jogjakarta leaders, tried to induce other unions to join the
strike; he was quickly detained and expelled from Java.
The PKI won a slight negative advantage; its support for
the strike cleared it of the charge of cowardice. But Malaka
and the PKI's Dutch grey eminence, Bergsma, evidently
did not appreciate the government's determination. They
made plans to issue a call for a general strike, were arrested
in mid-February and deported; the PKI was thus effectively
left headless. Leadership of the Pawnshop Workers' Union
now devolved on to Salim, who called a meeting of all its
members. Only a minority were in favour of the strike and
it was called off.

Playing by Ear

Meanwhile, Semaun was in Moscow, seeking guidance. Russian and therefore Comintern policy in the early 1920s displayed a general lack of interest in the east, striving to avoid revolutionary action and concerned to mend bridges with the western powers. The First Congress of the Peoples of the Far East, held in September 1920, attended by the newly expelled Sneevliet, had betrayed extreme animosity to nationalist movements in the colonies, though grudgingly admitting that the communist parties had no chance of success without their help. It had expressed opposition to both foreign and native capitalism, and had called for agrarian revolution and the establishment of workers' and peasants' soviets. But after this meeting there was little Russian interest in the east.

Less than a year later, the third Comintern congress was held in June and July 1921: this time it was Darsono who represented the PKI. Russia was then applying her New Economic Policy, which required cooperation with the west, and it was not intended that the situation in Asia would be discussed. The delegates from that part of the world, however, induced Lenin to create a Colonial Commission. This expressed two opposed views. On the one hand, bearing in mind Russia's interests in the near east, it was in favour of pan-Islam and an alliance of all classes against the western powers in that area. M. N. Roy, on the other hand, vehemently opposed cooperation with nationalism and with pan-Islam. No attempt was made to reconcile these opinions. The Comintern position, reflecting Russia's interests, was put by Zinoviev: support for any movement opposed to the west, however anti-communist. Though useful for Russian foreign policy, this principle was hardly likely to commend itself to the Asian communist parties. The fact was that the Comintern did not have much faith in Asian revolutions and its colonial strategy was cooperation with nationalism rather than encouraging imitations of the Bolshevik 'proletarian' revolution.

Semaun arrived in time to represent the Indonesian party at the 'First Congress of Toilers of the Far East', held at Irkutsk in November 1921 and in Moscow in January and February 1922. This was really a Russian riposte for not having been invited to the 1922 Washington conference on arms limitation in the Pacific. Russian opinion in the conference was now opposed to cooperation with 'bourgeois' nationalist movements but the Sarekat was not defined as such, presumably because the PKI still had hopes of controlling it. All this, however, was rather above Semaun's head, as he understood none of the languages used at the conference. The chief value of his stay in Russia lay in conversations he had with Lenin. The latter, evidently speaking as a Russian rather than as a communist, urged on him the need to create united anti-imperialist (that is, western imperialist) movements. He emphasised that the tactics of the Russian communists could not be duplicated by Asian parties, who faced quite different conditions; he expressed the same view at the Comintern fourth congress later in the same year. These words were music in Semaun's ears. He had never shown signs of any great enthusiasm for revolutionary action and Lenin's advice virtually told him to trust his own judgement.

Furthermore, the caution that Russian experience was no necessary guide may well explain a certain lack of faith evinced by the PKI in the pronouncements of the Comintern. For this was, as we have mentioned, simply an organ of Russian foreign policy, which at the time sought a 'united front from above' with a generally unmilitant approach in western Europe but an aggressive 'anti-imperialism' in the middle east. The Asian delegates at its fourth congress in November 1922, among whom was Tan Malaka on behalf of the PKI, heard this policy expounded and found themselves urged to participate in any movement that would give them access to the people while retaining their 'proletarian purity'. The congress even approved the PKI's 'bloc within' the Sarekat Islam, all ignorant of its ejection. It nevertheless refused to alter, despite Malaka's urging, the second congress's denunciation of pan-Islam, which the Russians saw as a threat in the Muslim parts of their empire. Tan Malaka forbore from dispelling the Comintern's ignorance about the Indies; he may well have thought that it was not really interested in situations which did not suit its books.

In May Semaun had returned to an Indies where the permitted limits of political activity had narrowed considerably. It will be remembered that Governor General van Limburg Stirum had promised a Revisional Commission at the time of the ill-founded reports of revolution in Holland in 1918. But in March 1922 the Minister of Colonies, Simon de Graff, declared that a revision of the Indies constitution was quite unnecessary. Shortly after, parliamentary elections in the Netherlands produced a more conservative government, which kept de Graff as minister of colonies. The Ethical Policy was now finally, if tacitly, abandoned.

Semaun's principal preoccupation, however, was to rebuild his shattered party. Its indulgence in direct action had had a debilitating effect, and the PKI's mainstay, the VSTP, which had been nearly seventeen thousand strong at the time of Semaun's departure for Moscow in October 1921, had fewer than eight thousand members on his return nine months later. So, when he spoke to a rally in Semarang in June, Semaun repeated the advice he had received from Lenin, and added that the party should abandon direct action in order to concentrate on organisation and propaganda. He put his own precepts into practice and in a few months had restored the PKI's labour strength, especially that of the VSTP. He could not have chosen a better time, for the SI's influence among labour had been virtually extinguished by the failure of the pawnshop workers' strike. In addition, the effects of the world depression of the time were being felt. So the PKI found no obstacle to establishing several other unions.

With his base consolidated, Semaun now sought to build up and influence a labour federation. While he had been in Moscow the previous December an attempt had been made by the Public Works Employees' Union, VIPBOW, to sponsor an Indies Labour Federation, *Persatuan Vakbond Hindia*, or PVH, in Madiun. It was intended to be politically neutral between the SI and the PKI, and its main function was to oppose the removal of the cost-of-living bonus granted to state employees, another of the government's economy measures. This federation had received no support from the SI- or PKI-led unions, and had vanished with the pawnshop strike. With the intention of reviving it, Semaun now, in June, courted VIPBOW. This body called a meeting of unions of state employees, which in September established a new grouping under the same name as its defunct predecessor. The new PVH, of some twenty-three thousand members, was composed almost entirely of government employees. It held its first congress in December and expressed itself opposed to capitalism. This was hardly surprising, given its bureaucratic membership, and that the largest union in the federation was the PKI's loyal VSTP. The situation was ideal in that it permitted the PKI to manipulate the PVH without appearing to do so. The latter could thus be represented as a symbol of cooperation between communists and non-communists in facing the imperialist enemy.

Ejection of the 'Bloc Within'

Simultaneously with extending its influence in the labour field, the PKI was attempting to reverse or at least to remedy the collapse of its 'block within the SI' policy. But it was now not dealing with political innocents, and even Tjokroaminoto seems to have understood that certain prices were too high for a PKI-dominated 'unity'. In May he had been released from detention, and in August finally acquitted of perjury in connection with the 'section B' investigations. He sought to unite Indonesian non-communist political movements on the basis of Islam. In November he chaired the first al-Islam congress, in order to promote the religion and to give politics more Islamic content. (Ironically, the PKI sent representatives to show their goodwill.) But this was only a preliminary to his plan to revamp the Sarekat Islam. In the last months of the year he called for cadres to be appointed within every Sarekat branch. They would be members of a new organisation to be called the *Partai Sarekat Islam,* which would eventually absorb the Central SI and all the branches. The object of the cadres was to guard the unity of the branch, while the political aim of the new *partai* was to be independence based upon the principles of the Koran. This scheme, obviously intended to ensure the ejection of the communists from the Sarekat Islam branches, was to be debated at the congress of the CSI to be held in February 1923, when the question of party discipline would again be raised.

He may well have been spurred to evolve this plan by the fact that even with the PKI ejected from the CSI, its influence was growing in the branches, especially through the spread of SI schools such as Tan Malaka had founded in Semarang. Most branches were not applying the CSI ruling on party discipline, and the cadres were intended to ensure they did so.

Meanwhile, however, the European-led Democratic Socialists had been attempting to form broad political groupings to promote national unity. In June 1922 the ISDP had organised, with the support of the Sarekat Hindia and the Sarekat Islam, an All-Indies congress. Taking inspiration from the Indian Congress Party, it showed a spirit of non-cooperation with the government, a natural result of the government's refusal to give more autonomy to the Indies.

Then, in November, the ISDP put together a new and broad 'Radical Grouping'. Unlike its predecessor of 1918 and a 'Political Grouping' in 1920, the present coalition was intended to apply pressure outside parliament on the authorities. It is worth noting that all these combinations were put together by a European-led party; the Indonesian leaders were too divided among themselves to band together even against the colonial power.

However, this ideal of unity played into the hands of the PKI, by preventing a total divorce between Jogjakarta and Semarang. The PKI attended the foundation meeting of the grouping and Semaun gave his strong support. He no doubt realised that this was probably his last chance of influencing the Indonesian political movements, as Tjokroaminoto's projected reorganisation of the Sarekat would preclude the possibility of re-inserting the 'bloc within'.

But matters went even worse than Semaun could have expected. The CSI congress held in Madiun between 17 and 20 February 1923 was notable for the fact that Tjokroaminoto worked closely with Salim, and the result was a foregone conclusion: Tjokroaminoto's plan for a disciplined Partai Sarekat Islam was accepted. The PKI was now definitely out. Open hostilities then broke out between the SI and the PKI; the casualties were the Radical Grouping and the PVH. The rank and file SI members, unable properly to assess the issues debated, were shaken at the dissensions among their leaders and left the association in large numbers. Yet, though Tjokroaminoto and Salim were not to know it, undoubtedly their action in preventing communist control saved the Indonesian nationalist movement. Had they not done so it is at least probable that the SI might have been implicated in the PKI revolt which was to take place only three years later, and proscribed in consequence. In that case not only the PKI but also Indonesian nationalism would have been lifeless at the end of Dutch rule.

Emphasis on Islam had rallied the Central Sarekat Islam against the communists, but it also led to the disintegration of the Sarekat as a whole. For the Islam in question was of the Modernist type, emphasising the sources of the Faith, and rejecting later, and therefore local interpretations, so discrediting the Islamic practices of the majority of Javanese. Also, the SI, in great contrast with the PKI, devoted its attention to broad and abstract issues; the latter followed its minimum programme tactic, played up local grievances and drew the greater numbers. Consequently the SI branches saw the decision on party discipline as an attempt to impose on them the irrelevant and Modernist Islam favoured by their leaders in Jogjakarta. They resisted both the discipline and the Islam, and even Jogjakarta itself split. A number of prominent members who had also belonged to the PKI now gave it their exclusive allegiance; among them were two men of later prominence, Alimin and Musso.

The PKI and the Red SI discussed their future, now they were out in the cold, at a congress held in Bandung on 4 March 1923. There were between two and three thousand people present, being delegates from fifteen PKI branches, thirteen Red SI branches and thirteen labour unions. Apart from proclaiming support for Islam (*pace* the second Comintern congress' condemnation of pan-Islam) and opposing state supervision of religious teachers (another application of the minimum/maximum strategy), they decided to set up *Sarekat Rakyat* (People's Unions) to be placed under the PKI itself but distinct from the party's own branches. They were also, oddly enough, to remain separate from the Red SI, which it was hoped would become Sarekat Rakyat.

This reorganisation was intended to achieve the object of controlling the mass base, or in other words a dictatorship of the proletariat by the communists; a situation known as the 'bloc above'. The reason for the change was obvious enough. The PKI leaders knew very well that the interests of the proletariat were not those of the party, or to put it in Leninist terms that the minimum programme was different from the maximum. Hence it felt the need to keep the mass on a very short rein. However, this decision deprived the Red SI's of much of the autonomy they had enjoyed as members of the Sarekat Islam, and was so very unpopular that it was put into effect only after the party congress of June 1923, some fifteen months later.

The unwillingness to accept discipline was a characteristic not limited to the Red SI. Indonesian political structure is perhaps best understood as groupings of leaders and their personal followings. This, of course, makes the leaders less willing to obey or compromise than they might otherwise be. We have already seen how the Sarekat Islam branches were reluctant to accept the party discipline decisions of their Central. The same problems were to afflict the PKI, and for much the same reason: the interests of the PKI were not those of the leaders of its branches.

Having been politically enfeebled by exclusion from the SI, Semaun and the PKI now lost control of events in the labour sphere. As part of its economy measures, the government reduced the cost-of-living bonus awarded to its employees with effect from 1 January 1923, while on the same day a private railway line announced reductions in wages and in personnel. This naturally heated the atmosphere at the VSTP congress in February 1923, and calls for strikes were made. Semaun was, as ever, strongly opposed to such action; he now had Darsono to support him. At the Comintern's bidding, the latter had reluctantly left his theoretical studies in Europe and arrived in Batavia in February 1923. He was just as much against direct action as Semaun, though for different reasons. He was convinced that a 'proletarian' revolution was imminent in Germany and would quickly spread to Holland, thus leading to independence for Indonesia (he evidently had not considered the fate of the Russian colonies in Asia after the revolution). Accordingly, he reasoned that the PKI's role was not to organise a revolt against Netherlands rule but to strengthen itself in order to prepare for the gift of independence from Dutch communists. For him 'world capitalism', not the Dutch, was the enemy, and therefore a common front with other Indonesian parties was undesirable.

All of which, it is clear, amounted to a rationalisation,

or a philosophy, depending on one's point of view, to do nothing but simply keep in being the PKI and its associated groups. There was to be neither an attempt at revolution nor organisation of a united front against the colonialists; the PKI was simply to stand and wait until the Dutch communists had done their work. Perhaps all this shows is simply that Darsono was not a man of action; unfortunately, the situation in the Indies to which he had just returned was inimical to passivity.

With the great spread of administrative services, the government had found the budget increasing rapidly. In order to keep it within bounds, it announced a new salary structure which, unlike the previous single scale of 1913, distinguished between Europeans and Indonesians, and of course aroused Indonesian opposition. So when in early March the VSTP leaders met in Bandung they over-rode Semaun's objections and went ahead with plans for a strike throughout the railway and tram network in the Indies.

Any tempering effect Semaun might have had on the strikers was eliminated when he himself was removed from the scene. Disregarding a warning from government to moderate his actions, he threatened a strike if any VSTP leaders were arrested. The government then placed him under detention; the strike began (at least in Java) and quickly ended in disaster. The government, supported by European opinion, dismissed all the strikers, placed the railways under military control, forbade the VSTP from meeting, and added a new law to the criminal code, outlawing strikes. Many VSTP and PKI leaders (reportedly 120, of whom 110 were communists) were arrested. The strike lingered on until July, then collapsed when the government announced its decision to ban Semaun. There were at the time some twenty thousand rail and tram employees in Java. The number involved in the strike has been variously estimated as between two and a half thousand and thirteen thousand. Membership of the VSTP at the time of the strike was about thirteen thousand; according to one account it then fell to five hundred.

With this lesson that the government would not brook opposition, the non-communist labour organisations now withdrew from politics and functioned as professional associations, while the non-communist political groupings disintegrated. Only the communists, devoted as they were to revolution, remained a coherent force. But their leader Semaun was not to be with them. He left for the Netherlands in August 1923, not to see Indonesia again for another thirty years. His attitude (and his grasp of reality) may be deduced from his answers to a government questionnaire in which he stated that he had expected the Netherlands Indies government itself to introduce communism with the help of an American loan!

6
Disintegration and Destruction

Revolutionary Airs

By 1924 the PKI was virtually the only coherent political movement but did not really replace the Sarekat as the Indonesian nationalist standard bearer. The PKI congress in June (when it was a thousand strong) still assumed that an 'overthrow' of 'world capitalism' was imminent and still hammered away at the class struggle, totally ignoring nationalism. In other words, it would not accept, ideologically at least, the Indonesian definition of the situation but held fast to the conceptions of European Leninists. However, as we shall see, these commitments were not allowed to intrude on the local level, where the PKI agitators told people exactly what they wanted to hear.

The congress changed the name of the party to *Partai Komunis Indonesia*, an indication that the party was now putatively disciplined and that the term Indonesia was gaining increasingly acceptance. It also voted to move to Batavia from Semarang, as a result of difficulties in Central Java. But the main emphasis was on discipline and indoctrination, thus marking an abandonment of Malaka's adventures and a return to Semaun's settled strategy before he was led astray by the hotheads of the VSTP. The new central branch now sought to dominate the entire organisation, a move which was strongly resisted by the local leaders, especially when it involved control over their newspapers. Discipline did not mean retrenchment; on the contrary, great efforts were now made to develop the Sarekat Rakyat, to involve more women in the PKI's activities, and to develop a Youth Front.

At the same conference an organisational change of some importance was made. Provision was made in the constitution for 'extraordinary membership', which permitted local associations to keep their own name whilst adding an indication of affiliation. This was simply a means of asserting PKI control over the Sarekat Rakyat so as to ensure its 'proletarian character', i.e. so that it would pursue not its own interests but those of the PKI. While this move was fully in accord with Leninist doctrine, it failed in its purpose, as we shall see.

The influence of the PKI increased considerably in West and Central Java, but this success was bound to be short lived, for the government was not content to sit idly by. It increased its pressure on the PKI, particularly after a governor general's conference with his senior officials in September 1924. The PKI reacted by reducing the number of its public rallies, and working more intensively among fewer people, but it still shrank from going underground. Its audience was largely illiterate and it therefore had to use cadres and travelling propagandists; their activities could not be hidden without much money and strict discipline, assets the PKI did not have.

The government measures back-fired, for they made the PKI appear as martyrs and swelled the number of recruits to the Sarekat Rakyat. But this expansion moved the party's centre of gravity and was a source of weakness rather than strength. For the Sarekat Rakyat grew at the expense of work among the urban proletariat; the organisers had to be redeployed from the towns to the country. This would not have mattered so much had the SR been a reliable and lucrative source of support. But it was neither. Its members, necessarily, could not be as tightly organised as urban workers; and their financial contributions were uncertain. Had the PKI allowed matters to continue unchecked they would have found their energies simultaneously depleted and dissipated.

Only three months after the SR had been made 'extraordinary members', the PKI executive meeting in September resolved that henceforth its main effort would be devoted to the urban workers, while its rural activities would cease to expand. This decision, however, was so much at variance with current policy that it met with strong objections in the party, and was then deferred to a special conference, which was held in December at Kutagede near Jogjakarta. There assembled some ninety-six delegates representing thirty-eight PKI sections with about eleven hundred members, and forty-six SR branches with a total strength of thirty-one thousand. The conference temporised and decided that the SR were indeed to be abandoned, but not immediately. Their present membership would be maintained while being sifted, and the chosen few would be allowed to join the PKI, increasing its membership to three thousand, while the SR would then cease to exist.

The decision to concentrate on urban workers had a purpose; for the meeting's most important resolution was to organise an uprising. For this purpose it was to reconstitute itself into ten-man cells, who would work underground. But here again the spirit of compromise intervened. There was to be no terrorism, but also 'democratic centralism' was to be abandoned. Local units were authorised to act independently, without informing the headquarters, as long as their decisions were in line with the PKI constitution and by-laws. Who, at the moment of decision, was to judge whether they met these criteria, was left unstated. This ambiguous situation was dignified by the contradic-

tory term of 'federative centralism'; it meant, as events
were to show, that the party could be led by the rear. It is
possible that government repression made impossible close
supervision by the executive. But the policy adopted meant
dooming the party.

The resolutions of the conference were put into force
without much delay. The PKI-led labour unions were
grouped into a (somewhat ineffective) 'Secretariat of Red
Indonesian Labour Unions' at Surabaya, the Indies' major
industrial centre. Seamen and dockers were united into one
union and greater efforts were directed at the PKI's main
support, the VSTP, as well as at other urban workers. Their
poverty, compounded by all this agitation, had the result
both of increasing the influence of the PKI unions and of
deluding them into believing their own revolutionary rhet-
oric.

External Critics

Neither the decision to dissolve the SR, nor the plans to
revolt, were in accord with the expressed wishes of the
Comintern and its associated bodies. The fourth Comintern
congress of 1922, as well as the 'Pacific Transport Workers'
Conference', held in Canton in June 1924, had indeed
urged greater 'proletarian' purity and more emphasis on
revolutionary trade unions. But it had also approved of
communist-controlled rural organisations of the SR type.
Indeed, the Comintern congress held the same month
specifically endorsed the Sarekat Rakyat.

Nor was this attitude limited to those without first-hand
experience in the Indies; it was shared by both Semaun
and Malaka. The former, on his expulsion from the Indies,
had arrived in the Netherlands on 20 September 1923 and
became the PKI's European representative. He deplored the
decision to abandon the SR as soon as he heard of it.
Malaka was banished from the Indies in March 1922.
He remained in Moscow for a year (during which he
wrote a book on the Indonesian situation for his Russian

patrons) and then, in mid-1923, was named supervisor for what was later to be called South-East Asia: namely Burma, Thailand, Vietnam, Malaya, Indonesia and the Philippines. He asserted that this appointment gave him the right of veto; a claim disputed by others, especially Semaun. However that may have been, Malaka was responsible not only to the Comintern, but also to the *Profintern,* or Red International of Labour Unions. His view of the December 1924 decisions fully supported that of his Comintern head office. He published a tract, *Naar de Republiek Indonesia* (Towards an Indonesian Republic) in which he set out his criticisms, and advised the communists to emphasise the goals they held in common with the rest of the population instead of insisting on a purely 'proletarian' programme. This part of his advice the party never took; they did, however, as we shall see, accept his strategic suggestions on how to make the revolution. He advised first an uprising in the Outer Islands; then, when the Dutch were weakened and distracted, terrorism should begin in Java. It is not clear how or why he expected the authorities to be so affected by a party with a mere handful of leaders and a thousand uncertain members; it is part of the general air of unrealism which pervades communist discussion and actions at this time.

When the PKI decided to dissolve the SR it knew the attitude of the Comintern but effectively rejected its leadership. Nor does the party seem to have been unduly disturbed by the condemnation of its strategy by the plenary session of the executive committee of the Comintern (ECCI) in March/April 1925, which declared that the SR should have been established as a mass organisation, formally independent, with the communists operating as a 'bloc within'.

All this advice showed only that while the onlooker may see most of the game he rarely can advise on how to play it. The policy the Comintern advocated would no doubt have helped Russian foreign policy. There would have been, on paper, a large rural organisation ready to agitate as and when required by Moscow; the PKI's policy meant only a small urban group of conspirators. But what the Comintern overlooked, perhaps, was the debilitating character of a rural organisation in Indonesian circumstances.

In any case, events were to show that the Comintern vision of a large docile rural army under PKI orders was an exercise in fantasy. For though the PKI did not put its own resolutions into effect, and retained the SR, this was effectively led by its own local men, who knew nothing of communist theory and whose allegiance to the PKI was more nominal than real. They led the uprooted and dissatisfied, who were not so much concerned with a communist revolution as with removing the Dutch, whom they saw as the authors of their discontents. So to keep their positions these leaders inevitably had to organise disturbances of one kind or another. This was very far indeed from Lenin's discipline; indeed, it was the very kind of uncoordinated terrorism he had condemned.

The PKI did go some way to meet the Comintern's wishes. Semaun had urged them to renew their ties with the Sarekat Islam and to unite all Indonesian organisations into one anti-imperialist front, while the ECCI also suggested nationalist-type demands. So, early in 1925 the PKI tried to resume its cooperation even with anti-communist groups—a foredoomed venture given the enmity between the Sarekat and the PKI. And while the PKI was now not opposed to nationalism as such (though it continued to believe it wrong), the party insisted that this be revolutionary—which would naturally have given it leadership. The other Indonesian parties were not interested. So the PKI tried to win over their individual members, with as little success.

Manifestly, then, the policies advocated by the Comintern were inapplicable to Indonesian conditions. This followed from the very poor links between the Comintern and its 'Indonesian secton', the PKI. In truth, South-East Asia was always peripheral to Russian interests; their concern was much more with first the west and then their eastern neighbour, China.

Despite the Comintern desire to see the Sarekat Rakyat maintained in being, it is revealing that the Peasant International, the *Krestintern*, was established in Moscow only in Autumn 1923 and then paid little attention to Asia. The fact is that not only were Comintern, Profintern and Krestintern primarily interested in prosecuting the aims of Russian foreign policy, but even in this they were stultified by the conflict then raging between Stalin and Trotsky. Moscow, i.e. Stalin, feared that to establish Asian centres of the international organisations would simply help the left opposition, i.e. Trotsky.

Sneevliet, alias Maring, who was sent in 1921 to be the first director of the Comintern's south China office at Shanghai, of course had a personal interest in the Indies. But in January 1923 he was moved to the Vladivostok office and at the end of the year he resigned, returning to Moscow. This left only Tan Malaka, poorly and with an ambiguous role, in Manila, and Semaun in Amsterdam, as the only Comintern officials in personal contact with the PKI.

In fact the major (but still very defective) link between the party and the Comintern was provided by the Communist Party of Holland. Its interest was first aroused on Sneevliet's return to the Netherlands in 1919, and quickened when Darsono attended its 1921 conference. His visit produced a message of sympathy to the PKI, the inclusion of the 'Liberation of Indonesia' on the party's programme, and a campaign to have the Netherlands Indies' government's 'extraordinary rights' abolished—they were the principal inhibitors of PKI growth.

The Dutch party, seeing itself as guide, counsellor and friend to the PKI, suggested that the latter establish a branch in Holland (which old Indies' hands among the Dutch communists would have joined). But the PKI, while welcoming the efforts of the CPH, had no desire to be led by its members; indeed Semaun accused them of racism.

So nothing came of the suggestion. In consequence the Dutch party depended for its information on expellees' memories of the situation, which of course gave an out-of-date and often misleading picture.

Semaun's opinions on PKI activities usually paralleled those of the Comintern, indicating perhaps that he too had lost touch with the situation in the Indies. This was not particularly his fault; he had suggested to both the CPH and the Comintern that PKI foreign headquarters (i.e. himself) be moved from Amsterdam to somewhere in the far-east, Singapore for example. The Comintern turned a deaf ear to the suggestion, however. Russia was then trying to achieve friendly relations with the west and did not wish to send new agitators to the eastern colonies, least of all Singapore. And just as important, with the Stalin-Trotsky feud then near its climax, it did not want Semaun, who was too independent for its liking, out of reach.

In brief, therefore, the PKI's links with the Comintern were so weak as to be useless. That body's advice, while reflecting the desiderata of Russian foreign policy, bore little if any relation to the problems facing the party. On the other side, because of the lack of a chain of communication, the Comintern was unable to intervene effectively in the Indies. Though nominally a 'section' of the Comintern, the party was in fact virtually autonomous. And, indeed, there was little to compel it to heed Comintern advice. It certainly received some money from one or other communist international organisation but it was not dependent on it. And when it came to the crunch, as we shall see, the Comintern proved unreliable.

On to Disaster

It is possible, though not certain, that more substantial Comintern intervention might have halted the PKI's head-long rush to destruction. Far from uniting all the disaffected under its wing, the party's methods of recruitment, including boycotts, threats and terrorism, had set up their own inevitable reaction. Beginning in the west of Java, anti-communist mutual aid associations, known as the *Sarekat Hidjau* (Green Association), spread over the island. They broke up meetings of the PKI and SR, destroyed communist property, maltreated party adherents, disrupted SR schools, and even sometimes drove PKI followers out of their villages. It seems probable that these Sarekat Hidjau were aided and abetted by members of the Javanese bureaucracy; what is known is that many members of this organisation had previously been press-ganged into the SR. Nor can it be assumed that they were opposed to the PKI on ideological grounds; they also attacked the Sarekat Islam. Indeed, the other Indonesian political parties condemned them as 'fascist'. It is doubtful if they had even that ideology. They probably were groupings of bandits, ever-present in Java, somewhat melodramatised in Javanese tradition, who in the general atmosphere of tension and defiance of authority cultivated by the PKI and SR found in attacking these organisations a new socially approved outlet for their energies.

To counter government opposition, the PKI in February 1925 decided to abandon altogether large public meetings and hold only small closed ones. The next month a conference of PKI leaders at Batavia applied the December 1924 decision and instructed party branches to form ten-man groups and to reorganise party activities on a cell basis. These were intended to subvert non-communist groups (the 'united front from below'). The conference also took a decision which was disastrous in its consequences. This was that outlaws were to be encouraged, in that they were opposed to authority; in particular, Sarekat Hidjau members were if possible to be cultivated and brought into the party. But this meant, of course, that the decisions of the December 1924 conference to concentrate on the urban workers were effectively abandoned; rural agitation was to continue as previously, with a dash of terrorism for good measure. Accordingly, communist

activity in the countryside increased in 1925 and 1926.
PKI propagandists offered to achieve every group's ambitions, no matter how opposed. To the poor they promised
wealth, to the rich they offered freedom from taxes. The
word was spread that rebellion was imminent, that foreign
liberators (Turks, Arabs, Japanese, Russians, Chinese) were
on their way, and that those who did not leap on the
bandwagon would be crushed beneath its wheels. Membership of both the PKI and SR was sold; so that membership figures represented insurance premiums paid rather
than converts gained. The only organisational principle
followed was the age-old one of personal leadership.

In June 1925 the party leaders decided that the constituent groups were to be composed of five men, not ten,
as part of a reorganisation of the party. Specific plans
were also laid for the revolt. There were to be strikes
where the PKI was strongest, namely the railways and
harbours, culminating in a general strike. How realistic
these schemes were is open to doubt. For the PKI had
made no secret of its decision of the preceding December
to seize power, and the authorities had intensified their
vigilance. In consequence, membership fees were declining,
contact between headquarters and the branches was weak,
the decisions of the December 1924 congress had not been
implemented, and all schemes for ten- or five-man cells
remained on paper only. But the point of no return had
been passed. The urban workers had been so agitated by
the PKI that they demanded that the communist-led unions
do something; to retain their credibility and their leadership the communists had to respond and in July a number
of PKI unions in Semarang staged major strikes.

That month, however, the government tightened the
screw still further when a governor general's conference
formulated a plan to curb the party. On 5 August the PKI
told its branches that 'world revolution' had been delayed
for a while by the stabilisation of the 'capitalist forces', and
that consequently the party should adopt tactics which recognised that circumstances were not favourable to revolu-

tion. But these were words on the wind; that very day the communist unions decided to convert their strikes into a general one. The government put its plan into effect and simply suspended the right of assembly. The unions were unable to plan the general strike and each was left to decide its own role. The result was predictable. The strike was broken, the strikers lost their jobs, and the unions disintegrated. Several leaders of the PKI were arrested. Alimin, the 'planner' of the revolt, took refuge in Singapore, where the PKI had opened an office earlier in the year, then went to Canton and eventually to join Tan Malaka in Manila. More positively, the government set up Dutch schools to draw children away from Malaka's creations. (An incidental ban on state employees buying communist journals as part of their duties brought the PKI daily, *Api*, close to bankruptcy!)

Playing Revolutionaries

The alternatives for the PKI were clearly closing; they had either to desist from agitating for revolution, or to rebel. To meet the expectations of their followers, the PKI leaders took the latter course. They might perhaps have been more successful had they been able to rely on a disciplined body of adherents. Instead, their local leaders ignored orders from headquarters and indulged in violence whenever they felt the occasion demanded it.

The failed strike in Semarang was followed by an even more disastrous one in Surabaya. This city, the most industrial in the Indies, harboured most of the communist unions. Following Marxist 'theory', the PKI had great expectations of its 'revolutionary' future. Unfortunately, it could not control the workers. A machinist's strike, intended to set off a general insurrection, broke out prematurely in September and continued until December, when it was finally suppressed by the police. (The PKI's image was not embellished when the Surabaya representative to the central executive of the party, one Sutigno, made

off with the strike funds!) Simultaneous strikes had been
organised in Batavia and Medan (North Sumatra) but
achieved no greater success. Those who suffered were the
ordinary union members. Employers blacklisted all workers
suspected of communism; often literacy was taken as sufficient evidence. The government shortly released all those it
imprisoned but then denied the right of assembly to all
communist organisations and the PKI was left with no recourse but to go underground.

On 25 December both the PKI and its trade union arm,
the VSTP, held important meetings, the one at Prambanan,
the other not far away at Surakarta, both in Central Java.
Final plans were drawn up for an insurrection. It was to begin in six months' time with strikes, and to culminate in
armed violence. Attempts were to be made to draw peasants
and soldiers in on the communist side. The PKI was to keep
hidden its hand in the strikes, which outwardly were to demand a general wage increase and express popular grievances. If they received much support, the PKI would then
launch its revolt, first in Padang (Central Sumatra) to
draw off Dutch troops from Java, then in Java itself. If they
did not, more preparations were to be made, and more
strikes, until the time was ripe. For its part, the VSTP decided to launch in May 1926 the rail strike which would
lead to revolution and to conduct a referendum on the strike
among its branches. All preparations for the revolt were to
be the responsibility of a Double or Dictatorial Organisation, which was to be the real, highly disciplined, party
leadership.

All this sounded very methodical and very brave. But the
party leaders knew, perhaps better than anyone else, that
their chances of success were slight in the extreme. Having
had two disastrous strike failures, they would have been singularly foolish to believe that their chances had now improved, with the right of assembly denied to them and with
most of their experienced leaders absent. Unable to accept
either passivity or defeat, they took refuge in the belief that
they would receive decisive help from abroad. As mentioned

above, the belief that foreign liberators would be imminently arriving to expel the Dutch had been sedulously cultivated in the countryside. The party leaders' own belief in the possibility of help from abroad was much encouraged by the very improbability of success through their own efforts. So they decided to appeal to Moscow for help and delegated as courier Alimin, the chief proponent of revolution.

At the end of 1925, however, the government cracked down. It banished three of the PKI's senior leaders. One, Darsono, was permitted to exile himself to Russia, the other two were sent to Western New Guinea, where they lived out their lives. Many others escaped the police and took refuge in Singapore, where they conferred and reasserted the decision to revolt. They despatched Alimin to the ailing Malaka in Manila to solicit Comintern assistance.

Malaka was aghast at what he considered the PKI's fool-hardy plans and firmly discouraged them. Alimin returned to Singapore but did not pass on Tan Malaka's views to the *émigré* leaders. They decided to appeal to Moscow direct themselves and to send Alimin and Musso there. If the International backed them, they would delay the revolt until support arrived; otherwise the PKI would engage in guerrilla and terrorist actions on its own. In other words, if they did not get the support they needed for a successful revolt they would launch one that was doomed.

Meanwhile, back in Java a meeting of party leaders at Batavia on 13 January 1926 affirmed that legal political activity was no longer possible, and followed this by the *non sequitur* that revolution was the only hope. They then proceeded to divide party members into soldiers, spies and propagandists, the aim being both to prepare for revolt and also to give members the feeling that they were involved; it was hoped this would encourage them to keep on paying their faltering dues.

Since 1 May was Labour Day, everybody, including the government, expected the PKI then to put into effect its threat to revolt. The party executive, wisely, decided not to have its activities determined by accidents of the calendar and instructed its branches not to celebrate May Day so as to avoid arrests. This did not save it much. The government strengthened the criminal code, with the effect that the revolutionary press ceased to publish and the PKI and the SR were formally disbanded. In the major cities of Java the PKI had been emasculated. Even the VSTP, the only PKI-led union still in existence, was rapidly disintegrating; all other unions were in a state of collapse.

In the general disorganisation, the PKI headquarters lost control over its branches, a process legitimised by the resolution on 'federative centralism' taken in December 1924. In some regions secret terrorist organisations were set up locally; there were sporadic incidents of violence and local party leaders were arrested. The police were dominant everywhere and to escape supervision in May the PKI moved its headquarters from Batavia to Bandung, some seventy-five miles to the south-east in the hills of West Java. There it finally set up its Dictatorial Organisation; but this was never important.

Retreat and Rout

Across the Java Sea, Malaka, doubting Alimin's trustworthiness, had hastened to Singapore as soon as his health allowed, and found his fears confirmed. He had thereupon called the party leaders to Singapore; and they had sent the vice chairman, Suprodjo. He arrived back in June, just when, at a headquarters conference, the branches had been unanimous in demanding an uprising in the near future though leaving for a few months the decision on the exact date. There was not to be such general agreement again. For when Suprodjo had conveyed Malaka's views the party chairman, Sardjono, had difficulty in preventing a rescinding of the Prambanan decision to revolt. Suprodjo then toured the branches in Java presenting Malaka's arguments; gradually they gained acceptance. At discussions in July between leaders of the party, once again it was decided not to set a deadline. The executive went further the next month when it finally agreed with Malaka that an uprising was not timely. He, however, insisted that the Prambanan decision to revolt be rescinded altogether. The executive began to go into reverse. It sent messengers to all its branches to review the situation and to discuss Malaka's proposals, warning that no action was to be taken to start an uprising and intimating that 'federative centralism' was to be abandoned.

But there was no longer a 'party' in any meaningful sense, for the headquarters was unable to prevent any branch taking action and involving other branches with it. In other words it could not stop the tail wagging the dog. Disintegration did not stop there, however; the branches themselves were incapable of ensuring that they followed their own decisions. This was well illustrated at Tegal, on the north coast of Java, a traditionally fanatical Muslim area. The PKI branch there was determined to launch a revolt, which simply meant murdering all Europeans and government officials. Despite a poll among branches which opposed independent action, after much bargaining the party executive and other branches on the north coast reluctantly agreed that they would neither support nor oppose Tegal, but that if it went it alone they would help in the ensuing struggle. This rather contradictory position was happily not supported by Tegal's organisational ability. Having arranged for a disturbance on 28 September, the signal that was to set it off was mistakenly given only the next day, when the rioters had dispersed!

The Batavia branch went further; it secretly set up a rival 'headquarters' for the party. It had been preaching imminent revolution for so long that when this did not materialise the party's followers began to turn on the communists who they felt had duped them. So to provide some interest the branch sponsored a few bomb-throwings. At the same time, the vice chairman, Sukrawinata, drew up his own plan for revolt and formed a 'Committee of the Revolution' which the next month, in September 1926, grew into a 'Committee of Supporters of the Indonesian Republic', with participation from members in Java and Sumatra. At the end of October this committee decided to revolt on 12 November; and on 8 November the VSTP leaders reluctantly agreed to strike in support on 13 November.

All these goings-on, of course, were kept secret from the headquarters at Bandung, but as is clear this was only nominally in charge. In addition to the Batavia committee there was also Malaka's group in Singapore, which was achieving success in converting the Bandung headquarters to its view. In the event, what passed for a revolt was in fact set off not by the official headquarters but by the Batavia bravoes.

But however much Bandung was in the dark, the authorities were not. Their informants had already provided them with the main outlines of the situation. If anything, it would seem that they did not take the preparations for the revolt with the seriousness which the communists would have felt was their due. Nevertheless, the government reaction was effective enough.

On 7 November, when a coded telegram was sent from the Batavia group to Pekalongan on the north coast of Java giving the date of the uprising, it was of course intercepted and, in the leisurely fashion salutary in the tropics, brought to the attention of the resident (the senior Dutch local government official). He promptly warned his superiors in Batavia and ordered the arrest of the communist leaders in his residency. There was no uprising in Pekalongan.

Nor was there any trouble elsewhere in Central Java, as the police there discovered the instructions for the rebellion and arrested all the communist leaders. The peace was broken only by a few brawls here and there, in Surakarta led by union members. In Batavia itself, though trouble was expected, the European and Indonesian administrators did not concert their actions sufficiently to prevent the outbreak. The rebels attacked policemen, nightwatchmen, and a prison, and seized the telephone exchange. Mobs three hundred strong roamed abroad in the suburbs, fought with police patrols and with passers-by for good measure, raised a few fires, and invaded a small police barracks. Needless to say, nothing was achieved by this; by morning life was back to normal.

Only in the west of Java, in Bantam and the highland area of the Priangan, did matters take a more serious turn. In Bantam, a prosperous, fanatic and anarchic area, the revolt assumed the appropriate garb of a holy war, one however fought only with knives, cutlasses, a few guns, and of course charms to ward off *kafir* (unbeliever) bullets. Only in the Priangan was a professional touch seen. Here communication lines were sabotaged, and armed groups assaulted village heads, police and lower officials and set fire to official buildings. But this too was of no avail.

The structure of the Indies government could not be said to have been much affected by the trouble in Java, the only European killed being a Dutch railway official. The revolt had been suppressed largely by the senior local government officials, the residents. Only on 17 November, when the uprising had been not so much crushed as waved away, did the attorney general order the arrest of all persons known to be communists. Large numbers of people were then detained and the PKI and its associates ceased to exist.

Paradoxically, only when all hope was lost did the communists in the Minangkabau area on the island of Sumatra decide to rebel. There was much disagreement on the date, while the leaders were picked up and detained by the police. Finally local branches settled on 1 January, mainly, it would appear, to put an end to the talk. Fighting spread rapidly, the rebels were better armed, and the fighting was heavier than on Java. Even so, the authorities obtained the upper hand by 4 January and the rebellion had collapsed by the 12th.

All in all, the government arrested some thirteen thousand, shot those responsible for murder, and put five thousand in preventive detention, of whom all but five hundred were sentenced to prison. Also, 1,308 detainees, who could not be charged under existing laws but whom the government held responsible for the outbreak, were sentenced to exile in Western New Guinea. None escaped and very few survived to take part in political activity after Indonesian independence.

Having been duped by the communists, who had so easily been slapped down by the authorities, the ordinary Indonesian decided to abstain from politics. Only Japan's victory over the allies, and the consequent encouragement the conquerors gave to Indonesian nationalism, brought him back.

Apathetic Ally

Meanwhile, Alimin and Musso's mission to the Comintern proved as irrelevant as that body's subsequent pronouncements on the Indonesian revolt. They arrived in Moscow in June 1926, and were taken before the executive committee together with Semaun who had come from Amsterdam, and Darsono, newly exiled from the Indies. Both then, and three months later when they saw the committee again, this time with Stalin present, they were told substantially the same thing. The world was too prosperous for revolutions and in any case Stalin was against disorganised attempts which were unlikely to succeed.

The two delegates returned to South-East Asia in leisurely fashion; there was no point in arriving in the Indies until after the success of the revolt, news of which reached them on their way. On 18 December 1926, well after the rising on Java had subsided, they were arrested in Johore with two and a half thousand dollars in American banknotes on them; it would appear to have been all the help the Comintern gave.

For the International's concern with the Indies was, as ever, dependent on more important Russian interests. The most pressing at the time was still the feud between Stalin and Trotsky. The latter had opposed Stalin's support of the Kuo Min Tang in China, and he seemed to be proved right when Chiang Kai-shek began turning against his communist allies (who formed a 'bloc within'). The Comintern decided on the one hand to continue its support for Chiang, hoping that though he might massacre the Chinese communists he would still maintain an alliance with Russia; on the other it prepared itself to oppose Chiang if necessary by claiming that a 'new revolutionary wave' was rising in the east. There was no evidence whatever to support this idea until, Marx be praised, the Javanese revolt broke out just before the Comintern's seventh plenary session. The Comintern professed to see this damp squib as a major conflagration; even poor Semaun declared that the revolt was a 'real civil war' (then hurried to Amsterdam to hand over control of the Indonesian revolutionary movement to the Indonesian student association in Holland, the *Perhimpunan Indonesia*; he was evidently not deceived by his own oratory). The Comintern went through all the proper motions; the Profintern on 25 November and 23 December, well after the revolts had fizzled out, called for support for them. But this make-believe did not save the Comintern's China policy; it was discredited by the Chiang Kai-shek coup which destroyed the Chinese Communist Party. By 1927 the International was reduced to arguing that the rebellion should have been better prepared. The following year, Alimin, who with Musso had shuttled back to Moscow after being expelled from Singapore, berated the Comintern for not giving the revolt enough support. This no doubt helped to explain the failure of his plan; it must however be doubted whether any help from abroad, short of a full-scale invasion, would have led the rag-tag-and-bobtail uprising to achieve any success whatever.

7
Communist Attractions

Leaders

The natural break in the narrative imposed by the destruction of the PKI in 1926 permits us to consider in greater detail its members and supporters. We remember that at the time the Indonesian societies, and particularly the Javanese, were in a state of disruption in consequence, largely, of the Netherlands Indies government's steps towards their modernisation. It was therefore inevitable that many people should be uprooted from their traditional groups and seek social support in new associations.

This general condition, however, does not by itself account for the recruitment specifically into the PKI. As we have noted, many other associations, and especially the Sarekat Islam, also arose about this time, no doubt in their own way responding to the needs of some at least of the estranged. We also know that for a long time many of them belonged to both the Sarekat and the PKI. If we are to discover the latter's peculiar attractions it may be helpful to discuss the characteristics of its members and the circumstances surrounding their adhesion to the party.

We may consider first the leaders, about whom a certain amount of biographical detail is available. In the period up to the revolt of 1926 the most prominent were Semaun, Alimin, Musso, Darsono and Tan Malaka.

Semaun was the son of a minor railway employee. He was born in 1899 near Surabaya and in due course followed in his father's footsteps. In 1914 he joined the Surabaya branch of the Sarekat Islam and soon got the job of secretary. Union work on the railways brought him to public notice as one of the Indies' first labour agitators. In the course of his work he met Sneevliet, then at the beginning of his work with the vstp, and consequently in 1915 joined the isdv as well. Here too he was quickly promoted and in 1916 became vice chairman of the Surabaya branch. That same year he was transferred by his employers from Surabaya to Semarang; he thus moved from the zone of influence of the Central Sarekat Islam to that of Sneevliet and his isdv and vstp. The Semarang branch of the si was radical and well organised; Semaun's arrival was profitable to both, enhancing his status and increasing its size, so that it began to rival the Surabaya headquarters. He rapidly acquired the reputation of the Indonesian best grounded in Leninist theory, and published an article on 'Communism in Indonesia' in the organ of the Comintern, *Communist International*, in the early 1920s. After his expulsion from Indonesia he is said to have gone to Paris and taught at the Sorbonne where he was awarded the degree of Doctor of Philosophy about 1924.

The principal instigator of the 1926 revolt, Alimin, was born in 1889 of the lesser nobility, as indicated by his title of *Mas*. He was fortunate enough to become, at the age of nine, the foster son of a Dutch official, G. A. J. Hazeu, who later became adviser for native affairs. Alimin was thus able to attend European schools in Batavia and acquired fluency in French, English and Dutch. His foster-father intended him for the Civil Service but Alimin opted for politics and journalism. He joined both Sarekat Islam and Insulinde, and organised various unions. For a time he worked for Mitsui, the Japanese firm, in Batavia; he was dismissed apparently at the insistence of the Indies government. He then joined the isdv, and in due course moved entirely into the pki orbit.

Musso was born in 1897 in Central Java, made his way up the educational ladder and attended secondary and teacher training schools in Batavia. He acquired Alimin's friendship, and became a protégé first of Hazeu and then of another Dutchman, the educator and reformer van Hinloopen Labberton. Like Alimin, he belonged to several associations—Insulinde, Sarekat Islam and the ISDV—and if anything was considered to be somewhat conservative. Harsh treatment in prison, however, followed by his rejection as a teacher of Indonesian languages by the Japanese government, probably because of his political record, turned him to revolutionary activity.

Darsono was also born in 1897, his title of *Raden* indicating his nobility. The son of a police official in Pati, he acquired a European-style primary education, attended the School of Agriculture in Sukabumi (West Java), and later taught agriculture in Bodjonegoro (East Java). He drifted to Semarang, attended Sneevliet's trial, and became so entranced with the accused's Marxist message that he was converted on the spot. This revealed the predominant trait in his character: he was a thorough intellectual in the unfortunate sense that his contact with reality was somewhat tenuous; indeed he acquired a reputation for having difficulty in adapting his Marxism to Indonesian conditions, a problem which would not perhaps have bothered Lenin, a man of quite another cast. Darsono was yet another uprooted intellectual, whose primary bonds had been considerably weakened by the social mobility involved in his education and for whom all-embracing verbal formulae such as are represented by Marxism represented a fatal attraction.

Tan Malaka, perhaps the best-known Indonesian communist, was born between 1893 and 1897 in the Minangkabau area of Central Sumatra. His family were considered gentry, his father was head of his village, and he too was one of the favoured few who enjoyed European-style schooling. He attended a teacher training school in Bukit Tinggi, and the Dutch assistant director persuaded the leading families of Malaka's home town to finance his further education in Holland. There, however, fog and flesh-pots conspired to give him a poor academic record. He did,

however, develop an enthusiasm for authoritarianism and its
obverse, revolution, but remained uncommitted until his return to Indonesia at the end of 1919. He found himself
compelled to earn a living by teaching the workers on a
Sumatran rubber estate, and little more than a year of this
decided him to enter politics and move to Java. At the
March 1921 PKI congress his knowledge of Marxism impressed Semaun, who invited him to establish a school at
Semarang. This was immediately successful, branches were
established in other cities, and Malaka became known as a
political figure. By publishing a book on parliamentary and
soviet government, favouring the latter, he also established
himself as a theoretician.

Certain points of interest emerge from the above. First,
none of these leaders could be considered as belonging to
the poor peasantry; all were in fortunate circumstances
coming from families with privileged status in their society.
It was this that directly or indirectly provided them with
their relatively high level of education. For at the time that
they were of school age, the 'first class native schools' initiated in 1893 were largely restricted to children of the
nobility; and without attendance at these schools they would
have been unable to acquire western lore including of
course Marxism. It is ironic that three of these five leaders
(Alimin, Musso, Tan Malaka) owed their educational promotion to Dutchmen who took a personal interest in them.

Despite their initial advantages, however, none of these
men had achieved the highest status. The stereotype, not
altogether incorrect, of the Indonesian political leader is of
a doctor or a lawyer. No communist leader in Indonesia
has been in this category. Those we have been considering
did not compare in this respect with, say, Dr Tjipto
Mangunkusumo of the Indisch Partij, a physician who had
been decorated for his services. The highest academic qual-
ification, indeed, seems to have been held by Darsono, but it
was in the poorly esteemed field of agriculture, not in law or
medicine.

It is also evident that, except in the case of Darsono, there
was neither blinding flash of light nor long-sought vocation;
these were no Indonesian Sneevliets. Typically the individ-

ual moved gradually through many changes of course, in response to personal circumstances, before finally entering the ISDV or PKI. Semaun joined Sneevliet only after he had begun his career as labour agitator (which had been a natural extension of his filial occupation); Alimin opted for the ISDV only after the government had secured his dismissal from Mitsui; and Musso turned to revolution only when the Japanese government rejected him as a teacher of languages.

The PKI and its associated organisations offered positions as school teachers, propagandists, and party, union and Sarekat Rakyat officials. These were badly paid but offered status higher than the village occupations. It may not be too fanciful to think that for those involved the movement represented primarily the most esteemed occupation open to them personally rather than a band of believers to whom they were irresistibly drawn. It was not so much a calling as a career.

Another attraction of the PKI was that it could look after its own. The leader of the Surabaya Red SI/Sarekat Rakyat, by name Prawirosardjono, explained to the CSI congress in August 1924 why he had chosen to exchange his allegiance to the Sarekat Islam for loyalty to the PKI. After emerging from detention for a political offence, he had needed money. The Sarekat had been unable to help, so he had gone to the PKI.

The PKI's peculiar distinctions perhaps emerge from the above. More intransigent than the nationalist organisations, it attracted the embittered. In addition, the party was stabler and better organised, and so able to offer greater support to those opposed to government.

Followers

In no organisation would one expect the rank and file to be of a higher socio-economic status than the leaders, and so it proves for the PKI at this period. A survey of the thousand people interviewed after the collapse of the 1926 revolt[1] is of great value in this connection.

[1] Mansvelt, 1928: 221–2.

First, it is important to place the interviewees in the organisation. Only 601 persons chose to answer questions on this score; even so, their answers should be taken with several grains of salt, as naturally they would not wish to incriminate themselves more than necessary. Between them these 601 people claimed to have held 747 positions, as some had two or more. These offices were:

Central administration	4
Terrorist leaders	4
Officials of the PKI	71
Officials of Sarekat Rakyat	53
Officials of labour unions	44
Members of the PKI	249
Members of Sarekat Rakyat	216
Members of labour unions	45
Propagandists	61

Whatever qualifications may therefore have to be made, it is probable that the thousand respondents were, for the most part, ordinary members of the PKI and its associate, the Sarekat Rakyat.

What was their level of education? Some 761 people of the thousand were literate, but only one had successfully completed secondary education. Their academic attainments are summarised below:

	ATTENDED	GRADUATED
University	—	—
Secondary schools	24	1
Vocational education	97	37
Primary education		
Primary only	640	396
Muslim religious	—	45
Village schools	40(?)	—
Second-class native	400+	250+
Dutch-native	128	67
European primary	32	10

Properly to assess these figures, it should be noted that only the secondary and Dutch-native primary schools of fered qualifications which gave access to western-type employment; and there are only sixty-eight of their graduates in this group. At the other end of the scale, only forty had attended village schools. This places the majority firmly in the category of the semi-westernised; there were few non-westernised, even fewer thoroughly westernised. Indeed, the largest single category was of those who had attended the second-class native schools, which provided some western education but did not qualify for entry into western schools. They gave their pupils sufficient westernisation to uproot them from native society but not enough to find a new home in the westernised sector of the Indies. It was only in 1921 that connecting schools (*Schakelschool*) were founded to permit students from the second-class schools to move into the westernised school system.

It should not be concluded, however, that all Indonesians so affected necessarily became communists. On the contrary; between 1914 and 1925 there were some twenty-three thousand graduates of Dutch-native or European primary schools, against only 77 among the 761 literate interviewees. And even the latter figure is a very small proportion of the seventy-nine thousand pupils attending Dutch-language primary schools in 1926. So clearly, while their dead-end educational experience may have been a predisposing circumstance it was by no means determining.

What had they done with their education? These respondents gave a list of some 1,907 occupations they had followed, or an average of about two per person. They were as follows:

Government service	518
Western industry and commerce	374
Native industry and commerce	858
Native society (teachers, journalists, etc.)	157
Unemployed for some time	108

Given the education of this group, one can be fairly sure that employment in native society was a *pis aller*, to be accepted only when government or other western jobs were denied. Equally with the 'unemployed'. This is not a category relevant to peasant societies such as the Indonesian;

it can only mean unemployed in the western sector. So less than half the jobs held by this group had used their western education, difficult to obtain though it had been.

There is no doubt that a too rapid dissemination of western education contributed to the creation of this pool of the unplaced. The desire for such schooling was widespread and growing; the capacity of the educational system was far below it. Nevertheless, around 1920 government service, the main employer of the educated, became more difficult to enter. As ever, the increased number of primary school graduates cheapened their qualifications; they were now no longer enough for entry into the lower ranks of the Civil Service. And even for those sufficiently qualified the outlook was bleak: government economies had reduced the intake.

Given both the widespread demand for education and the surplus of educated, it was inspired entrepreneurship on Semaun's part that suggested the creation of SR schools, which became Tan Malaka's special charge and raised him to prominence. These schools provided not only funds for the PKI but also jobs to attract supporters and party workers, as well as a means of spreading the Leninist message. They also produced even more educated unemployed who would gravitate towards the PKI. For the positions offered by the movement were a great attraction to those whose qualifications were not enough to permit them to enter the western sphere but who could not return to the native.

It is possible that some if not indeed several leaders as well as ordinary members had an ability above that of their educational qualifications and found that only party work gave scope to their talents. This should not be taken as meaning that PKI membership indicated a higher ability than average; we have no way of comparing the few in the party with the many outside who had identical educational qualifications. All that can be said is that perhaps some individuals whose ability was not adequately reflected in their educational qualifications found scope in the PKI; others, in like situation, found other outlets for their energies.

Finding Agitators

The growth of the PKI, either in its stronghold of Java or in the other islands, depended on the pool of socially un-placed, among whom it found its leaders, not on the masses of illiterate uprooted. In the towns and cities, such PKI-inclined agitators of course were found and cultivated in the labour unions (especially the VSTP); they included clerks, literate foremen and skilled workers as well as the semi-educated unemployed.

The picture was different in the rural areas and their ur-ban centres. Here leaders were sought among those some-what raised from the masses of peasantry and who felt dis-contented with the many changes occurring. Such were traders, cash-crop farmers, better-off villagers, religious teachers, local notables and officials. The method of leader-ship selection may be called that of notoriety; once an in-dividual had become involved in PKI activity at an early age he acquired a radical reputation which he could not dis-card.

Leaders were so scarce, and so sure of their followings, that the PKI, like every other political grouping in the coun-try, could not hope to impose discipline on them and devia-tions had to be tolerated. But the agitators were equally well aware that their followers wanted results. Hence whatever patient strategy Semaun and Darsono might envisage was quite out of tune with their supporters, who wanted Utopia now. This dilemma between discipline and a small party or a large party and indiscipline has continually dogged the PKI. Unfortunately for its survival, it has usually favoured popularity, with the consequence of indiscipline and disaster.

Ethnic Allegiances

For reasons no doubt embedded deep in social structure and culture, the PKI has always found its greatest response among the Javanese. In the period up to 1926 its base was the Rail-

way and Tram Workers' Union, the VSTP of Semarang, and
its influence followed the railway lines across Central Java.
After the section B affair it spread to the Sundanese of
West Java, and in the island as a whole its influence was
no longer limited to the urbanised but took advantage of
rural discontent as well.

In the early 1920s, too, it began to sprout branches outside Java, usually founded by members who had been to
that island. Indonesia being a sort of social confederation
of ethno-linguistic groups, the PKI branches were similarly
based. In many instances they were started by Javanese residents in the Outer Islands; such was the branch in the
Moluccas, in fact the first outside Java, founded in 1919.
But of course it was in Sumatra, then being rapidly opened
up to development, with consequent social disruption, that
the PKI was strongest outside Java.

However, there was a most important distinction between
Java and the Outer Islands. By and large, the administrators in Java tolerated the existence of the party; their
counterparts elsewhere did not. It was their habit to remove the PKI leaders; when this occurred, the party collapsed. It is of interest that the branch which survived this
treatment best was the Javanese based at Ternate. It, too,
collapsed in 1922 when its leaders were arrested but revived on their release. Elsewhere among the non-Javanese
peoples PKI influence was much more ephemeral.

Minimum Programmes

The general Indonesian intellectual climate was of course
very much in the PKI's favour. Many of its catchwords were
already in common use. 'Imperialism' was an everyday term,
and many newspapers adopted an 'anti-imperialist' stand;
given their Indonesian readership they could hardly do otherwise. Capitalism was taken as a synonym for colonialism;
the capitalists were the Dutch and therefore responsible for
the misfortunes from which Indonesians were suffering.
Muslims had always looked abroad for help against the

Europeans; in similar fashion, the PKI declared that their foreign friends would liberate Indonesia. Nor was this insincere; as we have noted above, the party's chief propagandist, Darsono, thought that independence would be the fruit of the efforts of Dutch communists.

However, when it came to more specific appeals, then it was the Leninist 'minimum programme' that was followed rather than Marxism. We have mentioned above the latter's dramatic script, with the 'workers' as the central actor and the 'revolution' as the great convulsion which would usher in Utopia in the shape of the dictatorship of 'the proletariat', i.e. the Communist Party. But this was a message tailored for the European intelligentsia of the nineteenth century; something else was required for Indonesians. And the PKI proved particularly adept at dyeing its coat according to the colour of its audience. We noted above how, in its message to the branches outside Java in 1920, the party insisted on the proletarian purity of membership. In practice, however, the party cultivated all levels of society: it had absorbed well Lenin's injunction to exploit local grievances. And while these differed in detail, they all represented essentially a resistance to change.

There were already signs of this conservatism before the emergence of the PKI. We already know the Saminists as a group who totally withdrew from the then modern dispensation and sought an idyllic past. As part of their rejection of state intervention, they refused to pay taxes. This agreed very well with one of the PKI slogans, and in the parts of Java where Saminism was strongest a mystical synthesis between it and communism emerged in 1924 in the shape of a Sarekat Rakyat. No closer union between the two movements occurred but the party was to prove adept at exploiting the sentiment expressed in Saminism.

The party's message, designed to harness in its cause this resentment at change, was not particularly Marxist. Thus, though the Father of the Faith had maintained that capitalism was an advance on feudalism, the PKI told the Javanese that capitalism was responsible for the worsening of their condition from the idyllic and feudal past. The revolution would not necessarily mean an armed struggle, but the coming of the *Ratu Adil*, or Just King, of Javanese folk myth. He would bring in a new era of freedom called communism; this was not a dictatorship of the proletariat but a classless society based on voluntary mutual aid!

A detailed study of the 'minimum programme' approach is provided by the report of the government committee of enquiry into PKI activities in the Minangkabau area of West Sumatra, where some of the most serious outbreaks of fighting occurred in early 1927. The area offered the PKI a fertile field. To begin with, it was in process of rapid modernisation; not very long before, it had been a sub-sistence economy with property communally owned by ma-trilineal extended families. The introduction of money and cash crops had brought about a rapid, if uneven, change in the social structure. Traditional customary law became in-creasingly honoured more in the breach than in the observ-ance. Undivided family property was being dispersed and in consequence economic differentiation was increasing. Mod-ern thought, introduced either through the schools or via Islamic Modernism from Mecca, gave rise to conflict be-tween the educated young and the traditional chiefs (*peng-hulu*). The position of the latter was therefore being eroded by many influences; it was further weakened by more intensive government administration, which put re-straints on the chiefs' customary powers and often removed them for all-too-frequent corruption.

These changes were largely the result of government de-cisions which had opened up the Minangkabau area to modern commerce. But the administration would not accept the consequences and was determined to keep the social structure unaltered. In particular, this involved supporting the native chiefs since these were its instruments of rule; unfortunately, the frequent government interventions hardly contributed to this end. The favourite method for shoring up the position of the *penghulu* was intimidation of all who wished for change, but the policy had also been pursued of reducing the available armed forces, so there was nothing to back up the threats.

All deviation from tradition was prone to be identified as 'communist', and was thereby often made so. The policy of upholding the chiefs involved an antipathy to all religious teachers (a mistaken application of Snouck Hurgronje's ideas); in consequence, all objection to any government measure, such as taxation, found a religious teacher able to give it chapter and verse in justification. The religious Modernists, who as we remember had been in the forefront of the struggle against the communists in the sı, were even more distrusted by the administration, especially by the Indonesian officials, and so no advantage was taken of important religious teachers who were opposed to the PKI. Generally speaking, any who wished for change were labelled *'kaum muda'* (Modernists) and were accordingly suspect.

However, it was not only the chiefs and the religious teachers who were disgruntled. The educated, especially the young, felt their social position did not match their schooling, while the ordinary people felt themselves caught in a money economy to which they found difficulty in adjusting.

Nevertheless, the PKI only turned to plough these fertile fields in 1926. At the end of 1924 most of the 660 members recruited into the Sarekat Rakyat were ex-government employees, especially railway workers, dismissed in the economy drive, and small tradesmen. The Marxist prophecy of impoverishment seemed to fit their misfortunes very well, and they blamed their fate on capitalism, which was coming to mean government by unbelievers. But the revival of economic activity in 1925 weakened their convictions and by the end of the year the movement had petered out. Unfortunately, the ranks of the leaders had been increased by individuals sent back from other areas in Sumatra; their only source of livelihood was their PKI appointment. They naturally sought to justify their existence and turned to exploit all possible grievances. They themselves, it should be noted, had their own. Predominantly, they were products of the new money economy, petty traders, and resentful of the privileges accorded to the traditional chiefs.

So from the beginning of 1926 there was a renewal of activity in the island under the general direction of *Sutan* Said Áli. Little attention was paid either to Marxism or to regular payment of membership subscriptions. Instead, emphasis was first placed on the benefits of joining the PKI, such as mutual aid and the availability of loans. If this failed to convince, then the attention of the audience was directed to their resentments. To quote Said Ali's own words: 'When talking to peasants, you must discuss the pressure of taxation and corvée-labour [a form of taxation in work]; when you speak to workers, discuss their wages and their work; and to traders you must stress their profits and taxes. In short, all grievances of the population must be stressed.'

Those prepared to listen were told that all would come right with liberty (*kemerdekaan*), which was interpreted according to the needs of each group but often meant a return to the past, before capitalism had disturbed the ideal condition of things. So for some it meant a return to the historic, almost legendary glory, for others freedom from tutelage. Some saw it as the absence of statute labour and taxation; others as a freedom from social restrictions, while yet others took it to carry a possibility of revenge for what they considered injustice.

However, if the cultivation of resentment failed to have the desired harvest, then threats were used, in particular that of the *bekot,* or boycott. For example, once the rice traders had become adherents of the cause, they refused to supply this staple foodstuff to any not carrying a red card to show their PKI allegiance.

For the really hard cases who failed to be subverted even by threats, resort was had to terror. This was the responsibility of the 'Double or Dictatorial Organisation', which was in effect an anarchic organisation of criminals prepared to use violence and murder against government officials. However, the lack of success of the other methods used gave the upper hand to the violent and eventually the PKI came to rely almost exclusively on intimidation to obtain support. (The Dutch scholar Schrieke reminds us of Danton's apposite phrase: '*Dans les révolutions, l'autorité reste aux scélérats.*') But these bandits were neither disciplined nor popular and effectively ensured that the insurrection did not enjoy general support. The PKI died by the same sword on which it had come to depend.

Muslim Communists

Though the fight against the PKI in the Sarekat Islam had been led by the religious Modernists centred on Jogjakarta, not all fervent Muslims were opposed to communism. On the contrary, Islam provided of itself an easily exploitable argument for revolt, namely that Muslims ought not to be ruled by unbelievers. This of course was easily linked to the desire for a return to the *status quo* before the coming of the Dutch. Hence, since the PKI was striving to remove the Dutch, to many fanatics it appeared as a natural ally.

Two prominent Muslims who adopted the PKI's cause as their own may be mentioned. One was Hadji Batuah, a man of rank among the Minangkabau. He appears to have been converted to communism in 1923, after a trip round northern Sumatra, and began preaching an Islam much influenced by Leninism. Batuah was a man of considerable influence in consequence of being a teacher in an Islamic school system known as the Tawalib, which followed the principle that the teachers taught only the highest classes, while their pupils were in charge of the lower. His preachings bore fruit in the form of wild rumours of intended violence against Europeans. Happily, this quickly created a reaction among his fellow-Minangkabau, who buried their differences to join in opposing the communist programmes of non-cooperation with government. Batuah and an accomplice, by name Natar Zainuddin, were arrested shortly afterwards and subsequently banished. However, since many Tawalib graduates were unable to find employment during the depression, their teachings continued to favour communism and the PKI in the Minangkabau area retained a strong religious orientation.

The other example is Hadji Misbach, who was responsible for the development of Islamic communism in the Surakarta area of Central Java. In his case, the resistance to change as the motive force is very clear. As part of its social policy, the government imposed certain requirements in house construction and maintenance. Misbach refused to repair his house on the grounds that this was an invasion of privacy and eventually simply abandoned it. He first joined the Sarekat Islam, then Insulinde, in 1919 took part in an uprising in Surakarta, was twice imprisoned, and on his release in August 1922 resumed the leadership of two Muslim periodicals inclined to communism. At the 1923 SI congress, which imposed party discipline, he opted for the PKI. Eventually, after bomb-throwing incidents in Surakarta later that year, he was exiled to Western New Guinea. Islamic communism continued to be propagated in the Surakarta area by the *Mu'alimin* movement, which interpreted the Koran along Islamic communist lines and opposed government interference in Islamic affairs. Like other minor Islamic communist groups, its chief characteristic was opposition to Modernism. It was almost as if, sensing the threat from Modernist Islam (which had come to dominate the Sarekat Islam), these traditionally oriented Muslim groupings turned to communism for support. For them, too, communism was a means of retaining the *status quo ante*.

The most lethal combination of Islam and Leninism, however, occurred among the Bantamese of West Java, whose involvement with the 1926 revolt was analysed in depth by another commission of enquiry. Bantam proved a fertile field for communist endeavours, though contrary to wisdom still conventional at the time of writing the area boasted a flourishing economy (in fact, only in the poorest part did the PKI evoke little response), and few great extremes of wealth—if anything the region was comparatively egalitarian. Indeed, the former chairman of the PKI section in the chief town, Serang, when asked to list grievances, could only mention taxation and the cost of living, matters perhaps not peculiar to this area or, indeed, to the Indies.

The susceptibility of the Bantamese to communist blandishments lay more in social than in economic circumstances. The people form an enclave of Javanese origin among the Sundanese of West Java, but perhaps because of their migration do not have the firm village structure typical of the Javanese areas of the island. They were described as living together with no attachment to one another, under not heads but underpaid overseers, usually of doubtful character, corrupt and sometimes criminal. Matters had not been helped by an administrative amalgamation of villages, which had had the result that most villagers refused to acknowledge the authority of the head of the village to which they had been attached. Above the village level, the internal administration, here as elsewhere in the hands of the nobility, was notorious for both intrigue and corruption.

Altogether the structure of local government was in no fit state to cope with the population, who were distinguished by their religious fanaticism and therefore opposed to all foreign rule, and saw all administrators, whether European or Indonesian, as representatives of an infidel government.

Such an unintegrated society was wide open to subversion. The PKI propagandists quickly adapted themselves to Bantamese social structure, and abandoning all their paper concepts of 'five-man' or 'ten-man' units, sought to influence specific groups of prominent people, especially when they were linked by family ties. Marxist arguments were not deployed but rather each group was offered whatever it desired. And once leaders had been won over they brought their personal followings with them.

Given the fanatical character of the region, the PKI propagandists exerted themselves to persuade the Muslim dignitaries, whether teachers (*guru*) or holy men (*kyayi*), to declare a holy war against the Dutch. No attempt was made at a concordance between Marxism and the Koran. Such matters were of concern only to intellectuals and there

was not one among the rebels. In any case, there was no
need for such arguments; the anarchic and hostile spirit of
the fanatics needed no rational inducement to embrace the
PKI's cause.

What was required to convince the holy men was an as-
surance of victory, for without it a holy war may not be
declared. Accordingly, the PKI propagandists exerted themselves to show that their movement was powerful and in-
vincible. Its success was to be guaranteed by foreign help;
only here it would come not from Russia or China, as
argued in other parts of Java, but from Mustafa Kemal of
Turkey! Such arguments were often persuasive, and the
kyayi then declared a holy war to their followers. These in
turn were enticed with the prospects of the glories of para-
dise, the reward which would await them as warriors vic-
torious in Allah's name, or as martyrs who died for his
cause.

In similar fashion, the PKI propagandists adapted their
arguments to each specific group of the population. The
better-off were promised a Utopia where they could keep
everything they possessed, would not have to pay taxes,
and would even be appointed to positions with the new
government. The descendants of the sultan and other title-
bearers were promised the establishment of a new sultanate
and 'their own sultan'; of course the religious orthodox were
told that the new state would be Islamic.

For obvious reasons, nothing much was said about the
distribution of property belonging to the better-off. Occasionally, the common man was given visions of equality,
but this was not usually necessary, as his support was assured once prominent men had been enlisted. However,
everyone was promised cheap or free rice and transport.

For those who remained unconvinced, here too stronger
arguments were used. Not only would Utopia be denied to
them but also they would be oppressed and their property
would be handed to the founders of the new community. If
such threats were still insufficient, the recalcitrant were

intimidated by ostracism, threats of violence, even occasionally murder.

Success crowned these 'minimum programmes'. The PKI gained far more members in Bantam, and in a shorter space of time, than elsewhere. But these were in no sense disciplined, leave alone convinced, communists, but rather men out for what they could get. They were impatient to see the promises made to them fulfilled and grew steadily more uncontrollable. As with the Minangkabau communists, their lack of discipline ensured their failure.

Means and End

In brief, then, the PKI member was semi-westernised, of indeterminate social status, and with insecure employment, a product of the stage of transition from peasant society to the modern commercial and industrial complex. Being a casualty of modernisation he was well placed to appeal to his fellow-countrymen who were also suffering the dislocations of change, and to urge them to reject it and its Dutch authors, promising in exchange for their allegiance a return to the ideal past with the help of his foreign friends.

His success depended on exploiting the existing grievances; themselves a product of social change. He was helped by the ineptitude of the administration. The reaction of the Netherlands Indies government, at the levels of both policy-making and execution, was simply to support those institutions representing the past state of affairs, not to encourage new ones which embodied the present. At the same time, however, its repressive services were insufficiently developed. In brief, the government gave no encouragement to positive tendencies which would have opposed disruption and itself failed to suppress it.

If the grievances were waiting to be exploited, and the socio-political situation permitted this to be done, the manner of its doing was very much the result of the activities of the PKI. Matters would have been quite different otherwise. This became obvious over the next couple of decades, when social change continued if anything at a more rapid pace and with no doubt its inevitable casualties. But with the PKI proscribed, and a much improved police apparatus, no uprising occurred.

And the means the PKI chose determined its catastrophic end. If there is some doubt about the PKI leaders' Marxist convictions, certainly those Indonesians who adhered to the party were not much interested in communism. What they sought was the equivalent of the act of *amok,* a sudden outburst of energy which would in one fell swoop bring back the past by getting rid of the Dutch. Realising the lack of appeal of Marxism, the PKI accepted their support on their terms, and very shortly lost all control over events. The revolt fell into the hands of criminals, bandits and desperadoes.

Needless to say, this had nothing to do with Leninism, leave alone Marxism. Lenin would certainly not have scrupled to use criminals and bandits but he would have had them controlled by his intellectuals in the party so that they served its cause. The reverse occurred in the PKI. In Leninist terms, the 'minimum programme' became the 'maximum', and destroyed the party.

8
The
Twilight
Years

National Communism

From the PKI's elimination in 1926 to the emergence of the
Indonesian republic in 1945, the Indonesian communists
pursued an illegal existence, hounded by the police and
prevented from organising an effective party. Those in authority during this period were of course not only the
Dutch; the Japanese occupied the country from early 1942.
But they were if anything even more concerned at the communist danger, and their cruel but efficient secret police,
the *Kempeitai*, ensured that it came to nothing.

This period also saw the emergence of a tradition of national communism at variance with that which followed
the motions of the Comintern. In Europe, two decades later
it was to take the form of Titoism; and in another ten
years the Chinese communist state was to assert its independence of Moscow. But in Indonesia it began with
Tan Malaka in the late 1920s.

Both groupings were Leninists; the difference was that
one band of communists sought to apply Lenin's strategy

and tactics in the light of their own interests; the other followed the Comintern interpretation and, as we know, this really meant supporting the aims of Russian foreign policy as they were adumbrated from time to time. This may have included accepting the death of a communist party if it was in the Russian interest; we have seen how Stalin was prepared to acquiesce in the elimination of the Chinese communists if only Chiang Kai-shek would remain allied to Russia. No truly independent communist party would, it is safe to say, be prepared to make such a sacrifice of itself for another.

Malaka, as mentioned above, was the representative of the Comintern in South-East Asia. The year after the 1926 debacle he set up with his two Singapore associates, Djamaludin Tamin and Subakat, a new party, Partai Republik Indonesia, or PARI, in Bangkok. Its task was to train yet others and so build up a secret organisation. Over the years the effort bore some fruit, especially in infiltrating youth organisations. Two of its most prominent leaders in this field were Adam Malik, Indonesian foreign minister at the time of writing, and Sukarni.

The creation of this new party, along with Malaka's opposition to the ill-conceived 1926 revolt, has been given by Moscow-led communists as evidence that he was a 'Trotskyist'; a term which may seem musty now but apparently at the time aroused the faithful to paroxysms of virulent moral indignation. In so far as Trotsky stood for a universal revolution, and Stalin for revolution in one country, there seems no ground for believing that Malaka followed the former; he was evidently not concerned with any country other than Indonesia. And to condemn him for opposing the 1926 revolt should also carry the corollary of condemning both Stalin and the Comintern, who discouraged such an evidently doomed venture until, as we have seen, the quarrel with Trotsky made it tactically opportune to support the revolt once it had broken out.

Neither can Malaka's founding of a new communist party be taken seriously as a ground for treating him as a heretic.

The old one had been destroyed, and the fact that the new did not designate itself as communist is neither here nor there; there is no requirement in the Twenty-one Principles that a communist party must call itself such, only that it accept the discipline of the Comintern. And at least at its foundation, there was no sign that PARI was to be independent.

But the sign was not long in coming and is probably the real reason for Malaka's being designated as a 'Trotskyist'. In the year following the foundation of PARI, 1928, the Comintern held its sixth congress. This was the first since 1924, previous to which these meetings had been held every year. In the interval, Stalin had beaten Trotsky, having had the wit to realise that the chances of revolution in the world were somewhat remote and had then re-interpreted the Leninist message accordingly. The convening of the sixth congress therefore signified that there was no further dispute to be aired; it was also to show, very quickly, that henceforth there would be no discussion in the Comintern. The Russian party, that is to say Stalin, would decide policy, and the Comintern would approve it. It is probably this new totalitarianism that Malaka could not take. While he intended to create a power machine on Leninist lines for Indonesia, he had no intention of subordinating it to Moscow. It is true that at the Comintern congress Malaka opposed an alliance between native 'bourgeoisie' and communists, proposed by Bukharin, whereupon the latter dubbed him a Trotskyist, intending this as an insult. But the theses adopted by the congress in fact demanded that communists in the colonies '. . . liberate the toiling masses from the influence of the bourgeoisie and national-reformism . . .'; Malaka could hardly be accused of rejecting this advice. The most plausible explanation of the split between Malaka and the Comintern is that it was the former who, seeing that that body was now to be the voice of Stalin, and dismayed at the latter's abysmal ignorance of Asian affairs (he thought that conditions in China and Egypt were similar!), decided that he was better off on his own. In brief, the soubriquet of 'Trotskyist' applied to Malaka implies simply that though a Leninist he was his own man; which of course the Comintern could not abide.

Muscovites

Tan Malaka's followers were not the only active communists. The same sixth congress of the Comintern, smarting under the defeats in the Indies and in China, enunciated the policy of opposing 'bourgeois' (i.e. non-communist) political movements. As part of that policy, Musso was sent from Moscow to Surabaya, where he is said to have remained a year before returning to Russia. He built up the 'Underground Indonesian Communist Party', of course Stalinist in its allegiance, with aspirant members being organised in the *Partai Komunis Muda,* or Party of Young Communists.

In the same year and the same city some communists, close associates of Musso, who had however kept their powder dry in 1926, formed an Indonesian Labour Federation (*Sarekat Kaum Buruh Indonesia*). Their intention was to infiltrate various unions with a view to control. It took a year for them to recruit seven hundred members; then the government, scenting what was afoot, dissolved the federation and arrested the leaders.

But neither Malaka's organisation nor Musso's achieved much success; the government's anti-subversive apparatus proved superior to both. So communist efforts were largely limited to penetrating other organisations. They entered the *Partai Nasional Indonesia,* founded by Sukarno in 1927; its successor, the *Partindo* of 1931, and the *Gerindo* of 1937. This last included two undeclared communists who were to achieve prominence in later years, Wikana and Amir Sjarifuddin.

But possibly the communists' greatest subversive success was not in the Indies but in Holland, where they eventually secured control of the *Perhimpunan Indonesia.* This association of Indonesian students, established in 1922, was the successor to the Indies Society of 1908, and much more politically motivated. It bred by far the largest number of Indonesian nationalist leaders, the single notable exception being Sukarno himself. Most of its members were not communists but its politics were strongly Marxist, as was to be expected of an organisation opposed to western imperialism, and it actively cooperated with the PKI representatives in Holland.

As intimated in a previous chapter Semaun signed (on 5 December 1926), as representative of the PKI, an agreement with Hatta, as chairman of the PI, which gave it full responsibility for the nationalist movement in Indonesia and stipulated that the PKI would not oppose the PI as long as it sought Indonesian independence.

But evidently Semaun had not by then fully grasped the changes in his paymaster's office; almost exactly a year later he recanted and repudiated the agreement, on the grounds that it would mean liquidation of the independent and leading role of the Communist Party. Nevertheless, the PI continued to maintain its links with the Stalinists, especially through the League Against Imperialism, another front organisation, set up in 1926; Hatta himself was for some time a member of the executive of the league. This marriage of convenience was ended not by the PI but by the Comintern, which at its sixth congress in 1928, when the doctrine of the united front from below was announced, renounced cooperation with 'bourgeois' nationalist movements in the colonies. Relations between the league and the PI consequently deteriorated rapidly, and in the latter half of 1929 the Perhimpunan left the league. But, as ever in organisations formed of members dependent on personal leadership, when Hatta returned to the Indies in 1932 the PI came under the control of two covert communists, Setiadjit and Abdulmadjid. Thereafter it became a faithful servant of Russian policy.

Meanwhile, back in the Indies, in 1936 the communists managed, in a style reminiscent of the 1919 'Red Guards', to provoke a mutiny on the Dutch warship *Zeven Pro-*

vincien, which was quickly brought to heel by the Dutch air force. One of the principal instigators, Sumarsono, was again to engage in violence over a decade later, with as little success.

The policy of opposing 'bourgeois' (i.e. non-communist) political movements, enunciated by the sixth congress of the Comintern, was violently reversed by the seventh, held in 1935. The Russians, recognising that the most serious, and indeed explicit, threat to their regime and even people came from the other totalitarianisms, namely that of nazism in Germany and to a lesser extent fascism in Italy, commanded their followers to form where possible 'United Fronts' against fascism and to cooperate with 'bourgeois' democratic elements. This came to be known as the Dimitrov doctrine. In Holland, the Perhimpunan Indonesia obediently right-wheeled, argued for cooperation with the Dutch, and attacked the nationalists, many its own previous members, in the Indies.

In 1942 the Netherlands Indies succumbed to the Japanese attack. Immediately before the collapse we again hear of Sjarifuddin, who in order to establish an anti-Japanese underground is given twenty-five thousand Dutch guilders by the governor of East Java, Charles van der Plas, a man with a reputation for political intrigue. Many of the members of the underground, of course, came to be drawn from the clandestine PKI. It did not have a long span of life. Sjarifuddin was arrested early in 1943, together with other leaders of his organisation. At the end of February 1944 he was sentenced to death; only the intervention of Sukarno, who was in very good standing with the Japanese, induced them to commute the sentence to life imprisonment. His followers, however, are said to have been responsible for a short-lived revolt later that year in Blitar, East Java, among the *Peta,* a Japanese-trained home guard.

The destruction of Sjarifuddin's underground effectively emasculated the Muscovites. A recrudescence of their activity was made all the more difficult by a change in policy on the part of the Japanese shortly afterwards. To obtain support for their war effort, in March 1943 the Japanese established an inclusive nationalist organisation, the *Putera*, and three months later appointed Sukarno and Hatta to head it. As time passed more and more concessions were made to Indonesian nationalism. This neatly pinioned the Muscovites. They could hardly support Japan, a member of the fascist axis, now that Moscow was at war with Germany. Yet if they opposed Japan they would alienate a great part of Indonesian nationalist sentiment. For most of the occupation, then, they did very little, if anything.

But however draconic the Japanese were against the Muscovites—they were, after all, allied with Germany, which was fighting Russia—they appear to have followed a completely different policy towards Tan Malaka's group. He himself, after spending a number of years in Japan, is said to have returned in 1942, at the beginning of the Japanese occupation, and to have taken a job in a Japanese-administered coal mine; presumably he was in better health than when he had been Comintern representative at Manila. He is reputed to have worked secretly for Admiral Maeda, who was chief of naval intelligence for Indonesia as well as deputy chief of staff, and for the Japanese Department of Propaganda, broadcasting from Bantam as the 'Voice of Radio Tokyo'. He is also alleged to have set up a clandestine organisation of his own, enrolling among others Adam Malik, Chaerul Saleh, Achmad Subardjo and Iwa Kusuma Sumantri.

Subardjo was to emerge on several occasions in later Indonesian history. In the mid-1920s he had been a student in Holland, one of those covert communists who infiltrated the Perhimpunan Indonesia, and was its most important leader before Hatta took over the chair. He then went to Moscow, to stay at least a year before returning to Indonesia. From there he went to Tokyo as correspondent for an Indonesian newspaper. It is possible that he there came into contact with Tan Malaka, though apparently he himself denied this.

It was no doubt his familiarity with the Japanese, not to mention other possible assistance he may have extended to them, that resulted in his being made chief of the Consulting Office on Political Affairs of the Japanese naval headquarters in Java. As such, he was responsible to Admiral Maeda. This officer appears to have been very sympathetic to Leninist ideas, though not necessarily to Stalin. In any case, in 1944 he set up, and Subardjo organised, the *Asrama Indonesia Merdeka*, or Hostel of Independent Indonesia. The head was the old PKI militant Wikana; one of the pupils was Muhammad Yusuf, who was later to revive the PKI; another was Aidit, who was to lead the PKI in the 1950s and 1960s. The courses run at the hostel were on international communism of the pre-Dimitrov era, i.e. there was no advocacy of a united front against fascism—naturally enough. The emphasis was entirely on opposition to 'capitalist imperialism', i.e. the powers opposed to Japan, namely Britain and the United States. The aim clearly was to steal Russia's clothes, namely to organise the disaffected and uprooted by means of Leninist ideology and techniques, not in Russia's interest but in Japan's. Several hundred men were graduated from this hostel by July 1945, and already from May Subardjo was asking many of them to join an underground movement he was organising. Of course, he described it as anti-Japanese; the writing on the wall was so clear, even in news-darkened Indonesia, that he could hardly have invited them to join the losing side.

There is some controversy whether this hostel, and Subardjo's underground, were composed of followers of Tan Malaka or of Musso. The truth probably is that neither the Japanese nor Subardjo minded much which variety of Leninism was favoured so long as they controlled the organisation. And, indeed, while they encouraged the growth of this Leninist body, they resolutely stamped out all activity on the part of the Muscovite underground PKI which was independent and opposed to them. While the PKI's own account of its activity during the occupation boasts that it led a number of scattered anti-Japanese organisations, there is no independent corroboration of such claims. Indeed, one survivor of the period has recently cast doubt on whether there was *any* activity by any underground group during the Japanese occupation.[1]

[1] Mangkupradja, 1968: 125.

9
Tan Malaka's
Coup Manqué

Manoeuvres

As the Japanese occupation drew to its close, it was clear that the Indonesian body politic had changed radically in the four years since the Dutch had left. Then, nearly all Indonesian politicians had been in opposition to the state structure, some openly, others underground. But now, in 1945, very many owed their positions to the occupying power, the most eminent of course being Sukarno and Hatta. Furthermore, in the Civil Service Indonesians had replaced Dutchmen and Eurasians from the beginning of the occupation; as it drew to its close they also replaced Japanese. In 1942 virtually the only Indonesians in the Dutch colonial army were the Christian Ambonese; by 1945 the Japanese had created a home army, the Peta, which was not only manned but also officered by Indonesians, and in due course became the *Tentara Nasional Indonesia*, or Indonesian National Army.

The beneficiaries of this Japanese-sponsored state structure stood to lose virtually all if the Dutch re-imposed their regime on the Indies; hence their determined and ultimately successful opposition to it. What is perhaps not so well appreciated is that they were equally opposed to any attack from within on their Japanese-authored legitimacy. This was to come from the various undergrounds. The Leninist and Stalinist groups, as we have seen, were fairly insignificant; the largest was that led by the socialist Sutan Sjahrir, who with Hatta had led a smallish nationalist party before the war. His organisation had attracted considerable support among the educated youth who had not found jobs in the Civil Service.

It was immediately clear, once the defeat of the Japanese became imminent, that if the Indonesian undergrounds were to obtain a share in power, it was essential that the new Indonesian state not derive its legitimacy from the Japanese; this would simply entrench the establishment and the undergrounds would be seen as hindrances to independence. Events soon precipitated a crisis. On 7 August 1945 an Independence Preparatory Committee was set up by the Japanese, and Sukarno, Hatta and friends were appointed to it. Four days later, at Dalat in Indochina, they were told by General Terauchi, whose command in South-East Asia was crumbling under him, that independence would be granted on 25 August. These events, of course, simply culminated a process set in motion over two years earlier when the Japanese appointed Sukarno and Hatta to head the Putera.

It was obvious that the undergrounds would have to move if they were to obtain any recognition at all. Already on 10 August, before the Dalat meeting, Sjahrir had urged Sukarno and Hatta to declare independence in terms of a strongly anti-Japanese statement he had prepared. He pleaded again, with no more success, on their return from Dalat on 14 August; he had heard that the Japanese had asked the allies for an armistice a couple of days earlier. To force their hands, a group of underground members kidnapped Sukarno and Hatta on 16 August. They again refused, as they still preferred to receive independence by arrangement with the Japanese. (They were released through the intervention of Subardjo and with the knowledge of Admiral Maeda.) Only when they had ascertained that the terms of the Japanese surrender to the allies precluded a transfer of power did they then on 17 August 1945 draw up (in Maeda's house) a declaration of independence which was in no way anti-Japanese but simply declared that the Indonesian people had now taken control of their destiny. (They now had a precious six weeks before British troops could arrive to take over.)

The underground were thus checked; clearly Sukarno and Hatta were not going to take any action which cut the ground from under their own feet. The cabinet that Sukarno and Hatta drew up then was composed mainly of collaborators with the Japanese, such as Subardjo, who was designated foreign minister, but also included members of the underground, among them Amir Sjarifuddin, still then an undeclared Stalinist. Sukarno offered a cabinet position to Sjahrir, who however declined. Only when a tour through Java convinced him that, collaborator or not, Sukarno enjoyed vastly greater popularity, did he decide to support him.

Tan Malaka now entered the scene and offered a compact to Sjahrir whereby they would together overthrow Sukarno, he (Malaka) would become president, and the cabinet would be dominated jointly by Sjahrir and Subardjo. Sjahrir refused, and suggested that if Tan Malaka fancied his chances against Sukarno he ought to go on a tour of Java such as he himself had just completed. Malaka did so, to find that a shadowy underground career was no substitute for official Japanese sponsorship. Only in a few parts of Java and of Sumatra did he enjoy greater support than Sukarno.

Malaka then thought of another scheme, namely that Sukarno designate him as sole heir, since there was a real possibility that the president might be despatched by the Dutch. When he suggested this, with Subardjo adding unctuous support, Sukarno agreed in principle but foiled

Malaka by designating three additional heirs, one of them Sjahrir.

While Subardjo was happy to support Malaka when it was to his advantage, he was also concerned to feather his own nest. The underground he had formed from Asrama graduates had now emerged into the largest political organisation in the embryonic republic, posing a distinct threat to Sukarno, Hatta and the rest of the presidential cabinet. This presented Sjahrir with his opportunity. Early in October Sukarno accepted his suggestion to change the Central National Committee (*Komite Nasional Indonesia Pusat* or KNIP), which had replaced the Independence Preparatory Committee on 29 August, from a body which advised the president to one which legislated. Out of self-preservation Sukarno accepted, and the committee was vested with full power jointly with him. Furthermore, it set up an executive body, called the Working Party, which would be in continuous session and concerned with broad outlines of policy. Sjahrir was elected chairman, and Sjarifuddin vice-chairman, with the right to select thirteen additional members. In a somewhat politically naive fashion, and in contrast with Sukarno's selection of his cabinet, Sjahrir chose all the new men from among his own supporters, mostly from the underground. Over the next few weeks he used his powers to set up a network of local national committees with a chairman appointed by himself. This gave the cabinet some control over local political development and a means of harnessing it to the national purpose. But Sjahrir went further; he also instituted a multi-party system. While this encouragement of latent fissiparous political tendencies had the desired effect of breaking Subardjo's organisation, over the years Indonesia has paid a heavy price for what became a vested interest in multiplicity of parties. When the parliamentary system failed to provide efficient government, Sukarno was able to point to the abandonment of the presidential cabinet under Sjahrir's urging as the cause of all Indonesia's misfortunes.

The destruction of Subardjo's mass support benefited principally Sjahrir and Sjarifuddin. For whilst the minority of his followers divided themselves between Malaka's group and the PKI, the majority became Sjahrir's para-military supporters. He now sought to move against the central establishment. At the end of October 1945 he published a pamphlet entitled 'Our Fight', making two principal points. The first was that Indonesia would have to live in the American-British sphere of influence. The second was that all collaborators with the Japanese should be thrown out of office. The implication was clear: if Indonesia was to be in good standing with Britain and the United States, then Sjahrir and his friends from the anti-Japanese underground should hold the reins of power. Unfortunately for Sjahrir, neither in the first nor in the later editions did he exclude Sukarno and Hatta from the ranks of those collaborators with the Japanese whom he anathematised. This was to lead to considerable political difficulties during the republic's struggles with the Dutch; it was also to make Sukarno his implacable enemy.

Immediately, however, the publication of this pamphlet had three consequences: it attracted to Sjahrir much support from the ex-underground and the students, it weakened Sukarno's position, and it aroused deep and abiding hatred of Sjahrir among the vast majority of the Indonesian elite who formed the Japanese-sponsored establishment. In effect, Sjahrir had tied his and his followers' political future to the need to remain in the good graces of the British and the Americans; once this was no longer necessary, they became expendable.

At the time, however, this set of circumstances gave Malaka an opportunity which he proceeded to exploit. He hoped at one and the same time to use Sjahrir's discrediting of Sukarno to remove him from office, and then to use the resentment aroused within the establishment by the pamphlet to eliminate the author himself. He thus foiled himself by making Sukarno and Sjahrir allies in self-preservation. He might just possibly have removed one of his enemies; he could not unseat both.

In October and November Malaka toured Java with a forged document designating himself as Sukarno's sole heir and alleging that Sukarno and Hatta were prisoners of the British in Dakarta; no doubt credibility was attached to this story by Sjahrir's emphasis on the two leaders' collaboration with the Japanese. This scheme was scotched when Sukarno toured Java in December and showed that he was still a free agent.

Malaka nevertheless continued to intrigue against Sukarno, but to no avail. Then, with Subardjo's support, he urged on Sjahrir the need for Sukarno and Hatta to resign, on the grounds that their standing had been so eroded they could no longer command national support. Sjahrir's counter-move was to introduce on 11 November 1945 the principle of cabinet responsibility to parliament. Since most of the cabinet were drawn from the collaborative group, it brought them under control and, by so doing, prevented his supporters from drifting to Malaka. Realising that he himself was as much threatened as Sjahrir, Sukarno appointed him prime minister. Immediately Sjahrir dismissed most of the cabinet, supporters of Malaka, and replaced them by his own men. Throughout, however, Amir Sjarifuddin remained minister of defence.

Crisis

The opposed camps were now marshalling their forces. In November Malaka's followers formed the *Partai Rakyat Djelata* (Common People's Party). The next month Sjahrir's men combined with those of Amir Sjarifuddin into the *Partai Sosialis,* or Socialist Party. In November the *Pesindo* (*Pemuda Sosialis Indonesia,* or Indonesian Young Socialists) had been formed in Jogjakarta from a number of youth organisations supporting the two men, with as one of their leaders Wikana, the ex-director of the Asrama. Their total armed strength in the first year of their existence probably amounted to some twenty-five thousand. The Pesindo was in a sense a counter to the establishment's *Barisan Banteng* (Buffalo Legion), which originally had been a Japanese-sponsored youth organisation called the *Barisan Pelopor* (Pioneer Legion); it changed its name in December. It vied with the Pesindo in strength and was the armed auxiliary for the establishment, politically represented by the PNI (*Partai Nasional Indonesia,* or Indonesian National Party), supported largely by civil servants and those they influenced, and Malaka's group.

The establishment also had its own Leninist Party. On 21 October Mohammed Yusuf established the PKI. He had no connection with either the pre-1926 party or with the absentee Musso's followers of 1935 onwards. During the occupation he had apparently led a communist front organisation called *Djoyoboyo,* which had collaborated with the Japanese, and as we have seen he had been a graduate of the Japanese-sponsored Asrama. He was, of course, as could be guessed from the preceding, a follower of Tan Malaka and worked closely with him, instigating peasant revolts against absentee landlords and creditors in north Central Java, with the 'sovietisation' of the land as its aim.

Malaka himself, foiled in his intrigues, now turned to build up mass backing. At the beginning of 1946 he convened a meeting at Purwokerto in Central Java of three hundred delegates from the military and political organisations of the republic, purportedly to further national solidarity in support of the government. He called for monolithic unity until independence was recognised, the abolition of political parties, and an end to all political division. He demanded that the negotiations recently begun with the Dutch be repudiated, and that all foreign properties be confiscated. This programme was guaranteed to appeal to the establishment, who had most to lose from any concessions made to the Dutch, which might result in their Japanese-granted powers being curtailed. It was also contrived to create a single political organisation with

Malaka at its head, thus making him leader of the republic.

The reader who has followed Indonesian developments will have noted the similarity between this programme and that espoused by Sukarno some dozen years later, which emerged in modified form as 'guided democracy'. The difference between the two men was emphatically not one of aims but simply of ambitions; there was only one presidency, Sukarno had it, and Tan Malaka wanted it.

Malaka's call met with an enthusiastic response and a mere ten days later an even greater number of delegates, meeting at Jogjakarta, established the *Persatuan Perdjuangan*, or Fighting Front. It garnered support and within a month 141 organisations had joined, including many of the armed bands then rife. Even more important, it received the endorsement of the commander-in-chief of the Indonesian army, General Sudirman. Included among the organisations, at least at the start, were the Socialist Party and its armed auxiliary, the Pesindo. The Working Party of the Chief National Committee went so far as to urge the whole population to join.

But having gained this very great advantage in his drive to power, Malaka then proceeded to whittle it away by precipitate action. The very next month he directed that the constituent parties were not to take part in the cabinet. He thus showed his hand. Having previously implied that the Persatuan was set up to support the government, he now indicated unmistakably his intention to replace it. Immediately the cabinet's principal supporters, namely the Socialist Party and the Pesindo, left the Persatuan. Nearly all the other organisations, however, remained, and so permitted the Persatuan to declare that it was now more representative than the Chief National Committee. Under this pressure, the Working Party handed in its resignation to that committee, which however did not accept it. The Persatuan then demanded the dismissal of Sjahrir's cabinet and its replacement by a national coalition cabinet. Sjahrir resigned and Sukarno handed the mandate to the leaders of the Persatuan. However, their internal jealousies, coupled with their fear that Malaka was really out to replace not merely the cabinet but Sukarno himself, who was the guarantee of their own positions, prevented agreement. This left Sukarno free to ask Sjahrir to form a cabinet, on condition that it be more widely based, that is to say not limited to Sjahrir's friends and ex-underground workers. This was done. None of the new cabinet members, however, was from the Persatuan, though Wikana, the ex-head of the Asrama and Pesindo leader, was taken in as minister without portfolio. Furthermore, the cabinet was raised in importance by being given equal status with the Working Party.

The Persatuan was put on the defensive. It called a large meeting in Madiun, declared the cabinet unacceptable, and resolved to take matters into its own hands. The cabinet moved quickly and on 17 March arrested and jailed Malaka and a number of other leaders of the Persatuan, including Sukarni.

While it was thus fighting off the challenge of the Persatuan in Java, the cabinet was also attempting to weaken it in Sumatra. As ever in Indonesia, it must not be assumed that an identity of name indicates similarity of content. The Sumatra Persatuan, principally based in East Sumatra and in the West Coast Residency, was not composed of establishment figures, included two Stalinists, Karim Marah Sultan and Luat Siregar, among its leaders, and appears to have adopted the name only as a sign of opposition to the cabinet. A republican government mission led by Amir Sjarifuddin set up a network of national committees which effectively weakened the Persatuan, just as in Java it had emasculated Subardjo's organisation, and in the East Coast Residency succeeded in arresting the Persatuan leaders.

In March, too, the PKI slipped from the hands of the establishment. After its foundation in October the party had been joined by a number of Stalinists returning from wartime exile in Holland and Australia. Indeed, the Dutch, displaying an endearing kind of naive Machiavellianism, flew them out from Holland free of charge, in the belief that the Dimitrov doctrine, still then official credo in the Comintern, would result in these Stalinists supporting the Dutch against the 'fascist-sponsored' republican government.

In the beleaguered republic they were welcomed. At the time the fact of common origin over-rode ideological differences, and for all except a handful of the most sophisticated Indonesians, communists were seen not so much as agents of a foreign power striving to establish a satellite totalitarian state but rather as a political grouping concerned, like all the others, to obtain independence, and with the added advantage of foreign support. The Indonesian Stalinists were nobody's fools, and once back on republican territory quickly sized up the situation; the republic was certainly Japanese-sponsored but equally it was under threat from Malaka and his supporters, who would certainly have no room for Stalinists in any political structure he created. Accordingly, their first task was to remove Yusuf, a supporter of Malaka, from the chair. This they did in March 1946 at the party congress in Jogjakarta. At a conference in Surakarta next month they chose as their leader Sardjono, who had been chairman of the PKI in 1926, had been arrested before the abortive revolt and exiled to the Boven Digul concentration camp. When in 1942 the Dutch had retreated before the Japanese they had removed him to Australia and put him to work in their information service until March 1946, when at the request of the Australian government all Indonesians were sent home.

Just as the PKI went from the hands of the establishment to the Stalinists, so also did the Indonesian Labour Party (*Partai Buruh Indonesia*). This was formed in November 1945 by Indonesians who had worked in the Labour Department of the Japanese occupation authorities. But later that year Setiadjit, newly returned from Holland, entered its ranks. It will be remembered that he and Abdulmadjid, both covert Stalinists, had taken over the Perhimpunan

Indonesia in Holland when Hatta left for Indonesia. In the middle 1930s they studied at the Lenin Institute in Moscow; during the war Setiadjit fought in the anti-nazi underground in Holland. His organisational abilities were far superior to those of the leaders of the Partai Buruh and early in 1946 he emerged as its leader.

Other returned Indonesian Stalinists moved into the ranks of the Socialist Party and of course the Pesindo; what they did not join, significantly, were organisations supporting the Persatuan Perdjuangan. They knew, too well, that Malaka, with his combination of extreme radicalism and nationalism, was their most potent threat; they could only, at best, lay claim to the first characteristic. And the organisations they joined were all united in support certainly of Sjahrir, who was no communist, but equally of Amir Sjarifuddin, a Stalinist like themselves.

The cabinet took further steps to consolidate its position. In the political field it set up a National Concentration (*Konsentrasi Nasional*) which drew away much of the floating strength of the Persatuan in Java. An important exception was the civil servants' party, the PNI. But the cabinet also needed reliable military support. Sjahrir's blunderbuss attack on the Japanese-sponsored establishment had been taken to include the army among its targets. So the Persatuan still enjoyed the support of the military as well as of many irregular armed organisations. To offset this, Sjahrir incorporated the irregular armed units into the army, assuring himself of their support by giving their leaders high rank, and also created a new division, the Siliwangi, and the Police Mobile Brigade, whose loyalties were primarily to him and only secondarily to the commander-in-chief, Sudirman.

Events now moved to a crisis. The principality of Surakarta was virtually in the hands of the Persatuan, holding the headquarters of Malaka's party, as well as the Barisan Banteng. In June 1946 the Persatuan mounted a coup which took over the government of the city from the ruling prince, the Susuhunan, and received the support of Sudirman. Sjahrir thereupon proclaimed a state of emergency and established a National Defence Council, which included, it is interesting to note, both Sudirman and Sardjono, the new PKI chairman.

Little more than a fortnight later, on 27 June, Malaka and the other jailed Persatuan leaders were released from Surakarta jail by a Major-General Sudarsono, and Sjahrir was kidnapped by troops of the third division of the army. The cabinet transferred its powers to Sukarno, and a state of war and siege was declared. Sjahrir's military supporters then went into action. Pesindo troops moved from Surabaya, took Madiun and threatened Surakarta. From Bandung the Siliwangi division moved east and camped outside Jogjakarta, ready to take it.

On 2 July Sudarsono and Mohamed Yamin, a leader of the Persatuan, called on Sukarno and demanded that the Sjahrir cabinet be disbanded and replaced by a Tan Malaka 'Supreme Political Council', with the transfer of Sukarno's military powers to Sudirman, the commander-in-chief. Sukarno's answer was to have his bodyguard arrest the emissaries. In Surakarta, Sjahrir was released by some of his military supporters, and Amir Sjarifuddin managed to escape kidnap by troops of the Barisan Banteng.

All this time, Sudirman had remained carefully poised on the fence. Eventually, with the threat of civil war looming, he yielded to Sukarno's pleas and supported Sjahrir but on condition that none of the Persatuan leaders concerned with kidnapping him were to be arrested. With the failure of his coup, Malaka returned to jail.

10

Musso's Runaway Revolt

Submerged Stalinists

It was not lost on Sukarno that Tan Malaka's coup had come somewhat close to success and that his own survival was due in no small part to the Socialist Party and its armed auxiliaries. For reasons both of gratitude and of insurance, therefore, he took steps to diminish the power of the establishment (who were generally sympathetic to Malaka) to the advantage of Sjahrir and his friends. He proposed an increase in the size of the republic's highest deliberative body, the KNIP, eventually from 200 members to 514, but with the greater membership so distributed that the establishment parties' representation would be virtually halved, that of the underground parties would remain about the same, and both together, who at the time accounted for a majority of the seats, would be reduced to a minority. He hoped thereby to lessen his dependence on the establishment, certainly, but also to increase his independence of all political parties. The remainder of the seats in the chamber were taken up by representatives of 'functional groups', regions, and minorities. These proposals met with strong resistance and were finally accepted in March 1947 only under the threat of resignation by Hatta and Sukarno.

In the meantime Sjahrir had formed a new cabinet (in October 1946) which gave much greater representation to the establishment parties, the PNI and Masjumi. However, and perhaps of greater consequence, it retained Amir Sjarifuddin as minister of defence, and gave seats to both Setiadjit and Wikana. It was this cabinet which was responsible for signing on 15 November the Linggadjati Agreement with the Dutch. This provided *inter alia* for the restoration to all non-Indonesians of their previous rights and property. Needless to say, the establishment parties were not prepared to accept this surrender of the advantages they had gained under the Japanese and since. So, very quickly, the Masjumi, the PNI and Malaka's supporters (he was still in jail) formed the *Benteng Republik* (Republican Fortress) to oppose the agreement, and their antagonists, namely the Socialist Party, the Pesindo, the Labour Party, and the PKI, formed themselves into a coalition called the *Sayap Kiri* (Left Wing). But it was not until Sukarno's reforms had been effected that the KNIP ratified the agreement, and it was formally signed on 25 March 1947. The Masjumi and PNI still maintained their opposition and this left Sjahrir dangerously exposed. Three months later, under threat of war, he accepted the principle of an interim government which would control all foreign relations, with the Dutch representative having the last word. He was immediately deserted by the three covert communist leaders in the Sayap Kiri, namely Abdulmadjid, Wikana and Sjarifuddin; he thereupon resigned. It was Sjarifuddin who formed the next cabinet, with himself as not only prime minister but also, again, minister of defence, Setiadjit as deputy prime minister, and including Abdulmadjid and Wikana. Though they had withdrawn their support from Sjahrir purportedly because of the concessions he was prepared to make to the Dutch, they now made even greater ones. This appeasement encouraged the Dutch to insist upon a joint gendarmerie which would operate in republican territory. Not even the Sjarifuddin group's desire to remain in power would permit them to agree to that, and on 20 July 1947 the Dutch attacked the republic. Some six months of sporadic fighting were ended by Sjarifuddin's acceptance of the Renville Agreement in January 1948. This provided for a military truce, for the Netherlands to retain sovereignty until it could be transferred to a United States of Indonesia in which the republic would be a constituent part, and for a plebiscite permitting the population to opt for either the usi or the republic.

Renville was opposed by not only the Masjumi and the pni but also Sjahrir's followers. Sjarifuddin had no alternative but to resign; Hatta, the vice-president, then became prime minister. Sjarifuddin and his followers were excluded from the cabinet; the Masjumi and the pni were dominant. Solaced now by office, the latter proceeded to put Renville into effect.

The new cabinet enjoyed Sjahrir's support, for his way had parted from Sjarifuddin's; the Stalinist world had taken another whirl. Stalin had dissolved the Comintern in 1943 when his country had needed the help of the western powers against Germany and Italy. Now he turned against his recent allies and in 1947 formed the Cominform, or Communist Information Bureau, as a successor to the Comintern. In September of that year this new mouthpiece laid down the Zhdanov line, which divided the world into two opposing camps, Russia and her allies, and the United States and hers, called the 'imperialists'. Russia was no longer threatened by Germany, there was no further need of 'united fronts', Dimitrov had served his purpose. Communists who had been content to work with democrats in opposing the axis were now given no option but to be loyal Stalinists and show hostility to the United States and any who sought friendship with her. One such was Amir Sjarifuddin. Already in December 1947 it had become clear to Sjahrir that Sjarifuddin was a Leninist; the

only question was whether he put his nationalism first or
second. Sjahrir himself was of course no Leninist, and in
any case gave priority to nationalism. Clearly, such opposed
allegiances could not long remain together and in February
Sjahrir and his friends left the Partai Sosialis and the
Sayap Kiri to form the *Partai Sosialis Indonesia*. The
original party remained firmly under the control of three
covert communists: Sjarifuddin, Tan Ling Djie and Abdulmadjid. The Sayap Kiri reconstituted itself as the *Front
Demokrasi Rakyat*. It had the same programme as Sjarifuddin but now angled for the support of labour and the
peasantry.

However, from 17 to 21 February 1948 the 'World
Federation of Democratic Youth', another organ of Russian
foreign policy, held a South-East Asian Youth Conference
in Calcutta. The delegates, among them members of the
PKI, were brought up to date on the Zhdanov twist. The
consequences did not take long to show themselves in the
republic. On 26 February the new FDR was supporting
Renville; in March it abruptly executed an about-turn. It
now demanded that the agreement be repudiated, that
negotiations with the Dutch be suspended until they withdrew from Indonesia, and that all foreign property be
nationalised without compensation. Amusingly enough, this
programme was identical with that for so long advocated
by Malaka and his followers. The difference was that they
were their own men, not Moscow's.

But Sjarifuddin's guile had given him and his followers
an advantage Malaka's men did not possess. He had been
minister of defence from 14 November 1945 to 27 June
1947. In that period Sjahrir had greatly increased the backing of the 'underground' parties, both in the military formations of the republic and in its political councils. Sjarifuddin had made the most of his opportunities, by putting
his supporters in senior positions in the army and by
secreting arms dumps, supposedly against the possibility
of Dutch attack, in places known only to himself and his
henchmen. In addition, he had ensured that the irregulars

of the republic were well indoctrinated with Stalinist ideas,
directed especially against the Masjumi. They, like the
Sarekat Islam before them, have ever been the special
targets of the Leninists, as being an organisation not only
with roots among the people but also free of Leninist
control. The third source of support for the FDR was the
amorphous Trade Union Congress of the Republic,
SOBSI, with a membership of between two and three hundred thousand, and run by Sjarifuddin's men.

It is hard to believe that all these preparations were not
a prelude to an attempt by Sjarifuddin and his friends
to seize power. Sjarifuddin's machinations as minister of
defence were an open secret, and the establishment parties
refused to permit him to regain that portfolio. A cabinet
was formed with the vice-president, Hatta, as prime minister and minister of defence, and in which the Masjumi
and PNI were dominant. Not only were Sjarifuddin and
his supporters now in opposition but also the cabinet began
to weaken their military support. The monetary inflation
was such that Hatta decided to cut the armed services
from an ineffective 450,000 to a more efficient 160,000,
with similar reductions in the civil administration. In the
nature of the case, the rationalisation threatened the pro-
fessionals less than the amateurs, namely those guerrillas
whom Sjahrir had incorporated into the army and who
provided Sjarifuddin with his personal supporters. The
threat of disbandment led to disaffection and reinforced
their personal allegiance to Sjarifuddin. His friends were
especially numerous in the army's fourth division, based on
Surakarta and commanded by a member of the PKI. Its
main components were Pesindo troops and Marines. As
the republic had now lost all its sea outlets to the Dutch,
the latter especially were obvious candidates for demobilisation, and they knew it.

In May another tweak on the string came from Moscow.
The republic had sent as its ambassador to the Russian
protectorates in eastern Europe one Suripno, a secret Stalinist. He had, with Sukarno's approval, suggested an ex-

change of consular representatives to Russia, which had expressed interest. The course of the negotiations with the Dutch, however, and the need to preserve American goodwill, compelled the republic to temporise over the matter. Suddenly, in May, Russia announced that it was unilaterally ratifying the consular agreement. It had evidently conceived this as a 'master-stroke' which would force the republic into a reciprocal ratification, wreck the negotiations with the Dutch, and put it in the bad graces of the United States. This gambit was foiled; the Hatta government simply recalled Suripno 'for consultations'. The FDR, however, immediately seized on the consular agreement to appeal to the Indonesian dream of liberation by external agency, and claimed Russia was sending vast amounts of aid to help the republic in its struggle. It thereby hoped to arouse public support for the Russians and for itself as their local representatives. For it had now made its plans to seize power. First, the FDR intended to mount a political campaign to replace the cabinet. If this failed, then massive demonstrations would be organised, followed by a general strike and outbreaks of violence. If the government still refused to go, revolt would be launched. The FDR's hopes of accomplishing this stage successfully were based on the calculation that it controlled some 35 per cent of the armed forces and influenced large proportions of other units.

The Stalinists made little headway. The strikes they fomented against the government met with only limited success. They then demanded a 'National Programme' which they hoped would lead to a coalition 'National Government', in which they held key ministries. This cunning scheme was spiked by the Hatta government's acceptance of the 'National Programme', or at least their interpretation of it. In addition, knowledge of the FDR plan to seize power had leaked out and the government began moving Sjarifuddin's men out of critical positions in the armed forces.

Nor was it only the government that was preparing against the FDR. Malaka's followers, whose noses were perhaps most sensitive to danger from the Stalinists, formed a grouping called the *Gerakan Revolusi Rakyat* (GRR) or People's Revolutionary Movement. Its programme was identical with that of the FDR, with the important exception that Malaka's men supported the Hatta government. But the aims were not important; these were two camps of Leninists, one national, the other Muscovite, for each of whom the other was its worst enemy.

Emissary from Moscow

Evidently, however, the FDR was thought to need a more experienced hand on the tiller. Suripno, the ambassador to eastern Europe, returned to Indonesia in August 1948, bringing with him a present from Moscow, namely Musso, who was said to have been last in the Indies in 1935 when he set up the 'Illegal PKI'. The Stalinists in Indonesia had always regarded him as their master and accordingly they quickly moved Sardjono aside and installed Musso as secretary of the PKI.

Events now moved into a higher gear. First, the Stalinists stood up to be counted. Sjarifuddin announced that he had been a communist ever since 1935 when he had joined Musso's party. Setiadjit of the Labour Party, and Abdulmadjid and Tan Ling Djie of the Socialist Party, also revealed their long-standing allegiance to Moscow. These affirmations of faith were very probably under instruction from Moscow. Precisely at that time the Cominform journal was berating the Yugoslav Titoists for submerging themselves in the 'People's Front' of that country.

Some doubts have been expressed on whether Sjarifuddin's admission was true; it is thought that since he was undoubtedly an opportunist he may have backed the gift horse from Moscow as a matter of expediency. But the evidence of his own actions does suggest that whether or not he was a convinced Stalinist from 1935, he thought it sufficiently in his interest to concert his activities with those of Musso's followers long before their master returned to Indonesia, while of course building up a following which owed a personal allegiance to him.

Musso's next step was to integrate all the constituent organisations of the FDR into the PKI. In a scheme very reminiscent of the merging of the Sarekat Rakyat of the 1920s into the PKI (p. 67 above), Musso planned to weed out some half of the sixty thousand members of the Socialist Party and about the same proportion of the Labour Party. On 1 September the new Politburo of the PKI was announced. Among them are to be found, of course, Musso, Tan Ling Djie, Wikana, Suripno, Amir Sjarifuddin, Alimin, Sardjono, but also names of younger men who were to achieve prominence later, such as Aidit, Lukman, and Nyoto.

Reincarnating the FDR as a greater PKI was not enough. In addition it had to be ritually reborn by abjuring the errors of its former life. These it duly admitted; principally they were the support of the Linggadjati and Renville agreements, and the failure to emphasise 'socialism'. All this meant was simply that the FDR had been following the Dimitrov line instead of foreshadowing the Zhdanov doctrine, which had not even been pronounced at the time of Linggadjati, when Sukarno and his supporters were being denounced by Moscow as Japanese collaborators. To let all Musso's supporters know exactly what Moscow expected of them, the press organs of the FDR in the early days of September expounded the Zhdanov line.

Musso had not been sent out from Moscow merely to renew acquaintanceships in his mature years (he was now fifty). His intention was to make a revolution. He described his scheme as a 'Gottwald Plan', referring to the method by which the Czechoslovak republic had been shanghaied into the Russian empire a little earlier. In fact, his ideas were very similar to those of the FDR, involving steadily increasing pressure on the government ending with, if necessary, a resort to violence. There was a certain urgency, as it was generally believed that a Dutch attack was imminent. The identity of the two schemes leads one to suspect that the FDR had been already receiving its instructions from Musso even before his second coming; their origin in the 'Gottwald Plan' makes one question Musso's grasp of reality. At the very least, the identification of Indonesians, grouped into personal followings of somewhat anarchic character, with docile, obedient Czechoslovak workers, leads one to ask whether Musso had not been away too long from Indonesia.

Early in September, Musso invited the Masjumi and PNI to a joint conference for 'building national unity'. This transparent Stalinist ploy met the response it deserved. But already before extending hospitality Musso, Sjarifuddin, Wikana and others had begun a speech-making tour intended to whip up support against the government. In very short order, however, the speaking had to stop. They who had intended to mount a revolution in November now found themselves obliged to fight in September. Something had gone wrong with the 'Gottwald Plan'.

However weak Musso's grasp of Indonesian political realities, this was not one of Sukarno's failings. Knowing the general intentions of the FDR, and being too well aware that if they seized power he would lose it, in his Independence Day speech of 17 August 1948 he announced the release of Malaka and his followers from their incarceration after the attempted coup of June and July 1946. To fight the greater threat he let slip the lesser. Subardjo and Iwa Kusuma Sumantri came out at once; Tan Malaka and Sukarni not until a month later, on 16 September. Their followers were now grouped into the GRR. But as, unlike Sjarifuddin, they had never been able to manipulate patronage, their organisation was smaller and less effective.

It may be no coincidence that trouble broke out early in September in Surakarta, where the pro-Musso and pro-Malaka forces faced one another. On Musso's side was the army's fourth division of some five thousand men, mainly marines and Pesindo. For Malaka was the Barisan Banteng, of some two to two and a half thousand troops. There was in addition one battalion of the Siliwangi division, the formation created by Sjahrir to protect the government.

Early in September senior officers supporting Musso began to disappear; the PKI accused the GRR of being responsible. Then on 13 September the leader of the Barisan Banteng was kidnapped, while marines of the fourth division stormed the Siliwangi barracks. Fighting became general between the Pesindo and the marines on the one side, and the Barisan Banteng and Siliwangi division on the other: it ended with the former being driven out of Surakarta by 17 September.

In the meanwhile, however, other of Musso's military supporters, no doubt intoxicated by the scent of cordite, took it into their heads to embark on the military stage of the FDR plan to seize power, and moving into the Madiun area took the town itself on 18 September. One of those in charge of the operation was Sumarsono, whom we last heard of organising the mutiny on the *Zeven Provincien* in 1936. That very night Musso and his debating team arrived at his house and the former found that, far from following any 'Gottwald Plan', his tail had wagged him into a brawl. The next day Sukarno asked the people to choose between him and Musso; the latter answered by accusing the government of truckling to the 'imperialists', western and Asian. His henchmen, including Tan Ling Djie and Abdulmadjid, were arrested in Jogjakarta that day, all innocent that a revolution had been launched. But this Stalinist version of an opera bouffe did not last long. The area held by Musso's men was steadily reduced until, on 30 September, Madiun itself was recaptured by the Siliwangi division. Sjarifuddin now led the remaining revolutionaries to his caches of weapons in the mountains. On the way they took their revenge on the villagers who had failed to support them, especially members of the Masjumi. But even this retreat did not save them; by 28 October the last large rebel military unit was captured; three days later Musso himself met his end in a skirmish. On 1 December Sjarifuddin and Suripno were caught and a week later the army announced the end of the rebellion. It had placed under arrest some thirty-five thousand persons, mostly from irregular military formations.

In 1948 as in 1926 we see the steady procession of events to predictable disaster. A 'plan' for revolution is hatched; but it is never carried out because subordinate leaders of the party take it into their heads to jump with their own guns, correctly assuming that they will thus embroil the whole party. Inevitably, such a botched attempt is put down with relative ease, whether by the Dutch or, even more tellingly, by the embryonic republic with its beleaguered and half-trained army. The element both revolts have in common is the many-headedness of the conspiracy; the nominal 'head' or 'executive' of the party may bear public responsibility but this is not paralleled by the powers he has over his wilful followers.

11

Communists in Disarray

The End of Tan Malaka

The elimination of Musso gave Tan Malaka an opening of which he was not slow to take advantage, and in October 1948 he formed the *Partai Murba* from the GRR. Malaka himself, though the presiding genius, held no office in the party; equally, the irregular fighting units who supported him, such as the Barisan Banteng, were kept distinct from it.

Malaka defined *Murba* as those who owned nothing but their mind and body but who, unlike the 'proletarian', lived in family units. The party was based on religion, nationalism, and socialism, a trinity we shall see re-emerge later. Murba's policy was consistently radical but, unlike the Stalinists', it was also nationalist. Nevertheless, it considered friendship with the Soviet Union, and opposition to 'imperialism', to be in the Indonesian national interest. Indeed, the date of its birth was set for 7 November, the anniversary of the Russian revolution.

With his political support reorganised, Malaka went on the offensive. It was not long before fortune gave him an opportunity for intrigue. Hatta, the prime minister, in the course of his negotiations with the Dutch, handed them a secret *aide-memoire* implying that the republic would recognise their sovereignty for an interim period. One of Malaka's sympathisers in the republican delegation imparted the contents to him, and he immediately passed them on to the army, who were naturally opposed to any Dutch control. The information also reached a group in the PNI, who as the party of civil servants were equally concerned; at the end of November they opposed further talks with the Dutch.

But Hatta was not in the mood to give Malaka much rope. On 1 December he banned *Murba,* the party's newspaper at Surakarta, and revoked the licence for its radio station. The party announced its intention of convoking a 'People's Congress' at Jogjakarta on 24 December and rumours began to circulate of a planned coup. So on 15 December Hatta instructed Colonel Nasution of the Siliwangi division to disarm the irregular formations supporting Malaka.

The internal struggle was bedevilled on 18 December by a Dutch attack on the republic, consequent on its refusal to accept Dutch sovereignty and control of its armed forces. Sukarno and Hatta were quickly captured by Dutch paratroopers dropped on Jogjakarta and control of the republic devolved on to a commissariat. Most of the Stalinist leaders captured after the failure of Musso's coup, among them Sjarifuddin and Sardjono, were executed in face of the Dutch advance; however, Alimin, Tan Ling Djie and Abdulmadjid escaped.

Thus the Dutch attack at one blow removed Malaka's principal opponents; Sukarno and Hatta on the one hand and the Stalinists on the other. He moved quickly. On 21 December, Radio Kediri, in territory still held by the republic, announced the arrival of the 'Father of the Republic'. His programme, as he announced it later, consisted of outright opposition to the Dutch and the Stalinists, based upon a united front of all parties and fighting organisations. Kediri fell to Dutch troops on 25 December 1948 but

Malaka himself escaped and quickly obtained great support in the countryside.

For while Dutch troops had rapidly occupied the cities and towns of the republic, they were not able to control the rural areas. And in any case their victory was short-lived. The rapid advance of the communists in China had induced the United States to exert itself more strongly to prevent the possibility of a communist Indonesia emerging from the guerrilla warfare then in progress. As for the Dutch, they had no seat on the security council, and thus were unable to prevent it discussing the Indonesian problem, as the French had done with regard to their war in Indochina. So on 28 January 1949 that council passed a resolution envisaging Indonesian sovereignty and, after much negotiation, on 7 May, Dutch and Indonesians agreed to it.

Within the republican areas the army remained firmly in control; there was never any acceptance of the principle of arming a 'people's army', or of having military units under a committee on which one or other kind of Leninist would be represented. The irregulars were authorised to act only under army control.

The PKI, attempting to retrieve its reputation after the failed coup, opposed the security council resolution and organised a few armed groups; they were used principally not to fight the Dutch or even the republican forces but to attack the supporters of the Masjumi and of Malaka. At one point Sukiman, a member of the commissariat, in fear of the PKI's bandits, surrendered to the Dutch. The same tactic, be it noted, had been followed by communist forces when they had been on the run. One can only conclude that both sides felt that the fate awaiting them at Dutch hands was more benign than that reserved for them by their fellow-revolutionaries.

In addition to the popular support he was receiving for his opposition to the Dutch, Malaka also enjoyed the backing of the fourth division of the republican army, based in East Java and led by Colonel Sungkono. Emboldened by his popularity, Malaka denounced Hatta and Nasution for accepting the security council resolution. Nasution, it will be remembered, had been charged by Hatta with disarming Malaka's irregular supporters; he began doing so shortly after the resolution was passed. But Malaka's intransigence, and Nasution's pressure on him, lost him the support of the senior officers in the fourth division. When in March one of its brigades defected to him, he was forthwith put under arrest near Blitar. After a fight between the division and its disloyal brigade, which destroyed the latter, he was put to death—by the very division which had supported him only a few months previously. The great popular support he had created was not bequeathed to the Murba Party; as in the case of nearly all Indonesian political leaders, his backing was personal and disappeared with him. But his ideas lived on and his ghost must have looked with amused eyebrows on Sukarno, a decade later, adopting policies and attitudes to which Malaka had given birth.

Sovereignty and Conflict

While the republic was integrating the guerrillas into the army on the one hand, it was also rapidly finding an accommodation with the Dutch on the other and thus depriving the extremists both of their military supporters and of a political rallying cause. Mohamed Rum, on behalf of the republic, and van Royen for the Netherlands, reached agreement in July 1949, Sukarno and Hatta were released from their imprisonment in Bangka, and a new cabinet, the third presidential, was installed on 4 August. The Rum-van Royen accord promised to end the fighting but also to confirm in power the establishment. So for different reasons it was opposed by both Sjahrir's socialists and the Leninists of various persuasions. Among the latter was a Mohamed Djoni. A Stalinist until 1947, he had then broken with the PKI in order to oppose the Linggadjati agreement and had founded his own political party, the 'Red PKI' to indicate it was more aggressive than the Stalinists themselves. To obtain support for his opposition to the Rum-van Royen agreement he capitalised on the natural resentment of the guerrillas scheduled for demobilisation, and convened a 'guerrilla congress' for 17 September 1949 at Prambanan, near Jogjakarta, choosing the location in order to commemorate the 1926 revolt. But the minister of defence, the sultan of Jogjakarta, was in no humour to put up with such nonsense. He ordered the congress to be disbanded and Djoni arrested.

In September, Malaka's supporters in East Java, as ever intransigent, attacked the Dutch in violation of the cease-fire agreement, no doubt hoping that this would involve the regular troops of the republic. Instead, they were brought to heel by those same forces at the end of October. Other Malaka supporters in Bantam in the west of Java, led by one Chaerul Saleh, announced the formation of a People's Army on 14 October, to fight against the 'Sukarno-Hatta compromise policy'. It was not until February of 1950 that Saleh was finally arrested and his organisation broken up. We shall, however, read of him again.

Hardly had the new cabinet been installed than the Stalinists were heard from. On 10 August 1949 Alimin emerged from hiding and in a press interview argued that the party as such was not responsible for the Madiun revolt, only irresponsible individuals were. In fact, of course, as we know the Madiun revolt was planned at least overtly by the FDR first, and then Musso, and perhaps entirely by the latter. The 'irresponsible individuals' were accountable only for the failure of the revolt and Alimin's argument was tantamount to saying that only the insubordinate should be punished, while those who had not acted prematurely, and would have enjoyed the benefits of success if all had gone according to plan, should be absolved from all blame.

At the same time Alimin showed the first signs of a reorientation to the new facts of life in Indonesia. Recognising that as a religion needs a devil, so communism needs imperialism, he propounded a new theory which would both serve Russian interests and take account of Indonesia's independence. Since the country was shortly to be no longer a colony, it was to be known as a semi-colony and the focus of animosity was to be expanded from the Dutch in particular to westerners in general and those who had links with them. Therefore not all Indonesian capitalists were bad; only those who had links with the west: these were called 'compradores'. (The similarity with the concept of 'sinful' or foreign capitalism is obvious.) National capitalists, petty 'bourgeoisie', peasants and workers were all equally virtuous and should form a united front against the 'compradores' and the west, known as 'foreign imperialists'. This was Alimin's adaptation of the 'four-class coalition' evolved by Mao Tse-tung in China; the medieval disputes about how many angels could dance on the point of a needle are paralleled by communist arguments on how many classes may be distinguished in a given society: Mao showed great virtuosity in producing as many as were tactically required at any one time.

Perhaps because it accepted Alimin's specious argument, perhaps because it wanted to show its neutrality in the cold war which had begun with the Zhdanov two-camp doctrine, on 7 September the government announced that it would pardon all participants in the Madiun coup who were not held for criminal offences. The PKI was thus permitted resurrection; and sanction was given to indiscipline within its ranks. For clearly, since attempts at revolution are of their nature uncertain in outcome, risks would be limited and benefits maximised if the entire party would not be identified with such adventures. If successful, of course, the whole party would assume the credit, but if unsuccessful only those caught red-handed would suffer. But this naturally meant that there would be no particular incentive for the party to discipline its hot-heads. Happily, as we shall see, neither Alimin nor this theory was to prevail.

The cabinet not only gave life to the PKI, they also gave it a cause, by permitting the Dutch to retain Western New Guinea. On 2 November 1949 the Round Table Conference in the Hague ended in agreement. Briefly, the Netherlands surrendered sovereignty over all the territory of the Netherlands Indies except for Western New Guinea; the new United States of Indonesia, formed from the republic and the various puppet states the Dutch had constituted from 1945 to 1949, assumed the debts of the Netherlands Indies and guaranteed Netherlands and other foreign investments in the country. A Netherlands-Indonesian Union was set up to facilitate consultation.

The negotiators from the republic, principally based on Java, were not disposed to quibble about Western New Guinea; the only objectors were the delegates from the Dutch-created states, especially those on the other islands. The Javanese were if anything too well aware that delay in acquiring sovereignty would work against them, strengthening the extremists behind their own lines and establishing the Dutch-created states so firmly that it would prove impossible to dissolve them. Unfortunately, the Dutch retention of Western New Guinea was to prove a godsend to all in Indonesia whose interests lay in xenophobia. Immediately after the conclusion of the conference a spokesman for the PKI Politburo (probably Alimin himself) declared that because of continuing Netherlands control of the territory the 'fight for freedom starts anew'.

The next month, in December, the PKI urged the Zhdanov doctrine on Indonesia. It called for 'national unity' against the west and the neutralists (who, not being for Russia, were in her eyes automatically against) and urged Indonesia to cooperate with the Russian bloc, called the 'anti-imperialist nations'. It also sought to obtain a foothold in the armed forces by arguing that its militia be incorporated into the new Indonesian army.

On 14 December the Indonesian parliament ratified the Hague agreement. The establishment, consisting of the PNI and the Masjumi, were opposed by the extremists, made up of the communists, Malaka supporters, and various others. Sjahrir's PSI, caught between two fires, simply abstained.

Now that independence was gained, the real and deep differences of interest between the protagonists could not

help emerging. Elections had been long promised and could
not be denied indefinitely. But the parties were not equally
equipped to face them. As already mentioned, the PNI's
support was predominantly from Javanese civil servants and
such popular roots as they could strike. The Masjumi was
more fortunate. At the time, it contained the *Nahdatul
Ulama,* or Muslim Scholars, an orthodox group whose appeal was virtually limited to Java; the Masjumi proper was
the only important Islamic party of the other islands. In
the nature of the case, Islam is a religion in the basic sense
of the word, namely that it binds its adherents together,
thus providing them with a strong sense of social integration.
The PNI was well aware that its own popular support did
not compare with that of the Masjumi. Sukarno himself
was no better off, having no party to muster his followers.
Neither could boast the solid organisational structure supporting the Masjumi and both lived in fear of its expected
massive election victory. The PNI would then be reduced
to impotence, while Sukarno could hardly hope to survive
for long as president of an Islamic state; he had made his
secularism too abundantly clear. In consequence both,
unable to depend on organised public support for their
continuance in power, tried to maintain their positions by
perpetuating the attitudes that had created them, namely
enmity to 'imperialism', broadening out from the Dutch to
attack, in due course, the whole western world. It was only
a matter of time before their interests would coincide with
others opposing the west, represented in Indonesia by the
PKI.

In January the Soviet Union recognised Indonesia and
the next month a mission left Djakarta for Moscow. It
arrived at the end of April but Moscow still regarded the
republic as an 'imperialist' creation and the delegation met
only a cold reception. In February the Chinese People's
Republic and Indonesia extended mutual recognition to
each other.

SOBSI, the confederation of trade unions, had meanwhile
acquired Nyono, a covert communist, as its chairman. He
immediately launched it on a series of strikes. Though a

moment's reflection is sufficient to show that a poverty-stricken country like Indonesia is quite unable to afford such disruption, it is paradoxically true that the strikes gained sympathy among the general mass of non-communist Indonesians. Irrationally, no doubt, they felt that since most of the country's capital was foreign-owned, strike action was a way of asserting their own control over labour and thus showing that they too had an influence over the economic product. It must be recorded that, amazingly enough, the impression was widespread in Indonesia in the early 1950s that foreign capital needed to invest in Indonesia more than Indonesia needed the capital to survive as a state; it took two decades of privation to attenuate the strength of this delusion. With the outbreak of the Korean war in June of 1950, of course, SOBSI had an added political motive for labour unrest, hoping that its strike actions would serve to impede the flow of supplies, especially rubber, to the United Nations forces. The Hatta government itself took the view that this was a cold war struggle from which Indonesia should remain aloof.

In the meantime, the republicans had been assiduously at work under Sukarno's leadership destroying the Dutch-created federal United States of Indonesia, to which sovereignty had been transferred. Though Indonesia's fragmented character and poor communications demand a large degree of decentralisation for effective government, the federal state's Dutch odour was undoubtedly repugnant to the greater part of the Indonesian political public. It was therefore quickly dissolved, and on 6 September the first cabinet of the unitarian republic of Indonesia took office. It was headed by Mohamed Natsir, a prominent leader of the Masjumi, and consisted of an alliance between his party and Sjahrir's PSI. The animosities were beginning to show: the PNI refused to enter the cabinet because it would not work with the PSI.

Already, at this early stage of sovereign Indonesia's life, the two main opponents were identifiable. On the one hand the Masjumi, at this time in government, supported by the army; on the other the PKI. In due course the Masjumi were to be moved out of power but the enmity of the army for the PKI, which was never in power, was to remain constant.

Revival of the PKI

Fortuitously, however, relations between the Netherlands and Indonesia were to develop in a way which considerably helped the cause of the PKI. The talks specified in the Round Table Conference agreement were duly held at the end of December; nothing came of them, the Dutch being, as usual, both obstinate and insensitive. Sukarno and the PNI lived in fear of the exclusion of Western New Guinea being used as an exemplar by some of the former federal states, and thus destroying the unity of the republic. He pleaded with the cabinet for stern action against the Dutch. Natsir and his colleagues, however, seem to have been unaware of the explosive potential of the issue and rejected his plea. Not so the PKI; they expressed their support for a PNI motion in parliament demanding that the Netherlands-Indonesian union be abrogated in reprisal for the Dutch refusal to hand over the territory.

For the Stalinists were reorganising. After Musso's failure, a provisional PKI central committee had tried to keep the flag flying and maintain an embryonic party organisation. Most party members, however, were unwilling to declare themselves for fear of suffering further penalties for Musso's revolt. As acting secretary general the party had one Ngadiman Hardjosubroto; when he was chosen to sit on the working committee of the KNIP in December 1949, he was replaced by Djaetun, who had participated in the 1926 revolt and consequently been exiled until 1946. But in fact during 1950 the PKI was three-faced, and Djaetun's official PKI was only one of them. Another was made up of the socialist and labour parties. The first was led by Tan Ling Djie, who had been elevated to the general secretariat of the PKI two years earlier by Musso; while the Labour Party was led by Asmu Sakirman. But these two faces of the party were in fact twitched by the hidden third, an 'illegal PKI', which also maintained an underground organisation. Thus, Musso's 'New Road' resolution, enjoining a single public PKI, had been abandoned in favour of the policy espoused by the men he had demoted, Alimin and Sardjono.

Alimin, who had been cleared of involvement in the 1948 coup, was now over sixty (he was born in 1889), but he still retained considerable prestige and was head of the Agitprop secretariat to which he had been relegated by Musso in 1948. In public speeches he criticised not only Musso but also Stalin! The public PKI leader, however, was undoubtedly Tan Ling Djie, who formally led the 'Socialist' Party. Ever present, of course, was the ex-director of the Asrama, Wikana; he had been made head of the Youth Section of the Politburo by Musso in 1948 and was now busy building the Youth Front (*Pemuda Rakyat*) which was to play a macabre role fifteen years later.

That this shadowy leadership had deviated from the 'New Road' resolution was no doubt the result of a judgement that discretion was the better part of valour. So soon after the 1948 debacle they felt it would be folly to have the PKI as a perpetual public reminder of the Stalinist stab in the back. Rather they wished to work through the Partai Sosialis as the principal front, concentrating on the minuscule urban working class and inveigling non-communist Marxists into it. They still retained the 'New Road' resolution and even the 'Gottwald Plan' as their long-term aim but felt that the time was not opportune to come out into the open and work among the masses of the country; more could be done by parliamentary manoeuvre.

This cautious policy, however, did not endear itself to the younger members in the leadership, in particular to Nyono, the SOBSI chairman, who was engaged in provoking as many strikes as possible and who was further encouraged by his undoubted success. Within a year after the transfer of sovereignty he had increased the membership of his organisation from two hundred thousand to over one million. His opposition to the official policy of self-effacement was soon to be supported by the return of another two members of Musso's Politburo, Aidit and Lukman.

Dipa Nusantara Aidit, to give him his full name, was born in 1924 in Sumatra, the son of a minor employee in the forestry department. He attended elementary school in his native province, then went to a secondary trade school in Djakarta, joining the Gerindo, Amir Sjarifuddin's organisation, in 1940 when he was sixteen. During the Japanese occupation he is said to have organised transport and pedicab drivers and to have entered Musso's underground PKI in 1943. After the proclamation of independence in 1945 he helped launch a youth organisation. He was captured in Djakarta by British forces and handed over to the Dutch, who detained him until mid-1946. On his release he made his way to republican territory and devoted himself to the work of the PKI. He was well thought of, and at the fourth congress in 1947 was elected a member of the central committee. In that year too he became a member of the KNIP and chairman of the PKI group in it. He was also a member of the executive of the Pesindo and of the FDR. A year later he became a member of the Politburo, when he was a mere twenty-four years old.

Lukman, born in 1920, was a second-generation communist whose father, a *hadji* (returned pilgrim from Mecca), had been a member of the Sarekat Islam and then of the Sarekat Rakyat. He took part in the 1926 revolt and was consequently exiled to Western New Guinea in 1929. Young Lukman left for Java nine years later and drifted from job to job. When the Japanese came he entered the youth groups and in 1945 took part in the kidnapping of Sukarno and Hatta. He joined Yusuf's PKI in 1945 but the next year dutifully switched his allegiance to Sardjono. In 1948, when Musso pushed Sardjono aside Lukman, like Aidit, moved on to the Politburo, as head of the Agitprop secretariat. Alimin and Sardjono, who had been leading the party before Musso's arrival, were demoted to membership of the Lukman secretariat.

Both Aidit and Lukman avoided arrest after the failure

of their mentor's revolt and left for a year's stay in east Asia. They are said to have fought with the Viet Minh guerrillas, to have gone to China where they attended the Asian-Australian Trade Union Conference in Peking in 1949, nominally representing SOBSI, and returned in July 1950. They found the party being led by Alimin, whom Musso had reduced to a position junior to themselves and dedicated to a policy at variance with his. It was not long before they set matters right in their own eyes.

12
Fattening
the
PKI

Aidit Takes Control

As Stalinists and followers of Musso, Aidit and Lukman
were not likely to support Alimin and Tan Ling Djie's deviation from the 'New Road'. On returning to Indonesia they
rejoined the Agitprop secretariat and, despite Tan's opposition, began in August to republish the party's periodical
Bintang Merah (Red Star). They were helped by another
young man, Nyoto, then twenty-five years old. He too is
said to have taken part in the communist underground
during the Japanese occupation, and then in November 1945
to have helped re-establish the PKI in the small East Javanese town of Bekasi, soon becoming its secretary general.
He later represented the PKI on the working committee of
the KNIP and became chairman of the PKI group on the committee. Like Aidit and Lukman, he had been elevated to
both the central committee and the Politburo by Musso in
1948.

This trio used the party organ to discredit the existing
leadership (evidently 'revolutionary discipline' was still ab-

sent). They later claimed that the periodical increased its circulation from three thousand to ten thousand at the end of the year, a considerable achievement since party membership at that time was only between three and five thousand. Simultaneously, they set in hand the re-establishment of the party organisation, shattered after the failure of the 1948 uprising, staffing it with their supporters.

Their first contest with the official leadership took place in September 1950. Against the advice of Tan and Alimin, but with the support of the younger leaders, the party re-buried the eleven PKI leaders who had been shot after the failure of Musso's coup. This was done despite many obstacles placed by the government, and marked the beginning of the PKI's climb back to respectability. It also showed, of course, that the need for caution had been exaggerated by the party's leaders. It was not long before their heads began to roll.

First, the 'Labour Party' was compelled to dissolve itself 'in accordance with Musso's plan', with the adjuration that the 'Socialist Party', led by Tan, do likewise. Wikana was removed from the executive committee of the Pemuda Rakyat, made to recant his views, and compelled to withdraw from a study group organised by the Murba Party, Tan Malaka's followers.

West Irian (as Western New Guinea is known in Indonesia) was pressed into service as a political weapon. The first targets were the opponents of the Aidit group within the party. In December, Ngadiman, the previous acting secretary general of the PKI, put out a statement in the name of the secretariat calling for a confederation between a 'Democratic Republic of Irian, free from the Round Table Conference agreement, and the Unitary State of the Republic of Indonesia not yet freed from the agreement'. This was entirely in line with Russian policy, which had condemned the treaty. But Ngadiman was denounced by the rising leadership in the central committee, removed as PKI member of parliament, and excluded from the leadership of the party.

The year 1951 opened with a plenary session of the central committee of the PKI, and in short order Aidit replaced Alimin as chairman of the Politburo, supported by Lukman and Njoto. Whether this was because Alimin was considered insufficiently compliant with Moscow's intentions, or simply because Aidit and Lukman as younger men were thought to be better leaders, remains a matter for conjecture. But once in charge, Aidit began impressing his own policy, however Moscow-based, on the party. Tan Ling Djie was ordered to abandon the plan to reconstruct the Socialist Party. Sukarno and independent Indonesia continued to be attacked as imperialist tools. And a campaign was initiated, which was to acquire increasing intensity as time went by, to portray the failed Madiun uprising as a 'provocation'. Throughout the country, local leaders were replaced by Aidit's henchmen.

It is perhaps opportune here to sketch the organisational structure the PKI developed. Formally, ultimate control of policy was held by the national congress (this had met in 1947 and was to meet again in 1954, 1959, 1962 and 1965). In fact, however, the major decisions were taken by the Politburo, which itself was a standing committee of the central committee. In 1951 the latter had fourteen members, and over the years witnessed a gradual growth to a total of thirty-five full members and eleven candidate members, though eleven of the 1951 members were still on the committee in 1965. In 1953 a central committee secretariat for routine daily work was instituted with seven members, with Aidit as secretary general. The Politburo held five members in 1951; four of these, Aidit, Lukman, Sudisman and Nyoto, remained to the end, but in 1963 it was enlarged to seven full members and two candidate members.

The organisation these policy-making bodies directed was made up of four levels. The lowest were the cells, based either on locality or place of work, and consisting of only a few people. They were responsible to 'resort committees', which also were based territorially or institutionally and held less than a hundred members each. These were the basic organisational units. Above them came the subsection committees, responsible for the administrative divisions known as districts and sub-districts, and the smaller towns. In turn, they answered to the section committees, which were responsible for the larger administrative units known as regencies and the larger towns. At the topmost level were to be found the large area committees, covering, for example, a province such as West Java; the island committees covering various islands, and the Djakarta committee, responsible for the capital. At the apex was the central committee.

With the party firmly in his grasp, Aidit quickly asserted himself. Where Alimin had queried the wisdom of the SOBSI campaign of strikes and disruption, Aidit intensified it. There was open looting in Medan and Surabaya, the head towns of the major plantation areas of East Sumatra and East Java, with European planters being killed as frequently as their counterparts in Malaya. All this, of course, was in support of the Chinese campaign in Korea, then in progress. By February some five hundred thousand estate workers were on strike in a determined attempt to stop supplies to that country. Then the prime minister, Natsir, decided to act and prohibited strikes in vital industries, which was interpreted to mean virtually the whole economy. A military campaign to root out the remnants of communist guerrillas in the mountains of Central Java, known as the Merapi-Merbabu complex, was intensified. And in an attempt to cut off supplies of recruits and money for the PKI, the government limited Chinese immigrants to only seven thousand a year.

The cabinet was replaced in April 1951 for one more to the president's liking; it turned out also to be more vigorously anti-Stalinist than its predecessor. It was headed by Sukiman from the Masjumi, with members drawn from both the PNI and the Masjumi but united only by their loyalty to the prime minister. As foreign minister it had Subardjo, whom we remember as a young leader of the Perhimpunan Indonesia in Holland, a close associate of

Admiral Maeda during the Japanese occupation and supporter of Tan Malaka in 1945–7. The minister of justice
was Yamin, also one of Tan Malaka's allies.

Shortly after the cabinet took office, the United Nations
declared an embargo on all raw materials to China, as a
consequence of her intervention in the Korean war. The
cabinet decided to comply with the ruling. The PKI, in support of China, then moved to the attack and abandoned its
previous adherence to the prohibition on strikes. SOBSI
launched a number which over the next few weeks paralysed the airways, motorbus lines, shipping companies, sugar
mills, oil installations and estates (most of which were
foreign-owned). The high peak of this campaign was
reached in August, when a hundred and fifty armed men
attacked a police post at Tandjong Priok, the port of
Djakarta. Eleven men were killed and several SOBSI leaders
were arrested. A hand grenade was thrown into the crowd
at Bogor, south of Djakarta, wounding eighty-six people.
The PKI then announced that it would observe Independence Day, 17 August, independently of government. When
the prime minister prohibited all unauthorised public demonstrations the PKI replied that they would ignore this order.

In reply, on 11 August Sukiman ordered the army and
police to curb the disorder on the estates in East Sumatra,
a province where the workers were under close PKI/SOBSI
control. Six hundred persons, belonging to the PKI and its
labour organisations, were arrested, and law and order
returned immediately. The prime minister then applied the
same remedy in the capital. Fifteen members of parliament,
mostly from the PKI were arrested; the headquarters of the
PKI and SOBSI were raided; the editors of *Sin Po*, a Chinese-
language communist daily, were detained. Alimin took refuge in the Chinese embassy; Aidit went into hiding.

The security raids continued, spreading to East Java,
where trouble had been rife. By the end of August more
than two thousand people had been detained and by the
end of November the number had risen to fifteen thousand.
Sukiman defended the 'razzia', as it was called, on the

grounds that he had believed that a revolution similar to the Madiun uprising was in the offing. However, as he failed to bring the detainees to trial, his charges lacked some credibility. He was nevertheless supported by the president in his Independence Day speech; the latter in November warned foreigners (meaning mainly the Chinese in the PKI) not to propagate communism or social revolution. At this time there was no love lost between president and communists. The party published a 'White Paper' on the Madiun affair in the party newspaper *Bintang Merah* (Red Star); both Sukarno and Hatta were held guilty of the destruction of the PKI.

The 'razzia' set back the work of reconstructing the party, but relief was in sight. Sukiman fell victim to machinations by, of all people, the PKI's enemies, the PSI, or Sjahrir's followers. They used the acceptance of American aid by Subardjo to bring down the cabinet in February 1952 in the hope, successful as it proved, of participating in the next government.

New Course

While the PKI had been fomenting trouble, however, its foreign headquarters had resolved on a new policy. The Zhdanov line, opposing the Russians and their satellites to the west, had not paid off, and Stalin in February 1951 declared that war was not inevitable, which may be translated as meaning that he considered the risks too great. In May, the Zhdanov line gave a last kick with the second spring offensive in Korea; this was defeated and in June the Russian foreign minister, Jacob Malik, asked for a truce. In September the Communist Party of India abandoned violence, and in October that of Malaya, thoroughly routed, followed suit.

In January 1952 came the turn of the PKI. At its national conference Aidit proposed a 'united national front, including the national bourgeoisie'. By the latter term Aidit meant, simply, the PNI, whom he saw correctly as much more malleable than the Masjumi. The latter he put into the 'compradore bourgeoisie' pigeonhole, thereby indicating the PKI's enmity; he knew that, as the SI congress of 1923 had shown, the organised Modernist Muslims would have no truck with communism.

In addition, Aidit announced a decisive change of policy. From being a small group of the dedicated (it had less than eight thousand members), the PKI was to become a mass party; membership was to be increased to a hundred thousand in six months. He also repudiated Musso's 1948 coup, declaring that it was important to eliminate sectarianism and adventurousness. He meant, as events were to show, that he desired a party both disciplined and law-abiding, the strategy he was to follow until the PKI's destruction fifteen years later. He is hardly to be blamed, considering the history of the PKI since its foundation, not to mention much more recent events, for concluding that the party was most unlikely to succeed in seizing power by force and that the principal cause of its abortive attempts to do so had been the indiscipline of subordinate leaders. This had been true both of the 1926 botch and the 1948 adventure. As he was to say in May 1953, the PKI based its decisions on the balance of social forces, and clearly this was against it. No doubt Aidit intended, as a good Leninist, to achieve power at some date in the future. His actions indicate, however, that his major preoccupation was to build (by Leninist methods of course) a large, well-run, legal organisation.

Aidit's plans required educating the party and in March 1951 the PKI began an intensive campaign of publication of Marxist/Leninst translated works; in July it began publishing its own newspaper, *Harian Rakyat*. In that year, too, the work of training party officials (cadres) was put in hand.

Crucial to Aidit's strategy was the assumption that power was attainable through the democratic process; elections were expected in the near future. Also, no doubt, he hoped that an increase in numbers would lead to greater control over the various social groups in Indonesian society, and so create a 'united front' led by the PKI.

Fortune smiled on the party at the formation of the next cabinet and enfeebled their principal opponent. The government which took office in April 1952 was led by Wilopo of the PNI, and was principally a Masjumi-PSI coalition. In retrospect, it was perhaps mainly significant for the fact that as the cabinet, including the Masjumi members, refused to give the ministry of religion to the Nahdatul Ulama (until then part of the Masjumi) on the grounds of their well-attested corrupt use of office, that party then withdrew from the Masjumi. Not only did this halve the latter's strength, it also produced an ignorant group of political religious leaders ripe for manipulation. The opportunity, as we shall see, was not missed.

But the PKI was not content to await the turn of fortune. In pursuit of its new policy, it announced its support for the new cabinet and SOBSI called off all strikes. The PKI then, in the person of Alimin, put out feelers to Sidik Djoyosukarto, secretary general of the PNI, for a joint 'unity of attitude' programme to commemorate one of the country's nationalist festivals, Budi Utomo, on 20 May. Sidik, who rather fancied himself as a calculating politician, responded favourably. He was well aware that in the proposed elections his party faced decimation at the hands of the Masjumi, who had the support of organised Muslims, while the PNI could rely only on the grudging allegiance of those whom its civil servant members could hope to influence. The party's parliamentary faction, however, was another matter; it was much more strongly influenced by Sukarno and he insisted that it have no truck with the PKI.

Neither the divergence between Sidik and Sukarno, nor the latter's antipathy to the PKI were to endure. In May the PKI held the thirty-second anniversary celebration of its foundation. There Aidit argued that each country should travel its own road to socialism and called for a national front. Alimin, to the consternation of the delegates, led the cheering for Sukarno. This marked the beginning of what may be called the nationalisation of Indonesian communism. Henceforward the symbols of nationalism were to be emphasised while those usually associated with communism were to be obscured or even abandoned. Typical of this approach was the adoption by sobsi of a new constitution in September 1952. This left out 'socialism', 'people's democracy', and 'class struggle'. The pki's youth front, the Pemuda Rakyat, followed suit.

Supporting the President

Events again played into the pki's hands and made both Sukarno and the pni its debtors. In August 1952 the Ministry of Defence, staffed by many Sjahrir sympathisers, produced a plan to reduce the army from 200,000 ineffectives to 120,000 fairly efficient troops. Those whom they proposed to axe, on grounds of unfitness and illiteracy, were irregulars on whom Sukarno, the pni and many 'radicals' depended for support. Their riposte was to propose a motion in parliament calling for changes in the Ministry of Defence and the high command; it was passed by an unholy alliance of the pni, the Nahdatul Ulama and the pki. The next day the army arranged for a 'spontaneous' demonstration demanding the dissolution of parliament and the holding of elections; it was successfully bluffed by the president into awaiting an expression of feeling from the outlying provinces, which gave him an opportunity to instigate mutinies in various army commands and so restore the situation in his favour.

It is perhaps from this incident that we may date Sukarno's *rapprochement* with the pki. Feeling himself naked before the power of the army, and with no popular organisation of his own, he cast about for one that would support him. The pni, though his ardent followers, could not meet this specification, while his steadfast advocacy of a secular constitution had alienated the Muslim parties. The pki, on the other hand, not only was close to him ideologically but was rapidly striking root among the people, or at least among the Javanese. At its thirty-third anniversary celebrations in May 1953, it was announced that the target of one hundred thousand members had already been reached. (Though

Aidit, aware of how little this really meant, was to urge the need for better discipline and organisation.) The PKI was also continuing to give public demonstration that it was abjuring its foreign allegiances and giving complete loyalty to the country (which Sukarno, like some other rulers, seemed to equate with himself). At the same anniversary congress, for example, portraits of Lenin, Stalin, and Mao were conspicuously absent. It is true that Aidit was completing a six months' stay in Moscow, but on his return that same month he confirmed that there was no change in his policy of a 'national front'. This had been given added point by including in the PKI's pantheon of 'Heroes of the Working Class' the late commander-in-chief, General Sudirman, who had crushed the PKI's 1948 attempt at revolt, as well as Tjipto Mangunkusumo, leader of the Eurasian-dominated Indische Partij of 1911.

Aidit for his part was only too anxious to woo Sukarno, and he turned to establish a claim on him by working for the removal of the vice president, Hatta. The partnership with Sukarno had been forced on the latter by the requirements of the nationalist uprising; they agreed on little. Nor was it only the desire to please the president that made the PKI attack Hatta. As a determined opponent of communism, whose earlier experience with the Perhimpunan Indonesia in Holland had given him an insight into Leninist methods which was too deep for Aidit's comfort, he was in any case an object of special animosity to the PKI. As we shall see, time and circumstance eventually satisfied both Sukarno and Aidit.

In the very next month the PKI gained ample reward for its 'national' policy. In the east coast of Sumatra, Chinese squatters resisted eviction from land required by the government for its land reform programme; in a consequent struggle with police six squatters, five Chinese and one Indonesian, were killed and sixteen wounded. The incident had probably been PKI-inspired, and in June a PNI fellow-traveller in parliament, Sidik Kertapati, moved a motion of no confidence in the cabinet's Sumatran land reform programme. Thanks to cooperation between Sukarno, the PNI and the PKI, the motion passed and the cabinet, offensive to them all, was defeated.

The PKI may be said finally to have surmounted the political odium attaching to its abortive 1948 coup during the next cabinet's term of office, which held office for two years from July 1953. It was led by Ali Sastroamidjoyo, and was based on a coalition between his party, the PNI, and the Nahdatul Ulama, with support in parliament from the PKI and behind the scenes from the president. Even the composition of the cabinet was a result of PKI efforts, for during the period of its formation the party applied pressure on the PNI not to enter into an agreement with the Masjumi.

The new cabinet was in a very real sense a Javanese coalition. Both the PNI and NU drew their main strength from the Javanese; the NU almost exclusively so. The PKI, equally, was based nearly entirely on the same ethnic group; while the president was of course a Javanese. Their principal opponents, the Masjumi and the PSI, however, drew much support from outside Java; the Masjumi had fair claim to being considered the only all-Indonesian party in the sense that its followers were to be found in substantial numbers in all the major ethnic groups in the country, though perhaps relatively weakly among the Javanese.

The government soon distinguished itself by its promotion of Javanese interests; Javanese officials, members of the PNI, were posted to the outer islands with the intention of diminishing the support for the Masjumi. Nor did the cabinet scruple to feather the nests of its members and friends; it quickly acquired a name for corruption, and even Aidit, though his party was supporting the cabinet, spoke out against the prevalent venality.

However, Aidit was more concerned with getting his foot in the door. The PKI's fifth national congress, held in March 1953, ratified the party programme drawn up some six months earlier in the new political atmosphere of the Ali cabinet. The programme asked for a government of a 'national united front . . . alliance of workers and peasants under the leadership of the working class—a government of dictatorship of the people—not socialist but democratic reforms'. 'Working class' of course meant the PKI while 'democratic reforms' is best understood as a soft sell to the other political parties, for in fact the PKI was demanding a share in government.

Whilst making these demands, Aidit was tightening his grasp on the party. Tan Ling Djie, until 1951 the leader of the Socialist Party, had supported the policy of developing militant labour unions and peasant organisations, fomenting strikes, and waging an intense parliamentary battle. Emphatically not a man who believed in a mass party, which he considered unreliable, he wished to return to the strategy of the popular front, the development of a small cadre party, and tactics of concealment and infiltration. Aidit was at the other end of the spectrum. He saw little value in parliamentary battles. His policy was to agitate, organise and mobilise the masses in order to develop a large movement which would not only work above ground but also hold the centre of the political stage.

In October 1953 a plenary meeting of the central committee was called, well staffed by now with Aidit's supporters. It expelled Tan from its ranks for 'subjectivism, legalism, and liquidationism', in plain English for not submitting to Aidit. The latter now became not only king but also high priest of the PKI; the sole official reader of theoretical entrails, paralleling in this respect the leaders of all other communist parties.

With Aidit supreme, his opponents were gradually removed. Alimin was dropped from the Politburo and then, six months later at the fifth party congress, from the central committee. The editor of the PKI daily *Harian Rakyat*, Siauw Giok Tjan, resigned from his post. It seems clear that both his and Tan's removal were at least in part precipitated by Aidit's desire to present his party as 'national' as possible, which of course precluded having members of a heartily disliked minority group in positions of prominence.

As proof of his managerial ability Aidit could point to a steady growth of enrolment in the party. By October 1953 it could claim 126,671 members and candidate members, while SOBSI had reported 1,561,757 members in 1952. To give substance to its new-found interest in the peasants (in a country 80 per cent rural) the PKI launched a peasant front, the *Barisan Tani Indonesia,* or BTI. By September 1953 this declared eight hundred thousand members. But of course these 'members' were anything but convinced communists. There is little doubt that they used the PKI as instrumentally as it was using them. But though they may have provided plausible evidence of the party's ability to garner support, from the point of view of creating a disciplined party they represented inflation rather than development, fat rather than muscle.

13
Turmoil
and
Triumph

Mass Nationalism

The general misgovernment from which the country was suffering could not but profit the PKI's cause, as a party out of power advocating reforms purported to bring instant welfare. Nor was it done any harm by the xenophobia whipped up by the cabinet to divert attention from its incompetence. Measures were introduced for the surveillance of foreigners, giving powers to the minister of justice (Yamin again) to detain suspected aliens for one year for investigation, and in February 1954 some thirty-two Dutch nationals, 'imperialists' in the PKI's lexicon, were held on trumped-up charges and duly exhibited at show trials. In August the cabinet brought about the dissolution of the still-born Netherlands-Indonesian Union; this was claimed as a famous nationalist victory.

The real focus for xenophobia, however, was the claim to Western New Guinea. Unfortunately, the general assembly of the United Nations in December 1954 failed to give Indonesia satisfaction and so provided a cause which united both Leninists and Stalinists and indeed most Indonesians. The Murba Party called for extreme measures against the Netherlands. With Sukarno's approval other political fanatics, among them some former Malaka supporters, grouped into a body called the '1945 Generation', demanded a 'return to the spirit of 1945'.

This *rapprochement* between Sukarno and the 'Generation' was to gather increasing importance as time went by. For those with eyes to see, Sukarno was emerging as either a national communist or a red fascist (a distinction without a difference, perhaps). In other words, he believed in (his own, *bien entendu*) authoritarian control of the society and the economy, rationalised in fashionable terms of the welfare of the poor. We have already noted that in many respects the aims and ambitions of Malaka and his followers were identical with those of the Stalinists, save only that the former did not follow the dictates of Moscow. And whatever criticisms may justifiably have been made of Sukarno, subservience to other minds was not one of them. In this he and Malaka were brothers under the skin.

The PKI's fifth congress was held in March 1954. It ratified Aidit's policy by approving the party programme affirming that the parliamentary struggle alone was not enough—the development of mass organisation was also necessary. For its part, the central committee declared in favour of cooperation with nationalist and religious parties (the very point on which Malaka had split with the Comintern so many years before).

After the congress, Aidit turned to assert the party's formal control over the mass organisations, including the peasant front (BTI), the youth front (Pemuda Rakyat), the women's organisation (*Gerwani*), and SOBSI. Rally followed rally to emphasise the PKI's concern with the national interest and to remove the stigma of the Madiun uprising. Interestingly, though Aidit generally followed Russian foreign policy, even here his concern to identify the party with Indonesian interests compelled a deviation. If the Russian and other communist parties cast the United States as the devil, the PKI reserved the part for the Dutch.

Of course this nationalism was not without its Leninist calculation. In November 1954, in a speech to the second plenary meeting of the central committee, Aidit made a point of which Lenin himself would have approved. The 'united front from above', namely the cooperation with other parties and organisations, was a short-term strategy. The long-term aim was a 'united front from below', that is the abduction of followers of other parties.

Signs of the increase of PKI influence were not lacking. The country was now actively engaged in preparing for elections and in June 1954 much consternation was caused when the official committee concerned announced that the hammer and sickle emblem would be used both by the PKI and by candidates without a party. This somewhat transparent ploy would have successfully confused the illiterate electorate to the advantage of the PKI. The Nahdatul Ulama, however (not the PNI), objected to this procedure and another symbol was chosen for those without political affiliation.

No doubt remembering Mao Tse-tung's phrase, 'politics begins with the mouth of a gun', the PKI came close to acquiring their own armed supporters under this cabinet. One of their (and Sukarno's) friends in the cabinet, of whom we have heard before, Iwa Kusuma Sumantri, on several occasions tried to create a para-military force from the 'ex-servicemen' who were in an association (PERBEPSI) under PKI control, which was said to have some hundred thousand members. Most of them were in fact also members of the Pemuda Rakyat. He was, however, foiled by the army, who refused to permit the creation of an armed organisation over which they would have no control.

Nor was it only in internal affairs that the wind blew fair. In January 1954 Djakarta was the venue for an international peace congress, another means for the pursuit of Russian foreign policy. Then in April 1955 the Asian-African conference was held at Bandung; its principal function was to provide the leaders of communist China with a venue to meet non-communist statesmen from the two continents.

The Stalinists were not the sole trouble-makers. In May 1954 a terrorist group oriented to Tan Malaka and known as *Bambu Runtjing*, who had been in operation since the struggle against the Dutch, surrendered to the army; they numbered some 1,500. A month later the army arrested Sidik Kertapati (the same whose motion of no-confidence had with PKI support toppled the previous cabinet) as the Bambu Runtjing's underground leader.

This was not a development particularly favourable to PKI interests. But it was perhaps overshadowed by a much more significant event. In February 1955 senior officers in the army signed a 'Charter of Unity' at Jogjakarta to mark the end of pro- and anti-Sukarno factions in the high command, a division that had existed at least since the 17 October 1952 'incident' if not earlier. Since Sukarno had attempted to weaken the threat from the army by intriguing within the officer corps, the new agreement was a contretemps. This became painfully evident when in June the army presented a united front against Iwa's attempt to install a chief-of-staff of Sukarno's choice and boycotted his investiture at the presidential palace (the hastily called Fire Brigade band had to provide music!). The disgrace forced the resignation first of Iwa, then of the entire cabinet, and gave Sukarno a sudden attack of religiosity—he departed on pilgrimage to Mecca. The PKI for its part cannot have been too upset. For while the possibilities of subverting the army via Sukarno had been diminished, he was in consequence in greater need of their support.

Electoral Victory

The fall of the cabinet was a setback to the PKI but it used the occasion to retreat from its goal of a people's democracy to that of a 'national coalition' government, which would of course include itself. However, with Sukarno away in

Mecca, Vice-President Hatta appointed Burhanuddin Harahap, a member of the Masjumi, as cabinet assembler, and in due course he emerged as prime minister, supported by members of his party and of the PSI. The PKI, in pursuit of its 'national' policy, declared its approval of the cabinet and at the same time increased its agitation, exploiting local grievances, and expressing support for Sukarno and opposition to the Masjumi.

The Harahap cabinet's task was largely the supervision of national elections, which were held for parliament in September and for the constituent assembly in December. The results showed that the previous (Ali) cabinet had done its work well: the PNI emerged as the largest party, ahead of the Masjumi, while the PSI had virtually ceased to exist. But the greatest relative advance was secured by the PKI, which obtained over six million votes and 16 per cent of the total cast, making it one of the four major parties (the third was the Nahdatul Ulama).

These results lent plausibility to Sukarno, now back from Mecca, in supporting the PKI's call for a 'national coalition', consisting of the PNI, Masjumi, NU, and PKI. This would, of course, give the Javanese parties a considerable majority in the cabinet and stifle the Masjumi, while Sukarno would profit from the very party rivalries he condemned. His demand met with considerable sympathy from the Indonesian political public at large. The impression had been obtained that government had been impaired by party rivalry and so denied the Utopia expected on achieving independence. It was therefore hoped that a coalition, by curbing political animosities, would lessen the general administrative incompetence.

Of course in putting forward suggestions to 'bury the parties', and for a coalition government, Sukarno was concerned to further his own interests. He had never been an advocate of parliamentary democracy; it will be remembered that this had been forced on him by Sjahrir in November 1945. It could be truly said of him, as events were to show, that what he objected to in Dutch colonial government was not the method but its foreign users. And he could see that time was running out. These first elections had drastically reduced the number of important political parties. The four major parties accounted for 90 per cent of the votes, and the remainder were distributed among twenty-four parties of no consequence. Sukarno did not have to rely on games theory to realise that the electoral process might well continue to reduce the number of significant parties and increase their size. The consequence could only be that his role would suffer diminution; and he was not by nature a passive constitutional president. Either the abolition of political parties, or the perpetuation of their rivalries in a coalition government, would equally serve the purpose of leaving him with the decisions.

However, the chances of a coalition government including the PKI were nil. If the other parties had been unwilling to accept the party when it was relatively unimportant, they were hardly likely to do so now when it was able to claim parity of standing with them. For it was not only the size of the electoral vote that was ominous; the party itself had increased its membership yet again and at the end of 1955 claimed to have one million adherents (mostly Javanese, as ever), without counting the millions in SOBSI and the BTI, and to have more money than at any time in its history. And whatever Aidit's protestations about putting nationalism first, and 'not socialist but democratic reforms', the other parties could not but have noticed that after his victory, and even while the elections for the constituent assembly were taking place in December, he took himself off to Moscow for the Russian party's twentieth congress. This was the now well-known occasion where Khruschev revealed to the delegates monstrosities about the Stalin regime which had long been known to western students of Russia, and which heralded the dissolution of the Cominform. On his return, in an address to the fourth plenary meeting of the central committee held in March 1956, Aidit argued that the fault lay not in the system but in Stalin. This most un-Marxist analysis was not unlike that of the tribesman whose faith in magic is unshaken whatever the witch-doctor's performance.

The business of forming a new cabinet based on the elections, to succeed Harahap's, was then in full swing. Aidit admitted that despite the PKI's electoral strength it was unlikely to enter government. And indeed, not even the PNI, who were most open to influence by Sukarno, would buy his nostrum of a coalition. Like the other non-communist parties, it refused to form a cabinet with the PKI and instead worked to form a united front against them. So the new government was formed of members from the PNI, Masjumi, and NU, with Ali Sastroamidjoyo as prime minister for the second time. Notwithstanding its exclusion, the PKI nevertheless gave the cabinet its support, consistent with the policy Aidit pursued since he became party leader. This was a sound move strategically, for unfortunately the rivalries between the parties were too great for the cabinet to overcome the very serious problems it had to face.

Principally they stemmed from the division between Javanese and other peoples in the country and from the favouring of the former by the first Ali cabinet. Facilities on the other islands had been allowed to deteriorate to a point where some roads became impassable except on foot. Though the provisional constitution of 1950, adopted after the assumption of a unitary form of state, had promised devolution of powers to the regions, the Javanese had always jealously guarded their control over the administration. Thus not only did the government do nothing itself, it prevented the people from remedying their own condition. Consequently, there was much unrest among the non-Javanese.

With the situation becoming gradually more tense, Sukarno escaped first in mid-May 1956 to the United States, and then between August and October to Russia and her protectorates in eastern Europe, and to China. Before he left on the latter tour he took the precaution of denouncing the British-French-Israeli Suez adventure, but not the Russian invasion of Hungary; only in November did Indonesia, under pressure to give evidence of its 'neutralism', express its official regrets over the latter aggression. On his return, Sukarno used the Chinese example to argue for a 'burial' of political parties. On 10 November he went further and suggested a 'guided democracy', without explaining the term (though nobody had much doubt of who was intended for the role of guide).

All this was of considerable encouragement to the PKI. In July Aidit had voiced his doubts that a 'people's democracy' would be achieved by parliamentary means; however, he dismissed the alternative of revolution. The correct strategy, he argued, was to arouse, mobilise and organise the masses. Exactly how this would bring about a people's democracy he left unclear; it is probably fair to surmise, however, that he was looking to the president, having buried parliamentary democracy, to yield to the magic of numbers and admit the PKI to government.

Sukarno himself, however, was more concerned with the maintenance of his own position and Javanese dominance. He saw clearly that the continuance of a parliamentary democracy in Indonesia would mean not only the diminution of his own position but also the satisfaction at least to some extent of the demands of the non-Javanese, which could only be at the expense of the Javanese.

Observing the trend of events, Hatta on 30 November 1956 resigned his office of vice-president. His presence there had been seen by the non-Javanese as some guarantee that their interests would not be over-ridden, and clearly he had only been prepared to remain in office so long as his views were given due weight. But with Sukarno's reversion to autocracy this was not the case.

Since Hatta was one of the most determined of the PKI's opponents, his resignation was a cause of jubilation to them. But on the other side of the balance sheet, out of the limelight, the PKI suffered a serious loss. Beginning in December, the PKI-controlled ex-soldiers' federation, PERBEPSI, was gradually merged into an ex-soldiers' legion under army leadership. The army had clearly not forgotten

Iwa Kusuma Sumantri's attempts, during the first Ali cabinet, to arm this association, and had deftly removed it from the PKI's grasp. Had the party but known it, it was a foretaste of things to come.

The significance of the vice-president's resignation was not lost on the non-Javanese. In December the commanders of three military regions in Sumatra seized power. All declared their loyalty to the country but appealed for a return of Hatta to office, called for more regional autonomy, and for the extirpation of communists from government. However, the North Sumatra commander, Colonel Simbolon, was quickly overthrown by his deputy who, interestingly enough, used armed Javanese estate workers to re-establish the cabinet's authority.

The PKI, in any case overwhelmingly Javanese, immediately denounced the rebels as 'fascist' and of course proposed a 'united front'. It did not achieve this aim but events soon gave it a more prominent role. In January 1957 the Masjumi withdrew from its uneasy alliance with the PNI and NU and demanded that Hatta be premier. Well supported in the non-Javanese regions of the country, it had been unable to help them due to its relatively weak position in the cabinet and resignation seemed the more honest course. The Nahdatul Ulama did not follow its coreligionists; blood was much thicker than faith. The PNI decided to maintain the cabinet with PKI support; in effect this meant that the government was now entirely Javanese and based on the Javanese; the non-Javanese were in opposition in the shape of the Masjumi. Of course this development was to the benefit of the PKI; this second Ali cabinet, like the first, depended on it. If the party was not in government it was well able to exert influence on it. And with Sukarno supporting the PKI for his own purposes, all seemed set fair.

14
The
Old Order
Changes

Dying Democracy

As Sukarno continued to argue for his concept of 'guided democracy', its totalitarian character became clear from the support it attracted. Not only did the PKI give the idea their blessing but so also did the 'Generation of 1945'. Indeed, they now moved to set up a formal organisation by that name; naming as their general chairman Chaerul Saleh.

Nevertheless, the president received no approval of his desire to 'bury the parties'. Neither the PNI nor the PKI wished such a fate for themselves; and they were his principal political supporters. So he now proposed, in February 1957, a *'gotong-royong'*, or cooperative, cabinet and a national council which would be composed of 'functional groups', which are best understood as the social categories he discerned, e.g. Labour, Youth, Peasants, Intellectuals, National Entrepeneurs and (in April 1959) the Generation of 1945. It was evident from the start that the groups to be included, and their representatives, were to be chosen by the president himself.

As part of his strategy Sukarno was maintaining the demand for Western New Guinea. But he was having little success in convincing the rest of the world. In February 1957 the twelfth general assembly of the United Nations rejected a resolution favouring Indonesia. The PKI seized the opportunity to demonstrate their 'patriotism' in Djakarta and continued until an order banning further demonstrations was issued by Colonel Nasution, who under the Harahap government had resumed the office he had lost after the 17 October 1952 incident, of chief-of-staff of the army.

But neither presidential panaceas nor PKI prancing did much to dispel the gathering crisis in the country, which took a further turn when in March the military commander of East Indonesia, an area stretching from east of Bali to Western New Guinea, assumed control of the civil administration in his territory. For the cabinet this was the last straw; they resigned. Sukarno thereupon proclaimed a 'State of War and Siege' and formed a cabinet himself from members of the PNI, NU, a number of fellow-travellers, and some of the 'Generation of 1945', and headed by a non-party man, Djuanda Kartawidjaya. In retrospect, the proclamation, and the cabinet it legitimised, marked the beginning of the steady attrition which was to leave the PKI powerless, while of course ever vociferous and active. For the proclamation gave army commanders throughout the country wide authority over political activities and the civil administration. The powers of Sukarno, the PKI's protector, were correspondingly curtailed in favour of the army command as personified in the chief-of-staff, Colonel Nasution. While Sukarno remained formally commander-in-chief, events were to show that PKI activities could be repressed by local and national military leaders. Nasution himself, though no democrat, had never forgotten the treachery of the abortive 1948 coup.

The cabinet itself was an expression of the new balance of power. Ministers were chosen primarily for their amenability to Sukarno's wishes and acceptability to the army, secondarily for their relative competence. The president's pleas that government comprise the PKI remained unanswered in his own cabinet; evidently his partners in government had exercised their veto. Equally significant was the inclusion of members of the 'Generation of 1945'. Since this group was not a political party and had no seats in parliament, its presence underlined in unmistakable fashion the abandonment of representative government in the sense of the embodiment of popular interests. Thus, though Sukarno had to share power with the army, he had achieved his aim of breaching the principle of representative and responsible government. Even those members of the cabinet who had been elected were in fact dependent on him, and not parliament, for their place in government.

But Sukarno's gain was Aidit's loss; the rug had been pulled from under the PKI's feet. Their strategy had been entirely conceived on the democratic premise that representation would be in accord with electoral support: the greater the number of votes cast for the party, the more swollen the size of its front organisations, the more valid its claim to be included in government. The inclusion of the 'Generation of 1945' and the exclusion of the PKI showed this assumption to be false. All that was to matter now was acceptability to the ruling elite. The PKI did not meet this criterion. Sukarno was able to admit national Leninists to his cabinet but not their Muscovite counterparts, however useful they were to him as a counterpose to the army.

True to his past policy, however, Aidit simply bowed his head and the Politburo he dominated endorsed the cabinet. To do otherwise, fully to absorb the lesson spelt out, would have meant admitting that Aidit's policy had been overoptimistic, and given a lever to his enemies, such as Alimin, with which to prise him from office.

Sukarno emphasised the policy on which he had now embarked by touring the country and holding up for emulation Russia's 'guiding of the masses'. This may perhaps have caused some surprise among those who remembered his 1948 appeal to choose between him and Musso, the PKI leader; they may have reflected that they had been asked to prefer the smudged copy to the original. His change of position was a response to the post-independence situation and indicated his future policy. As the external pressure from the Dutch had weakened, so the inherent divisions between the peoples of Indonesia had come to the fore. Sukarno's only cement for the cracks was an appeal for unity against an external enemy. This demanded on the one hand the creation of a xenophobic fury and on the other a rigid political control, in its turn justified by the imagined enemy. Over the next few years Sukarno turned to seek the external threats he needed, and also to raise to positions of influence those who were simultaneously xenophobic and authoritarian. These included both camps of Leninists, those who followed Tan Malaka's ideas as well as those who followed Moscow's, and also those who, like Iwa Kusuma Sumantri, Leninists in their youth, were now simply both xenophobic and authoritarian, without much disturbance of ideology.

Sukarno first put into effect his idea of a national advisory council, which was part of the short-lived 1945 constitution. It was to be composed of the 'functional groups' previously described and was empowered to offer 'advice' to the cabinet through the president: it also had veto power over the government. In effect it was a way of shifting political decisions from the cabinet to the council. Sukarno selected (with the cabinet's approval!) forty-five members for the council. It was dominated by members of the '1945 Generation', i.e. Tan Malaka Leninists and similar persons, including Iwa Kusuma Sumantri, with only a dozen known communists and fellow-travellers. Even worse, included in this coalition of anti-democratic forces were the PKI's enemies the chiefs of the army, as well as those of the navy, air force, and state police. Whether intentionally or otherwise, the inauguration of the council coincided with the arrival on 6 May 1957 of Marshal Voroshilov, the Russian president, on a state visit.

The PKI achieved considerable success in the local and regional elections held between June and August of the same year (1957). It emerged as the largest party, with over 27 per cent of the votes cast, having drawn away much of the PNI's support in Java, and with nearly a thousand councillors. Of ominous portent, though entirely in line with historical experience, was the fact that the PKI had been unable to make any inroads into the ranks of organised Islam; the figures of voters for the Masjumi and the NU remained largely static. The victory had been gained by, among other things, an attack on the PNI for corruption; something not voiced since 1952. After the voters had bolted, the PNI attempted to close the door by denouncing its pact with the PKI.

Aidit, for his part, ascribed the victory to his policy of support for Sukarno and took it to show that communists could attain power by parliamentary means. This is perhaps best interpreted as meaning that there was no need for the 'adventurousness' which would destroy the large organisation he had built up. He had not yet grasped that under the new dispensation elections were irrelevant.

And the PKI's enemies were active. In July bombs were exploded outside the headquarters of both the PKI and SOBSI, probably arranged by a dissident ex-chief of army intelligence, Colonel Lubis, and the Darul Islam of West Java. Then in September the Nahdatul Ulama followed the example of the PNI and an all-Indonesian conference of Muslim scholars proposed a ban on the PKI.

But these signs of hostility to the PKI, though they boded ill for the future, were soon forgotten in the rush of events. In July Sukarno installed a Youth-Military Cooperation Body (BKSPM), including members of the Pemuda Rakyat, the purpose of which was stated in September to be the rekindling of the revolutionary spirit to bring the outside world to a sense of reality; i.e. to startle it by displays of xenophobia. The PKI wished a direct attack on Western New Guinea, calculating that this demand would serve its purposes best. War was then too formidable and dangerous an undertaking, so recourse was had to an attack on the unprotected Dutch community and economic in-

terests in Indonesia. On 28 September with Sukarno's encouragement a 'liberate Irian' campaign was launched; this
was the signal for the assorted hooligans assembled into
the Youth-Military Cooperation Body to go on the rampage
in Djakarta, molesting Dutch and other European civilians
and wrecking Dutch business houses.

Sukarno himself came on to the scene in November,
delivering an inflammatory speech threatening dire penalties on the Dutch if the general assembly of the United
Nations did not compel them to transfer Western New
Guinea to Indonesia. Then two events in quick succession
embittered an already sour atmosphere. On 29 November
the general assembly failed to vote in Indonesia's favour;
the next day an attempt was made on Sukarno's life. Again
Colonel Lubis was assumed to be the author of the plot,
with much non-Javanese participation. On 1 December the
government declared a twenty-four-hour general strike,
hoping to damage Dutch enterprise in this way, as well
as a ban on Dutch publications, followed four days later
by an order closing Dutch consulates and expelling the
Dutch.

But events now began to move out of the control both
of the government and of the PKI, which otherwise had
been looking on approvingly. On 4 December the labour
union of the KPM, the Dutch inter-insular shipping line,
seized the main office, to the surprise of Aidit and his
party; the next day, Dutch estates, banks and trading companies were grabbed by other unions in SOBSI. This trade
union federation had always, even in the days of Alimin's
leadership of the PKI, been considerably more militant than
the party itself; it is quite probable that, as is common in
Indonesia, it saw itself as the tail that would wag the dog.
It did not quite achieve the result it intended.

First, on 13 December, Nasution ordered a complete
halt to the seizures of Dutch property. SOBSI unions ignored the order and the army then arrested several of their
leaders. Faced with a situation where he either had to
stand by his colleagues in SOBSI or follow the path of

prudence, Aidit, with many communist precedents to guide him, left them in the lurch. It is of course true that they had departed from the policy he had laid down of avoiding adventurousness and sectarianism; as events were to show, his restraint was to pay his party great dividends.

Revolt

The xenophobic campaign was mounted, as has been made clear, to divert attention from the fissures inside the Indonesian body politic. Instead, it widened them. For a number of political leaders, principally from the Masjumi and the PSI, criticised the senseless act of cutting off the Indonesian economic nose to spite the Dutch face. They then became the targets of Sukarno's bravoes; some were set upon. Not surprisingly they fled the capital, and took refuge in Padang, the centre of the autonomous region of Central Sumatra. Among the most prominent were ex-Premier Mohamed Natsir and Sjaffruddin Prawiranegara, who had been head of the Bank of Indonesia.

From Padang, on 10 February 1958, the dissidents demanded that the Djuanda government resign, that a new cabinet be established by ex-Vice-President Hatta and the Sultan of Jogjakarta (one of the few eminent Javanese equally acceptable both to his own and to the other peoples of Indonesia), and that Sukarno resume his constitutional status. Djuanda immediately rejected the ultimatum and on 15 February the dissidents proclaimed a 'Revolutionary Government of the Republic of Indonesia' (PRRI). In a last-minute attempt to prevent a total break, Hatta and Sukarno conferred between 20 February and 4 March; Sukarno was as ever unwilling to permit the non-Javanese to share power and no agreement was reached.

The failure of the conference was the signal for the unleashing of military repression on the dissident provinces. On 11 March Javanese troops attacked Central Sumatra, the troops under PRRI command refused to fight, on 6 May the chief town of the province, Bukittinggi, was taken, and Sjaffruddin fled into the jungle.

The only other area which had rallied to the PRRI was North Celebes. Javanese troops invaded this province on 9 June; fighting here was intense and bitter but on 26 June Menado, the chief town, was occupied. The reasons for the failure of the rebellion need not detain us; in addition to the divisions between the non-Javanese peoples, which are as great as those which divide them from the Javanese, there was also demonstrated a great lack of professionalism in the creation of a government and in the training of its supporters.

Of greater interest to our story is the influence of this short-lived revolt on the fortunes of the PKI. The PRRI, in its hope of attracting support from the western powers, emphasised that it wished to eliminate the communist influence on government; it further elaborated that it had no intention of dismembering the country. The government for its part refused to accept the notion that it was subject to communist influence and insisted that the struggle was of nationalism versus anti-nationalism. Precisely this line was also emphasised by the PKI, who were concerned to play down any suspicion of their power.

The PRRI did have some success with its propaganda. Both the United States and Britain provided some assistance, which was rapidly ended when the recipients' failure became manifest. But it was enough to draw the fire of the PKI. On May Day 1958 the PKI planned a massive anti-American demonstration, which was abruptly cancelled by the prime minister, Djuanda, and the army authorities. Nor did the army rest content with that. It then prohibited all parades, censored speeches, and banned the use of the red flag. The party had held the sixth plenary session of its central committee from 3 March to 4 April 1958, and formed as the supreme body of the party an executive committee, to include Aidit, Lukman, Nyoto and Sudisman, but Aidit remained firmly in control. He showed his prudence and submitted to the restrictions. A little later the army even prohibited an elaborate PKI welcome at the airport for the new Russian ambassador; he was to be left in no doubt as to who was master.

The army did not limit itself to repression. It also took steps to create institutions which would replace PKI-dominated organisations. The Action Committee for the Liberation of West Irian, which was in the hands of Leninists of both persuasions, was dissolved and replaced by the West Irian National Liberation Front, chaired by no other than Nasution, now a general and minister of defence. Next the army, having completed the task of setting up an Indonesian Ex-Servicemen's Legion, proscribed all others, including of course the PKI's PERBEPSI. Nor was this ligature temporary: henceforth all May Day rallies were controlled by the authorities. All this, of course, was against the background of the firm economic base which xenophobia had placed under the army. The former Dutch properties were in its care and were administered by some four thousand of its officers. It is perhaps ironic that the bellicose policies Sukarno needed to retain his position were the very ones that increased the size, effectiveness, resources and powers of the army he feared.

As a means of escaping the army's restrictions, in September 1958 Nyoto, after a meeting of the party's central committee, declared that the struggle for Western New Guinea would consolidate a 'national united front', which naturally included the PKI as an integral part. He was still hoping that the increased numbers of PKI supporters would give it at least a primary role in government. In a decade the party had grown from less than eight thousand members to two million, distributed in 272 branches. In addition, its various 'fronts' had more than ten million members, including four million peasants in the BTI. It is true that the PKI was most heavily represented among the Javanese but after all they were the centre of power in the archipelago.

PKI expectations, however, received a considerable setback when in September 1958 the prime minister, Djuanda, postponed the elections for a year. The PKI responded a month later by demanding a '100 per cent implementation of the Sukarno concept', including the formation of a *gotong royong* cabinet with PKI participation, and in November the central committee at its seventh plenary meeting proposed special powers for Sukarno so that he could carry out his plan, emphasising that it completely supported the line he was pursuing. In January 1959 Aidit asserted that the Indonesian 'revolution' (the term used to describe the president's various manipulations designed to ensure his retention of power) was 'national and democratic' in character, and therefore praiseworthy by current communist criteria. His goal, he reminded his audience, was the same as that of Mao Tse-tung in China after 1936, namely the creation of a national front composed of workers, peasants, the petty bourgeoisie and the national bourgeoisie; i.e. all except those who had links with the west, an aim not fundamentally dissimilar from Sukarno's. He emphasised that thoughts of instant revolution were to be dismissed out of hand, as this would turn the 'national bourgeoisie', by which he meant the PNI and Sukarno, against the PKI. Since the party's growth had been largely due to the benevolence of the 'national bourgeoisie' so defined, Aidit's vehemence was understandable.

The next month, February, the congruence of interest between Sukarno and the army in ending the parliamentary system expressed itself in unmistakable fashion. Apparently at the suggestion of Nasution, Sukarno called on the nation to abandon the parliamentary cabinet adopted in 1945 at Sjahrir's urging, and to return to the original constitution of that year with its presidential cabinet. The PKI gave its support, reluctant at first when it feared that political parties would be prohibited, then enthusiastic when it realised that its only protection against the army was Sukarno. It was as if the PKI considered it more important to remain in being than to achieve its goal. Only false optimism could have led it to believe that it would now achieve power through the ballot box; the signs were there to see that Sukarno, in his own interest, did not want elections.

In April the president submitted his proposal to the constituent assembly then sitting, assuring the political parties that they would not be dissolved and the army that it would retain a prominent role. The next month Aidit declared that his party would resist a military dictatorship if one were set up. It soon became clear, however, that the army had considerable say in whether political activity was to continue, for in June Nasution prohibited it.

The assembly, however, refused to accept the president's proposal and he thereupon, in July, dismissed it and decreed a return to the 1945 constitution. This incident, which barely elicited surprise at the time, shows how weak indeed are the roots of democracy in the country. With the constitution changed, the prime minister, Djuanda, of course resigned and Sukarno immediately formed an 'inner cabinet' with himself as prime minister, retaining Djuanda as chief minister and minister of finance. Once again he gave no power to the PKI; it was fobbed off with two fellow-travellers, one of them Iwa Kusuma Sumantri, who was at least as much the president's man as he was the PKI's. There were, however, seven officers in the cabinet; it was the sword (or at least the pistol), and neither the hammer nor the sickle, that now lay firmly on the cabinet table.

15

Emasculating
the
PKI

Sukarnocracy

The new government declared its aims to be the restoration of security, the provision of sufficient food and clothing, and the reclamation of Western New Guinea. As ever compliant, Aidit immediately announced that his party would do everything possible to support the programme; but a month later he expressed himself dissatisfied, understandably enough, with the composition of the cabinet.

Sukarno next appointed forty-six members to the provisional supreme advisory council whose functions, it will be remembered, were limited to advising the cabinet through the president. Among the new members of this body, which had the appearance of responsibility but an absence of power, Sukarno included Aidit, Nyoto and other PKI leaders but also some of the 'Generation of 1945' now so close to him.

Lastly, Sukarno named a 'National Planning Council' of seventy-seven members. Here too the PKI was awarded a consolation prize; Semaun, its leader in the early 1920s, now elderly, was included as a member. The worth of this body is best reflected in the 'plan' it produced, which we shall have occasion to mention below.

His structure complete, Sukarno on 31 July authorised parliament to continue until the elections. Just in case it was not already sufficiently clear that the new structure was to be democratic only in form, not substance, the elections were simultaneously postponed until 1962. The army then lifted the ban on political activity. To reduce the power of the political parties even further, in that month all senior government officials were compelled to resign from them. This blow fell most heavily on the PNI, but it equally ensured that the PKI did not have overt sympathisers in positions of responsibility.

These changes, while they stultified the PKI's hopes, did not dash them completely. Aidit was therefore still able to argue that his policy was correct. That he had critics within the party was evident at its 39th anniversary celebrations that same month. He emphasised the importance of theoretical knowledge so as to know that the present stage of Indonesian development was 'bourgeois-democratic'; in other words his followers were to trust holy writ (of course as interpreted by Aidit), not their own impressions, and avoid rocking the boat he steered.

Sukarno's skill as a politician lay in retaining the semblance of a democracy with the content of a corporate state. Had he also adopted the form of the latter, the opposition to Aidit within the party might have had an effective argument to remove him or at least demand that the policy be changed. But Sukarno was far too intelligent to play into his political competitors' hands and in any case needed the PKI's stage army to overawe the military.

With the resumption of political activity, the PKI was able to convene, from 5 to 7 August, the eighth plenary meeting of the central committee, preparatory to the sixth party congress to be held a fortnight later. The principal item discussed was the army. The committee concluded the obvious, namely that it was certainly no friend of the

PKI. However, refuge was taken in the hope that the party's bitterest military opponents might be eliminated. Evidently this was not imminent, for the army ordered the party to cancel its congress. Aidit, apparently unable to discern the lie of the new land, decided to ignore the order; Sukarno saved him by ordering the congress not cancelled, but postponed. When it did meet, in September, it was under strict military control. It did little more than adopt a revised constitution that emphasised discipline and organisation; qualities which were to be shown sadly lacking. The magic of numbers was as ever potent: the party announced that 270,000 officials and activists had graduated from its schools or finished a party course as part of its three-year training plan initiated in August 1956. It also nearly doubled the size of its central committee, from eighteen to thirty-five, with eleven candidate members, principally as a ploy to increase its 'All-Indonesian' appearance: half of the new members and ten of the candidates came from outside Java. The congress also went on record as opposing dictatorship (by others, presumably).

The president provided some balm by coming to address the congress, and maintained that he had been a long-standing friend of the PKI. The members must have wondered how this squared with his actions at the time of Madiun. Nor was he able to provide much protection for the party, since that month the government announced that heads of local government units would be appointed, not elected as formerly, and would resign from parties. With one stroke of the pen the PKI's great gains in the local and provincial elections were thus largely nullified; the decisions would be taken not by representatives, whether carrying the PKI or other party label, but by officials. The bureaucracy gained, the politicians lost.

However, the PKI was not Sukarno's predominant concern, least of all at this time. He was too busy manufacturing 'concepts' and slogans to garnish his new structure of state. On 17 August, Independence Day 1959, he launched

MANIPOL, or the Political Manifesto, which set out the five main principles of state policy, which in turn were represented by the acronym USDEK, the initial letters of the Indonesian words for the 1945 constitution, socialism, guided democracy, guided economy, and the Indonesian identity. Obediently, two months later on 10 November the 'Supreme Advisory Council' adopted MANIPOL as the basis of state policy. Sukarno embarked on further alphabetical adventures and evolved RESOPIM, standing for 'Revolution, Socialism, and Leadership', and NASAKOM, or 'Nationalism, Religion, and Communism', these being what Sukarno professed to believe were the three main currents of opinion in Indonesian society. RESOPIM would base itself on NASAKOM, and put MANIPOL into effect so as to lead the people into USDEK.

This weaving of words to cover a lack of representation in the embryonic corporate state was perhaps not altogether distasteful to the PKI; certainly they supported NASAKOM. And it was an aspect of a consistent endeavour of the ruling elite over the next few years; namely, whenever possible to steal the PKI thunder. That same month, for instance, the parliament approved a government bill which provided for an equal division of the crop between share-croppers and landlords. This was the official response to a PKI agitation, begun at the 'First National Peasants' Conference' in April, for a division of the crop 6:4 in the share-cropper's favour, in the hope that this would incite the peasants against the landowners.

This was not the only embarrassment the PKI suffered. More serious was the promulgation of a presidential regulation which forbade aliens (i.e. mainly the Chinese) from retail trade in the countryside with effect from 1 January 1960. This was yet another blow visited upon the unfortunate Chinese communities in Indonesia. Imported by the Dutch into the Indies to act as middlemen in trade, a role the native Indonesians could not or would not fill, when the country achieved independence they had found themselves an unwanted minority of two million or so.

The Round Table Conference in 1949 had agreed that the
Chinese would acquire Indonesian nationality after the
transfer of sovereignty unless they rejected it within two
years. At least a quarter of the two million did so. When
the Chinese Communist Party gained control in China,
Indonesia recognised the new government and those Chinese in Indonesia who had not accepted Indonesian nationality, and did not now shift their allegiance to the
new Chinese People's Republic (CPR), became stateless.
That government, for its part, maintained the claim all its
predecessors had made since 1896, namely that the children
of Chinese fathers, wherever born, remained Chinese. At
the Bandung conference in April 1955, however, a treaty
was signed between Indonesia and the CPR providing that
Chinese who had not become Indonesian citizens would
have to choose between the two nationalities within two
years; if they did not, their citizenship would follow their
paternity. This reversed the position of 1949. Now inertia
would result in a Chinese remaining an alien. The truth
is that Indonesia did not want this thrifty and industrious
minority to become citizens, fearing their preponderant economic strength. Even this new treaty had to overcome
much resistance from the Indonesian parliament and was
ratified only in December 1957. Its effect was to make it
very difficult for Chinese to acquire Indonesian citizenship,
and therefore to give legitimacy to their treatment as
'aliens', no matter for how many generations they had lived
in Indonesia. The new presidential regulation was designed
simply to remove them as a source of competition for
Indonesian petty traders. It was successful. Chinese fled or
were evicted; by mid-1960 some forty thousand had been
repatriated, to China's embarrassment. She lodged a protest
against her nationals being suddenly deprived of their
livelihood in this summary fashion, but eventually accepted
the regulation. The PKI now had to choose between supporting the presidential regulation or the Chinese (who
provided a large part of its finances); it opted for the
latter. But popular animosity to the minority was too great

for Sukarno to heed any PKI objections, even had he been
so minded.

In any case, Aidit departed for Europe in December
1959 and in Hungary met Mr Khruschev, the Russian
prime minister, whom he is said to have convinced of the
need to visit South-East Asia in February. His deputy, Lukman, set the various PKI fronts in motion to protest against
the government's economic measures, a demonstration rather
limited, as ever, to the PKI's base in Java. They were
brought to a halt in January by the party's arch-enemy,
Nasution, the minister of defence. Sukarno's contribution
was to indulge in a conspiracy theory and urge the death
penalty for 'economic saboteurs'.

But while the party's agitation was no doubt heartening
its supporters, at the beginning of the year it faced a much
more serious moral problem. On 12 January 1960 the
president promulgated a law on the 'Conditions and Sim-
plification of the Party System'. The law decreed that
political parties must accept and defend the 1945 constitution, accept the Pantja Sila, and must use peaceful
and democratic methods. The challenge was fundamental.
One of the cardinal tenets of the Pantja Sila was belief in
God; historical materialism has distinguished communist
parties since their inception. Equally, it certainly was no
part of Leninism to accept 'peaceful and democratic' methods in the pursuit of power. Indeed, in the present day
not only Leninists but also zealots of many factions, especially those with moral pretensions, embrace violence as
a means to impose their will on the unwilling majority.

Given the choice of keeping their integrity or maintaining themselves in existence, the PKI took the Leninist
course and altered their constitution to accord with the
new law. Whether they were aware of it or not, by so
doing they had lost their distinctive character and begun
to query the ideological need for their existence.

Aidit returned from his trip to Europe on 10 February
and demonstrations against the cost of living were resumed.
But again behind the brouhaha the screw was tightened

still further on the PKI, as part of the process of continuing authoritarian control. The government decreed that newsprint was to be withheld from publications not supporting MANIPOL. Effectively this meant that all organs of opinion, including of course the PKI's, were henceforth not permitted to criticise the new dispensation. Once again the PKI simply accepted this; there is no record of any underground publication which might have offset their official publication's modulated voice.

Into this atmosphere of increasing tyranny came Mr Khruschev on his state visit. For our present purposes his stay was marked by a speech at the University of Gadjah Mada at Jogjakarta. He approved Aidit's patient and prudent approach but also reminded him that numbers alone were not enough. 'The communist movement is not a grocery store where the more customers you attract, the more soap, rotten herring, or other spoiled goods you sell, the more you gain.' He was in effect telling Aidit that numbers by themselves did not matter; quality of membership did. There is no sign that Aidit altered his policies in consequence.

Khruschev in any case had not come to guide the PKI but as a guest of Sukarno, who obtained his expected reward. At the end of his visit the Russian prime minister both supported the Indonesian claim to Western New Guinea and lent the country two hundred and fifty million dollars at the low rate of interest of 2½ per cent.

Thus encouraged, Sukarno proceeded on his autocratic way. The parliament had refused to approve his budget. Its right to do so had been maintained by the PKI; naturally enough, since parliament was one of the few centres of power where the party could exert influence. But on 5 March, Sukarno, exasperated by this obstacle to his wishes, dissolved the assembly. Four days later his palace was attacked from the air by an air force pilot; a solitary and ineffective protest.

In his efforts towards the establishment of a corporate state fuelled by xenophobia, the president cast the 'Generation of 1945' for a major role. Fifteen hundred of their 'representatives' held a 'Greater All-Indonesian Conference' between 15 and 19 March. Sukarno exhorted them to 'complete the revolution' and 'attain Indonesian socialism'. His next step, taken at the end of the month, was to appoint a 'People's Congress', which was empowered to dissolve parties, to inspect them, and to establish a national front. Very quickly, a 'National Front Preparatory Committee' was installed which included the chairman of the major parties, among them of course Aidit.

At virtually the same time, Sukarno established a *gotong royong* parliament of 261 members (which included the 'Generation of 1945'). It held 131 members from 'functional groups', including 35 from the armed forces; and 130 from the political parties (excluding the banned Masjumi and PSI), 30 being from the PKI. This parliament, with the lesson of the elected body's fate before it, was guaranteed to mind its p's and q's; even so, Sukarno made sure that the army and the PKI balanced one another.

Sukarno's suppression of democratic institutions did not go unchallenged. On 24 March a number of representatives of the Masjumi, PSI and most other parties apart from the PKI formed a 'Democratic League', opposed to Sukarno's flouting of democracy. It enjoyed military support and quickly established several branches. The League was opposed by, as might be expected, authoritarians of all persuasions, the 'Generation of 1945', and the PKI.

The party itself, however, was concerned less with the League than with the army. On May Day 1960 it launched a new offensive, opposing the increase in 'fascist army influence' and the curtailment in civil liberties (often by the army) which restricted its scope. To curry public favour it also condemned the rise in the cost of living and proposed 'mass actions' in protest. It may well have been encouraged into these displays of valour by murmuring among its members, for that month Sakirman of the Politburo admitted members' doubts about the party's support for guided democracy. His answer was, simply, that the party knew best, and they were not to cause trouble. The campaign continued into June, when Nyoto and other PKI and SOBSI officials toured Java to obtain support for their campaign. At the same time there were reports of minor armed clashes between communists and non-communists in the PKI base area of Central and East Java. It was also said that the triangle formed by Jogjakarta, Surakarta and Semarang had been formed into a retreat in the event of a showdown, and that Sudisman had been authorised to form a clandestine organisation. While most of this was probably smoke, there may have been a few tongues of flame, as events were to suggest.

Sukarno returned from another trip round the world on 24 June and installed his parliament. The Democratic League, whose success had been of the 'mice will play' variety, was totally ignored despite its military support.

Whatever satisfaction the PKI obtained from its representation in parliament was soon dispelled by a further turn of the autocratic screw. Having established the appointive system for parliament, Sukarno proceeded to apply it, against PKI opposition, to the local government councils and to the senior officials of the country's administrative divisions. The PKI thus lost the last vestiges of its great gains at the local elections of 1957. As a result of this measure not only were PKI voices in these assemblies rendered powerless but also their numbers were sharply reduced.

Military Masters

Their further weakening did rouse the PKI to some form of protest. In July the Politburo put out a statement arguing that the cabinet had failed in its tasks and should be reshuffled. Naturally it did not criticise the president—that would have been foolhardy—but it attacked several ministers. It also selected as scapegoats the 'bureaucratic capitalists', a term covering army officers and civil servants in charge of the former Dutch enterprises. Apparently, despite all outward appearances these did not form part of the 'national bourgeoisie' the PKI had blessed not long before.

Its temerity earned the party a sharp lesson. The army immediately banned the PKI newspaper *Harian Rakyat* and suppressed the Politburo's declaration. Aidit, Lukman, Nyoto, Sudisman and Sakirman were detained and interrogated between 16 and 30 July. They were asked 679 questions and their answers covered 190 typed pages!

Despite the bitterness between the PKI and the army, they found a common interest in the campaign for the acquisition of Western New Guinea. At a meeting on 21 July 1960 of the supreme advisory council, attended by Sukarno, Nasution and Aidit, the principle of state policy was declared to be confrontation of all Indonesian forces with 'Dutch imperialism and colonialism', a term used to describe the vestigial Netherlands presence in the territory. This morally justified aim was convenient in that it was virtually all that held the three men together; without it, as events were to show, Sukarno and Aidit would have fallen out with Nasution. Indeed, on 25 July, while the army was still engaged in grilling the PKI leaders, Sukarno addressed the ninth congress of the PNI and emphasised the similarity between his views and those of the PKI; three days later, receiving the Lenin Prize, he made an oblique attack on the army by attacking 'communist-phobia'. They responded by sponsoring demonstrations at Palembang, South Sumatra, and Bandjermasin, South Kalimantan, demanding a ban on the PKI. Both these, it will be noted, were non-Javanese areas where the PKI was therefore weak, despite Javanese colonists in South Sumatra.

Aidit emerged from eight consecutive days of military interrogation on 2 August. The same month, he published an article proposing an alliance between Sukarno and the PKI's various mass organisations in order to bring about a revolution (of a communist character, naturally). Otherwise he feared that the communists could not be restrained. This threat was of course bluff, as events were tragically to show. Of greater interest is the proposal of revolution from above, reminiscent of Semaun's assertion in 1923 (see above, p. 64) that he wished the Netherlands Indies government to introduce communism with the help of an American loan! Aidit's proposal was perhaps a little more realistic; what both showed was an awareness that communism would not come to the islands through the efforts of the PKI but only as an act of authority. No doubt, too, Aidit calculated that Sukarno's espousal of communist revolution would weaken the army, by arraigning his military supporters against the anti-communists.

The president, however, was more interested in his own political changes than in the PKI's ambitions. In his Independence Day speech of 17 August 1960 he declared that relations with the Netherlands had been broken off and made two points of some interest. First, he described as a 'crime' the institution of parliamentary democracy in November 1945 as a result of Sjahrir's urging. It had betrayed the spirit of Mutual Help and thus impaired the unity of the nation. This foreshadowed what became the real meaning of Mutual Help; complete acquiescence in the government's pronouncements on doctrine. To add point to his declamations, he announced the PSI and Masjumi parties dissolved, and banned the Democratic League and 'imported' organisations such as the Boy Scouts.

Secondly, the president declared land reform to be an essential part of the 'Indonesian Revolution'. He stated his aim to be the abolition of all foreign rights and colonial land concessions, the gradual termination of feudal exploitation, and the strengthening and extension of land ownership for the entire Indonesian people. Of these, only the elimination of the foreign-owned plantations had any serious content. The extension of land ownership, on the other hand, was no more than a political slogan, since in Indonesia large-scale indigenous land holdings have never been significant and the amount of arable land available is very small.

Two main laws were promulgated in 1960 to give effect to the intentions expressed in the speech. One, the Sharecropping Act (UUPBH), enacted the government bill mentioned above. The other, the Basic Agrarian Law (UUPA), based the right to land on hereditary individual ownership (previously, it had all in theory belonged to the state) and set limits to the amount of land which could be owned by an individual, varying with the local population density, subject to a minimum of two hectares (five acres) of agricultural land. The emptiness of the intentions behind the speech and legislation was obvious to those who knew the agrarian situation, and became generally evident when it was revealed that if all the arable land were parcelled out in the minimum holdings, it would provide for barely half the rural population! Nevertheless, as we shall see, it gave the PKI an area in which they could agitate strongly with presidential approval. It is of note that whereas the PKI of 1920 rejected the Comintern call for land redistribution on the grounds that it had no relevance in Indonesia, the PKI of the 1960s was to agitate strongly for Sukarno's land reforms. With the military in control of most major enterprises, and severe restrictions on the organisation and agitation of workers, the only missionary field still open to the PKI's disruptive endeavours was among the rural landless.

Towards the end of August the army sought to right the balance by banning the PKI and its fronts, including the trade union federation, SOBSI, in the three non-Javanese areas of South Kalimantan, South Sumatra, and South Sulawesi. Only at Sukarno's insistence was the ban lifted. In another non-Javanese area, West Java, the army brought to light a 'double organisation' in Tasikmalaya; the PKI had set up 'liberated' villages with taxing powers. A number of leaders of the PKI and its peasant front, the BTI, were placed under arrest.

With PKI activity checked in virtually every direction, it was not surprising that Alimin now attacked Aidit for 'right-wing opportunism', or failing to pursue revolutionary policy. Aidit dismissed this attack as crude and amusing.

His hold on the party was such that he could afford to
ignore criticism; Alimin in any case was principally remembered as the author of the unsuccessful 1926 revolt. But it
may well have been better for the survival of the party if
there had been more internal opposition.

Aidit was much more concerned to protect himself and
his party from the army's thrust, and in a private meeting
with Sukarno in September urged him to accelerate the
Western New Guinea campaign. He was, of course, preaching to the converted; Sukarno was well aware of the
need of an external focus for animosity in order to ensure
his continuing rule. Nor, incidentally, was the army leadership averse to the strategy. Led by Nasution, it evidently
reasoned that just as the campaign provided a rationale for
Sukarno to unite all political forces under his leadership, so
also it provided them with sufficient justification to reconcile
the dissidents within the army.

So Sukarno, Aidit and Nasution went in October 1960 to
attend the meeting of the general assembly of the United
Nations in New York. The assembly did not give them
what they asked for, namely a request to the Netherlands
to give up Western New Guinea. Neither did the Pentagon
give Nasution what he wanted, which was heavy weapons
for the campaign; they merely agreed to supply small arms
for his four hundred thousand men, the largest army in
South-East Asia.

Back in Indonesia, the president continued with his
measures to crush any opposition. On 30 September he
banned by decree all overt political activities by the parties.
This was quickly followed in October by a denial of permits
for publication of all seven periodicals published by the
PKI. This was not directed at the PKI particularly; it was
part of a disciplinary measure designed to ensure that all
publications supported the government on all major issues.
Only at the end of October did Sukarno's personal intervention save the PKI's daily, *Harian Rakyat*.

But this was only a small bone thrown to the dog. For

towards the end of the year all political parties were required to present government with a list of branches and particulars of all members, showing address, date of entry, and position in the party. Here again the PKI was faced with a moral choice. It was being virtually asked to denounce its members to the authorities. Once the list was compiled and submitted to the government there was little doubt that its members, like those perhaps of other parties, would come under the surveillance of the secret police. Nevertheless, on 4 February 1961 the PKI duly handed over the list.

The army next sought to fuse SOBSI and the Pemuda Rakyat into a tame, all-embracing organisation, much as they had merged PERBEPSI into a federation under their own control. Their efforts continued into 1961 and were frustrated only by Sukarno, who perceived that this would so attenuate the PKI's strength that it would be of little use to him. For the monopoly of virtually every SOBSI union in its particular sphere had been broken by the rise of other unions, some tied to various political parties, some to Muslim and other religious groupings, and others sponsored by government commercial concerns.

From New York, Aidit had gone to Moscow for the twenty-second congress of the Russian Communist Party, at which it abandoned its claims to be the official Marxist augur and gave all other parties, including most especially the Chinese, equal rights of prophecy. At the end of December the PKI central committee heard Aidit's report on the meeting; he appealed to Moscow and Peking to compose their differences. Throughout his leadership of the PKI Aidit consistently refused to take sides in the Moscow-Peking dispute over leadership of the other communist parties. In turn, they found no ground for disagreement over the ideological pigeonhole into which Indonesia was to be placed. Both agreed that it was an 'independent national democracy' (i.e. not communist, but unfriendly to the west) with good prospects of becoming a communist state. Aidit, for his part, had that year attempted to appease his supporters by publishing his argument that Indonesia was in the first ('bourgeois democratic') state of a two-stage revolution—the second would be 'proletarian socialist'. Otherwise put, since the old firm was bound to be trading profitably in the near future, the backers and shareholders should not interfere with its working now.

16

Being Kept in Place

Frustrations for the PKI

The regime now turned to make preparations for war. In January 1961 Nasution went to Moscow and obtained a credit worth $450 million for the heavy arms he had been refused in Washington; an amount later increased to $1,000 million. Its military supplies assured, the government next organised the political side. On 20 January, Sukarno installed the National Front, which we remember included the leaders of all authorised political parties (not, of course, the Masjumi and PSI). It quickly absorbed the 'West Irian Liberation Front', thus removing it from the army's exclusive control. Then, in March, the Front was relieved from the need to participate in future elections and, like its author Sukarno, made totally irresponsible. It proceeded to establish branches throughout the country, and over the next few months the president created labour, youth, peasant, and women's organisations within the front, each one including the appropriate PKI organisation. He was building a national political organisation under his control which would include all others; and the PKI had lost a little more of its autonomy.

All was now ready for belligerence, and in March 1961 the first paratroopers were dropped into Western New Guinea; they were quickly captured. But while the army were thus assisting Sukarno, they were also pursuing their purpose of using the national claim to unite all military factions. The army were particularly concerned with their brother officers who had supported the PRRI. And the rallying call became effectively that of opposition to the PKI, since this had been one of the declared motives of the PRRI rebellion in the first place. It was the main reason for the surrender in April of the highly respected Colonel Kawilarang, a Christian from the Celebes. But the real return came after Nasution toured the former rebel areas in May, calling for vigilance against 'certain elements', which everyone knew meant simply the PKI. Then in June and July, Colonels Hussein and Simbolon, leaders on Sumatra, surrendered. On Independence Day, 17 August, Nasution and Djuanda, the chief minister, compelled Sukarno to issue a 'last appeal' to the rebels, offering a general amnesty to all who gave themselves up by 5 October. Now not only military men, but also politicians, gave themselves up. By the end of September Sjaffruddin, the rebel prime minister, Burhanuddin Harahap, and Mohamed Natsir, all of the Masjumi, had surrendered. On 5 October the rebellion was declared officially over.

These developments were hardly to the liking of the PKI, but their reaction was cautious. The Politburo were told in April that the matter of their attack on the cabinet of July 1960 was now 'frozen', that is to say that no further action would be taken against them so long as they and the other members of the central committee refrained from similar action in future. This must be one of the rare cases of a communist party being put on probation. So their statements were now somewhat muted; they warned against the re-integration into public life of those they alleged to be 'traitors', i.e. the anti-communists of the PRRI. Since Sukarno himself had only accepted the amnesty scheme with reluctance, the PKI's protests were fairly safe.

But clearly the party's militants were not as well aware as Aidit of the situation. In July, on the pretext of Belgian action in the Congo, SOBSI tobacco workers tried to take over Belgian estates and factories. The authorities, backed by the army, quickly imprisoned nine hundred of them. The same month some party members attempted to seize control of villages in West Java; the only result was that seventy-two of them were gaoled. With the campaign for Western New Guinea as a reason, the government banned all strikes in vital enterprises; and the phrase was again, as in 1951, interpreted to cover all businesses. This meant, of course, that the PKI and its industrial front, SOBSI, were now deprived of any means of providing rewards for their supporters; both militant actions and more peaceful strikes would meet with sanctions.

Furthermore, both PKI and SOBSI soon found themselves manoeuvred into a position of responsibility without power in the economic field. Since the complement of 'guided democracy' was a 'guided economy', SOBSI under Nyono revived a proposal that workers' councils be formed in all state productive and trading enterprises. This was then demanded by all the main PKI fronts—it would naturally have given the party a foothold in all major undertakings. The government was no more prepared to allow this than any other PKI intrusion into decision-making bodies. On 12 October 1961 it issued rules governing the creation of 'enterprise councils' in government undertakings. These were to include a majority of worker and peasant representatives. However, their task was purely advisory, and in any case limited to increasing production. The PKI had again been trumped. Their SOBSI members were placed in positions where they could be held somehow responsible for management, whilst in fact they had no control over it, and in any case they were not to try to improve the wages and conditions of their members but to find ways of making them produce more, by no means the same thing. SOBSI members on the councils would be faced with the choice between advocating measures to increase production with the danger of losing their supporters' allegiance, and championing the workers' claims at the risk of being penalised for abuse of office. However, the sadder truth appears to be that these councils succeeded admirably in the government aim, consistent with 'guided democracy', of giving the illusion of power but not the reality; they remained facades.

The PKI hoped that the campaign for Western New Guinea would keep the army off its back. Indeed, with the enlistment of a large number of volunteers, many influenced by the PKI, the party hoped to acquire some armed strength. It was disappointed; the new recruits remained firmly under army control. Meanwhile, the build-up of arms continued. In July the arrival of TU 16 jet bombers marked the beginning of a continuous flow of heavy Russian war materials, complete with technicians and instructors. A force of MIG 19s and MIG 21s was assembled. On Independence Day, Sukarno declared that the dispute had entered a decisive stage.

The next month the president attended the Belgrade Conference of Non-Aligned States and returned encouraged in his campaign against the Dutch. However, it had become clear to them, despite their obduracy, that the game was lost. They now engaged in a number of diversionary tactics, designed solely to save face. In October they proposed that the territory be 'internationalised' under the United Nations, a suggestion which might have been sincere in 1950 but was simply hypocritical in 1961. With his Russian munitions behind him, Sukarno treated this with the contempt it deserved, and on 10 November announced that Indonesia would fight for the territory. Three weeks later he informed the world that 'the decisive moment' (he was fond both of drama and of repetition) was at hand. Of greater importance, perhaps, he also announced that the world was divided between the 'emerging new forces' and the 'established old forces', with Indonesia of course being among the former. This historicist perspective was kin to the myth of the inevitability of communist revolution, so sedulously propagated by Marxist parties in general and therefore the PKI. It provided further evidence, if any were needed, that Sukarno's mind, while firmly nationalist, was nevertheless of a Marxist disposition.

His Master's Voice

Aidit, for his part, was at about the same time demonstrating his own nationalism. In October he attended the twenty-second congress of the Russian party, a famous occasion when it attacked the Albanian Worker's Party, the mouthpiece of the Chinese communists. Aidit refused to join in the criticism there being expressed of Stalin and Albania; he argued that conflicts within the communist movement should be solved by 'discussion and consensus'. Shorn of the jargon, he was saying that his support for Sukarno did not permit him to accept the Russians' attempt to reach an accommodation with the west; and in any case he rejected foreign communist leadership.

In his absence, the PKI had had another rush of militancy to the head. In November some of its officials (cadres) encouraged squatters to resist eviction from government land in East Java. The only result was that some squatters were shot, and several were arrested and imprisoned. The lesson was again spelt out: the authorities would permit no militancy whatever.

While the PKI was thus being smartly chastised, the army was rapidly pacifying the country. By the second half of 1961 most rebel leaders had surrendered, including Kahar Muzakkar in the Celebes, whose own uprising dated from the early 1950s. The rebels were either re-incorporated in the army or settled with their families in Sumatra.

The Dutch now indulged in a further entertainment. They changed the name of Western New Guinea to West Papua, unfurled a Papuan flag and went through other motions of a somewhat magical character designed as prayers to the god of nationalism in order to avert the Indonesian wrath. The United States president, Kennedy, was not deceived. On 9 December he appealed to Sukarno for a peaceful settlement. To the latter, it was confirmation of the wisdom of his political strategy, evolved during the fighting against the Dutch. If the west would not support him at first, it would do so as soon as he turned to the Soviet Union and appeared about to 'go communist'. Nor did the United States wish South-East Asia to become an arena of conflict between two minor powers backed by the two major ones.

With American intervention it was a foregone conclusion that the Dutch would abandon Western New Guinea. Nevertheless, when on 14 December Mr Nehru, the Indian prime minister, attacked the Portuguese enclaves of Goa and Diu, Sukarno produced his own echo five days later by ordering 'total mobilisation'.

However favourable to Sukarno American intervention was, it could hardly be to the PKI's liking. Even so, now that the battle was won, it hastened to do its patriotic duty. On 23 December Aidit offered the PKI's two million members for active service. The Pemuda Rakyat announced that it was ready to receive military training. Quite apart from suspicion about motives, it must be doubted if the high command, already having to cope with a hypertrophied army, would have welcomed any further growth. In the event, only a few thousand 'volunteers' received any training.

The PKI therefore did not achieve any significant result in its attempt to put weapons in the hands of its supporters. Towards the end of the year Sukarno effectively deprived it of any claim to have a unique ideology. In a speech on 26 December he defined the 'marhaenism' which had long been his slogan, as well as that of the PNI. Marhaenism, from the Indonesian *marhaen*, a term for the ordinary poor man, he said meant 'Marxism practised or applied in Indonesia. . . . Those who call themselves marhaenists but do not practise Marxism in Indonesia. . . . are only pseudo-marhaenists.' The remark was of course addressed to those nationalists who were opposed to the PKI. By the same token, however, it raised the question of the need for the PKI. What was their ideology if not Marxism practised or applied in Indonesia?

Paradoxically, at about the same time Aidit raised the same question, no doubt unwittingly. Speaking to the central committee of his party he told them to put the national interest before class or party. This was a radically new doctrine. If a communist party is not to put the interest of the working class, ideally the international working class, first, but the nation, how is its existence justified? Other Indonesian parties, and especially the PNI, could have made perhaps more credible claims to put the national interest first.

Thus both Sukarno and Aidit were implying that there was no need in Indonesia for a communist party as usually understood. Sukarno, no doubt, spoke with intent. In his oblique way he was implying that since he was both Marxist and revolutionary, revolutionary Marxists, that is the communists, should accept him as their leader. And Aidit, perhaps without being aware of the implications, was arguing that his followers should serve the national cause first and the revolutionary Marxism second. This could only mean they should accept Sukarno as their leader and himself as next in command.

Aidit justified this radical departure from communist policy by arguing that every communist party should have complete freedom to determine its own policies. In other words he, and not the high priests in the Kremlin, was the arbiter of the correct policy for the PKI, even if this went against all previously accepted definitions of communism. Autonomy was perhaps not novel among communist parties; central control from Moscow had really ended in 1948 with the Yugoslav party's revolt against dictation, though it took some time for the Russians to recognise the fact. What was new was a denial of the central tenet of Leninist activity, namely that the interests of the 'workers', as defined by the communist party, are paramount.

So, by the end of 1961 Aidit's PKI had under compulsion

abjured its original historical materialism, forsworn violent change, and given the authorities a list of its members and branches. It had seen its front organisations absorbed into national structures, and thus smothered the party itself was carefully excluded from all real power. It could publish in its organs only what the military permitted; its representatives in parliament and the supreme advisory council could say only what Sukarno was prepared to hear. Whatever initiative it had taken had been either capped or frustrated by the authorities. Wherever it had extended an organisational hand the authorities had covered it with their own; where the fist had been clenched, it had been smartly smacked.

Now, to cap everything, the PKI found its leader saying that it had no ideological reason for existence, and by the same token its past was a mistake. That there was indiscipline at the lower levels of the party and in the associated organisations, as shown by the militant actions recounted above, and about which Aidit complained, is hardly surprising.

Sound and Fury

United States support for the claim to Western New Guinea did not lead to any abatement in Indonesian war preparations. These were considerably assisted when in the middle of January 1962 Indonesian torpedo boats were fired upon as they tried to break into Western New Guinea territorial waters. A crisis ensued in Djakarta, always somewhat excitable, and Sukarno took advantage of the situation to lock up his political enemies from the dissolved Masjumi and PSI parties, among them his arch-enemy Sutan Sjahrir. Hatta sent a strongly worded letter of protest to Sukarno, who simply ignored it.

The PKI was much more concerned to offer its own remedies for the economic crisis. For Sukarnocracy had exacted a heavy price in popular welfare. An indication of the cost is provided by an index compiled by the Central Bureau of

Statistics, based on the prices of nineteen foodstuffs on the free market in Djakarta. Taking 1952 as the base year, i.e. 100, by the first quarter of 1962 the index had climbed to 1,287!

This inflation had already made nonsense of the eight-year development plan, published in 1960 and intended to run from 1961 to 1969. It is principally known for the fact that its chapters, volumes and pages represented the date of the declaration of independence, 17 August 1945. However, its long-term virtue was that it made clear to its authors, the National Planning Council (on which we remember Semaun sat), that Indonesia's prosperity, even perhaps its survival, depended on attracting foreign capital. In the nature of the case this could only be western capital and the PKI was much exercised to exclude it. Its general theme in 1962 and 1963 was that Indonesia, with only minor economic aid preferably from 'socialist' countries, could overcome its own problems. In February 1962 it launched a 'grow more food' campaign and its peasant arm, the BTI, took part in a government conference to discuss agricultural productivity; the theme was duly taken up by the other PKI fronts.

There is no sign that their activities had much effect either in increasing food production, or (at least until late 1964) in influencing government policy in this field. A similar observation could be made about the elevation, on 9 March 1962, of Aidit and Lukman to the cabinet as ministers without portfolio; they were to be figureheads in positions of prominence but excluded from the 'inner cabinet', which held the levers of power. Indeed, at the seventh national congress of the PKI, held in March and April 1962, Aidit admitted that his party had had no effect on government policy. The main dish at this congress was humble pie. The preamble to the PKI constitution of 1959 was amended so as to accept the Pantja Sila with its affirmation of a belief in one God, as demanded by the Presidential Decisions mentioned above (p. 194).

No doubt as a reward for their acceptance of Sukarnoc-

racy, Aidit and his henchmen were invited to address staff
and command schools of the three fighting services as well
as the Police Academy, while on the other hand some of the
most virulently anti-communist officers were shunted aside.
But the army still remained very much in control of the
campaign for Western New Guinea, which was now reach-
ing its end. Russia agreed to sell more arms in February and
again in May, and Indonesia continued to land guerrillas in
the disputed territory with, as ever, little effect. However,
talks with the Netherlands were continuing through an official American intermediary, Mr Ellsworth Bunker, and
finally in June both parties agreed to a plan that would save
the Netherlands' face by transferring authority to the
United Nations, with Indonesia receiving it only six months
later. The agreement was signed on 15 August 1962 and a
ceasefire called immediately, just after a few hundred Indonesian paratroops had been dropped into the jungles of
Western New Guinea. The United Nations assumed control
on 1 October.

It was now only a matter of months before Indonesia, on
1 May 1963, formally acquired control over the long-desired
worthless territory. But the political machines were not so
easily put into reverse. In the month the ceasefire was announced over two hundred political parties, mass organisations and functional groups were said to have joined the National Front, with a total membership of thirty-three million.
This was Sukarno's dream come true, of a monolithic political organisation under his leadership with the PKI given
important representation. Collectivist activity best thrives in
a situation of threat, real or contrived, and the settlement
of the claim to Western New Guinea risked shaking loose
the mortar that held the political bricks of Sukarnocracy
together. Those who need enemies usually find them and
in less than a month after the ceasefire Subandrio, Sukarno's
disciple and foreign minister, expressed Indonesian hostility
to the project to form a new state of Malaysia from Malaya
and the British colonies of Sarawak, North Borneo and
Brunei. (In November of the previous year he had declared

to the United Nations general assembly that Indonesia had
no objection to the plan.) He was simply following the lead
set by the PKI the preceding December when an end to the
Western New Guinea campaign had just come into view.
Then, the central committee at its plenary meeting passed a
resolution condemning the projected federation. This was
the prelude to a campaign by the PKI newspaper, *Harian
Rakyat,* which was maintained over the next several months.
To some extent this attack was stimulated by the communist
or communist-influenced groups in Malaya and the adjoining British colonies, who sought the PKI's help against a
structure they knew would weaken their position. But in
any case the PKI was bound to object to the formation of a
state, in all likelihood friendly to the west, which would be
stronger than the small dispersed colonies from which it
was formed. That, for their own purposes, the leaders of the
Indonesian regime now took up the same position, was a
source of great gratification to the PKI. Even more was this
the case when Indonesia embarked on a theatrical show of
force, known as 'confrontation', with Indonesian warships
patrolling the Malayan coast and aircraft lying along its
borders, while a government-sponsored committee was set
up, with PKI participation, to arouse the Indonesian people
to the grave neo-colonialist danger threatening them, i.e. to
evoke some enthusiasm for the regime's policies.

The PKI also looked forward to increased scope in another
direction. The end of the campaign for Western New
Guinea provided an argument for ending the 'State of War
and Siege' which had obtained since March 1957 and given
ultimate power to the local military commanders, most of
whom had used it against the party. In October 1962 the
government announced that the regulations would be withdrawn by 1 May 1963 and appointed a seventeen-man committee, including Aidit, to formulate proposals on how this
should be done. Withdrawal of the regulations would mean,
of course, the end of the army's control over PKI activities,
and mark a signal defeat for the military at Sukarno's hands,
an achievement made possible only by the success of his

New Guinea campaign strategy to which, ironically, the army had lent some credibility.

But the PKI was only too well aware that it was being given only token representation in government and that unless it entered the inner cabinet it would be at risk—the army's suspicion was obvious—and would certainly be in no position to guide events. In October 1962 a Politburo statement, echoing Sukarno, demanded an eradication of all 'communist-phobia', 'worker-phobia', and 'people-phobia' in the state administration. This launched a massive campaign for 're-tooling', i.e. the dismissal of officials unsympathetic to the PKI, and 'a Nasakom cabinet', namely one which included the party. Though this campaign continued into 1963 it had no effect on government; there was neither 're-tooling' nor a cabinet reshuffle. This is surprising in view of Sukarno's own demands for precisely these changes. It is proof once again that though he could have his way in many fields, he was unable to prevail against his military partners' opposition to the PKI.

17

Merging
with
Sukarno

The Road from Moscow

The continuing dispute between Russia and China over leadership of the communist states now began to cast deeper shadows on the PKI. Aidit always scrupulously followed the policy that every party was entitled to work out its own policy, hence there was no call for 'leadership' in the old Comintern or Cominform sense. But the PKI was to find that its support for Sukarnocracy was to leave it little option but to follow Chinese policy in world events. In November 1962 Khruschev agreed to withdraw the missiles he had placed in Cuba rather than risk war with the United States. This met with PKI disapproval, for clearly they could not be less xenophobic than the regime they supported and the violently anti-western attitude of the Sukarno regime meant that the PKI could not welcome any accommodation with the west.

To discover the true state of feeling in the eastern European protectorates of the Soviet Union, Nyoto and Yusup Adjitorop, a candidate member of the Politburo, toured them at the end of the year. Evidently their meetings did not change the PKI's policy, for its message to the sixth congress of the German Socialist Unity Party, in January 1963, declared that: '. . . whoever attempts to unite the revolutionary movement with the right opportunists will himself fall into the meshes of right opportunism.' (In the communist lexicon, 'coexistence' and 'right opportunism' mean the same thing, namely cooperation with the democracies, but express different attitudes to it.) The cynic might well wonder if this was not the pot calling the kettle black, since to characterise Aidit's policy it would be hard to find a better word than 'opportunism', though of course it was not 'right'.

More immediately, however, new excitements were developing in South-East Asia. In December 1962 an anti-Malaysia revolt broke out in Brunei and Sarawak, led by one Azahari, who had fought on the Indonesian side against the Dutch in the struggle for independence. President Sukarno immediately broadcast an appeal for help and Indonesian territory adjoining these two British colonies was opened for use as a sanctuary by the rebels. The PKI was of course extremely pleased by this turn of events. The scapegoats, however, were not the fellow South-East Asians (anthropologically, even fellow Malays) of Malaya, but the British, who were considered responsible for the scheme and who, being western, were predestined for castigation. So from December 1962 SOBSI trade unions engaged in various boycotts against British ships, airlines and firms working in or passing through Indonesia.

At the beginning of the year Aidit was given another figurehead appointment, being made on 18 January 1963 one of the thirteen members of the council of assistants to the revolutionary leadership. This body had no executive power, since the revolutionary leadership was none other than the president. Less than a week later, on 24 January 1963, the supreme advisory council established an eleven-man committee, including Aidit and two other PKI members, to formulate proposals on economic stabilisation. This was a shrewd move on the government's part. The deepening economic privation consequent on belligerence had led to much discontent, on which the PKI had tried to capitalise by voicing criticisms of the administration of the economy. Placing PKI members on this body gave them an appearance of public responsibility for the economic state of the country. The principal remedy required, namely an abandonment of bellicosity and 'confrontation' with Malaya, was of course not one that the PKI could accept, any more than could the regime itself.

The party's frustration was well expressed at the meeting in February 1963 of its central committee. Here Aidit regretted that the PKI was not in government, while admitting that state policy was identical with the PKI's. Once again, without apparently being aware of it, he was asking whether there was any ideological reason for the party's existence. Similarly with another of his claims, that 'we communists represent the new emerging forces'. Since Sukarno himself had already declared that Indonesia was among those angels, it was not clear how Indonesian communists were distinguished from their compatriots in this respect.

Indeed, Aidit in his report showed an acute awareness that the survival of the PKI, at least in its then form, required that the policies of the regime be successful. Since they were manifestly not so in the economic field he criticised members of Sukarno's cabinet, but of course not the president himself, no doubt on the principle that the prince can do no wrong. Lukman for his part urged the committee to win the national businessmen and industrialists to the party's side; a somewhat forlorn hope in view of the treatment of their counterparts by the Chinese party. But the reason for this appeal was in Aidit's address. He emphasised that unless the country's economic difficulties were overcome, then foreign investment and western aid were inevitable. This was of course anathema for the PKI. Unfortunately for it, the courses pursued by the government, with the party's support, ensured that the economic difficulties would be exacerbated.

Paradoxically, Aidit simultaneously rejected the only other source of material support, Russia. He declared that its use of economic aid to non-aligned countries was in effect supporting the non-communist regimes in power, making the communist parties subservient to them, a policy he dubbed 'modern economism', as indicating that it placed economic development and not political change as its first priority.

The same emphasis on politics emerged in his discussion of the forthcoming end of the state of war and siege on 1 May 1963. He asserted that on that date the political leadership of the 'revolution' must truly lead those with rifles but warned that the military were attempting to retain the powers they were about to lose. Internally, Aidit claimed, as he had done a year earlier, that party discipline was much improved but should be strengthened still further. Indeed, throughout this year the PKI was concerned to 'steel' its mass support, in other words to rouse it from its customary apathy.

At this meeting of the central committee, the Politburo was expanded to seven members. Yusup Adjitorop and Nyono were made full members; two others were made candidate members. But the five members of the Politburo, namely Aidit, Lukman, Nyoto, Sudisman and Sakirman, who had gained their positions between 1951 and 1953, remained unchanged as the directing centre of the party.

The theme of the meeting may be summed up as an expression of the political will to survive as an organisation and its desire to participate in government. But as if with sardonic amusement, the day following the meeting, on 13 February 1963, Sukarno announced a five-point programme for his National Front. This, as we have seen, embraced all political and functional organisations; perhaps it was distinguished from a United Front of communist textbook strategy principally in that the president, and not the PKI, dominated it. The policy was to consolidate past

victories, including the return of West Irian and the maintenance of security; to help increase production; to continue
the struggle against · imperialism and neo-colonialism; to
effect political indoctrination; and to carry out a 're-tooling'
of the state apparatus. To none of these objectives could a
'United Front' have taken objection, and may not have
been able to improve on them. Once again, even unwittingly, Sukarno had posed the question whether the PKI
was politically necessary, since everything they could do he
could do better. He showed this very convincingly by
ordering, a little over a year later, on 16 March 1964,
that the local governing committees known as the *Tjatur
Tunggal* (or Four in One) consisting of the military commander, police chief, civil governor, and the district attorney, should become a *Pantja Tunggal* (i.e. Five in One)
by including a representative of the National Front, so that
even at the local level there would be felt the influence of
his national political organisation (in which of course the
PKI was included).

The PKI's true function and ability as ever lay in muster-
ing the masses. In April 1963 it was announced that since
July 1959 membership of the PKI had increased from one
and a half million to over two million, with the four major
PKI fronts (SOBSI, BTI, Pemuda Rakyat and Gerwani) having raised their joint numbers from 7.8 million to 12
million. However, the party knew only too well that these
were far from disciplined revolutionaries, but much more
like 'rice communists'. It simultaneously announced that
its second three-year plan for training cadres had been completed but admitted that discipline was somewhat lacking,
especially in the all-important matter of paying subscriptions.

On 1 May 1963 the regulations of the state of war and
siege, under which military commanders held their powers,
came to an end and the PKI was free to embark on a new
contest of strength with the army. But the PKI quickly discovered that their protector, President Sukarno, was his own
man and not subject to ideological constraints. Having been
elected president for life by the Provisional People's Con-

sultative Assembly, the highest deliberative body, Sukarno at the end of May received Tunku Abul Rahman, the Malayan prime minister, and as a consequence the three foreign ministers of Indonesia, Malaya and the Philippines met from 7 to 11 June, discussed how to bridge their differences over Malaysia (the Philippines were claiming North Borneo), and agreed to work towards close and formalised relations among their three countries. The PKI was thus presented with the *fait accompli* of Indonesia cooperating with two free-enterprise countries, both under the protective wing of the west. Aidit could only have mused that his complaint that the PKI had little influence on government still remained true.

The *rapprochement*, to the party's relief, did not last. When the agreement creating Malaysia was signed in London on 8 July, Sukarno accused the Tunku of bad faith, though there is no evidence that the latter ever promised to arrest the formation of the new state. Nevertheless, Sukarno, the Tunku and President Macapagal of the Philippines met in Manila from 30 July to 5 August 1963 and resolved to request a United Nations verification of whether the people in British North Borneo and Sarawak wanted to join Malaysia, and to accept its findings. They also agreed to set up a confederation of their three countries, to be called 'Maphilindo'.

However, when the United Nations carried out the survey requested and announced on 14 September 1963 that most respondents did indeed want to join Malaysia, Sukarno refused to believe the result, and therefore to recognise the new state when it came into being on 16 September. Malaysia immediately broke off diplomatic relations with Indonesia and the PKI came into its own again. Mobs in Djakarta, led by Pemuda Rakyat members, stormed the Malaysian and burnt the British Embassy, and went on to destroy British property. SOBSI unions seized British firms which were then, following a now established routine, taken over by government 'supervisory commissions'. British subjects and other foreigners left the country.

A trade war against Malaysia was launched and Indonesian troops were concentrated on the border with Sarawak. The Indonesian army organised and trained raiding parties, eventually amounting to between sixty and one hundred men, composed of young Chinese from urban areas in Sarawak, with regular Indonesian NCOs in charge and helped by small units of Indonesian paratroopers. In its military activities, as in its political, the regime was proving itself adept at using the communists for its own purposes. One of the principal objects of these excursions was to link up with communist Chinese banded together in the '*Pergerakan Gerilya Rakyat Sarawak*', (PGRS) or Sarawak People's Guerrilla Movement, around Sibu in that territory, and so establish a 'government' in a 'liberated area'. They failed. In Sabah, as North Borneo was now called, Indonesian agents had no greater success in building up a fifth column among the seventeen thousand Indonesians employed, mostly non-Javanese.

The PKI itself was concerned much more with indoctrination. In August 1963 it produced a four-year plan for culture, ideology and organisation. As ever, its preoccupation was with numbers; it intended to double them within four years and to improve discipline, in particular to make members pay their subscriptions. It was only too well aware the majority barely knew the name of the game. To this end, in a scheme reminiscent of Tan Malaka's schools (see above, p. 92), it organised *Universitas Rakyat*, teaching Marxism and economics in the major cities, as well as in secondary schools organised by the PKI in the smaller towns, and in elementary schools in the villages. The party hoped that by the end of the four-year plan, its older members would be literate. It was also organising Regional Training Centres for all its officials, where they would be at once indoctrinated and familiarised with the economic and social features of their regions.

Aidit himself was at the time in foreign parts, visiting Cuba, East Germany, Russia, North Korea, and China. Having been snubbed by the Russians, he was made an honorary member of the Chinese Academy of Sciences, the first foreigner to be thus distinguished. On 2 September 1963 he argued to his Chinese hosts that, on the evidence of Sukarno's Political Manifesto, Indonesia had now joined the 'world socialist revolution', i.e. was on the Chinese side (and, by implication, Russia's dispute with China was alienating 'non-aligned' countries like Indonesia). A couple of days later he maintained that the first stage of revolution could only be achieved through a 'national united front government led by the working class and based on a worker-peasant alliance'. What he did not say, but must have known, was that Sukarno's supreme advisory council in its comments on the Political Manifesto had also emphasised that the 'revolution' (whatever that meant for them) was based on the workers and farmers. And since there already was a 'National Front' doing much the same service as a 'United Front', all that was lacking was leadership by the 'working class', alias the PKI. But Aidit was baying for the moon and was doubtless aware of it; it was highly unlikely that Sukarno would make him leader.

Aidit's report to the central committee of the PKI on his return to Indonesia was notable for two points. First, he emphasised the Indonesian character of the PKI, and singled out the North Korean party for special praise for having stood on its own feet without help from larger communist states. It was clear that this was his own policy too; he rejected the 'baton of any other communist party'. At the same time he emphasised that the PKI was a 'Marxist-Leninist' party, that is to say not revisionist. And in flat contradiction with Russian communist theory he declared that 'socialism' could be achieved by the party's own efforts, in which external assistance from the Russian-led states would at best be a contributory factor. He denounced the Russians' attempts to muzzle opposition to their policies by economic bribes to other communist parties, and nailed his colours firmly to the Chinese mast by declaring that 'socialism' could be achieved in the newly independent countries only 'through a fundamental change in the political system that is effected in a revolutionary way', not, that is, in the gradualist manner advocated by Russian communist theorists. Presumably, this 'fundamental change' implied something more than 'guided democracy' to date. But the president was still to be courted. During the year Aidit had re-published an article by Sukarno, originally written in 1926, which urged cooperation between nationalists, religious, and communist elements (or NASAKOM). In addition, now discussing the Madiun uprising, he absolved Sukarno from all blame for repressing it; Hatta alone was culpable!

Aidit was also able to announce to his central committee further progress in building up the organisation. Not only did it now claim two and a half million members (with similar growth in its associated fronts), but also every province in the country, with the exception of West Irian, now had a 'greater regional committee'. There were also 'section committees' in 93 per cent of regencies and larger towns, 'subsection committees' in 83 per cent of districts and smaller towns, and 'rural committees' in 62 per cent of villages.

All this was very impressive. But acute observers[1] at the time had noted that, as with the early Indonesian communists (see p. 89 above), for many of the PKI officials their functions had become jobs like any other bureaucratic ones. The opening of new 'committees', with their attendant official paraphernalia, no doubt attracted many who hoped to secure white-collar jobs thereby. This in no way implied a desire to overturn Sukarnocracy—or for that matter any other authority.

At the time, in any case, the PKI saw Sukarno as their protector against the army. Nasution in November had declared that Indonesia had in principle accepted Malaysia as a *fait accompli*. This of course made nonsense of any further confrontation, and was not Sukarno's view, who continued to chant that Malaysia must be crushed. For-

[1] E.g., Hindley, 1966: 302.

tuitously, that very month Djuanda, the first minister, died. Sukarno thereupon reshuffled the cabinet so as to demote Nasution, and so reduce the influence of the armed forces.

The PKI, of course, could only be gratified at this development, for evidently they feared the army. In December 1963 *Harian Rakyat* published an article by Aidit discussing three possible approaches to the Malaysia 'problem'. He rejected the reformist solution, which expected the British and Malaysians to come to some arrangement with Indonesia. Equally undesirable was the adventurist approach (i.e. the launching of open war), for this would provoke British attack, create panic in Indonesia and unseat Sukarno. The only correct approach was a long-drawn-out confrontation in all fields, appeals for support to 'new emerging forces', recognition of the rebel movements in North Borneo, and expropriation of British enterprises.

This argument reveals, more clearly than anything Aidit previously uttered, his dependence on Sukarno. He was evidently hoping that by maintaining a constant state of emergency the PKI would be able to prosper under Sukarno's wing. Yet he must have been aware that virtually the only, and certainly the best, opportunities for communist parties have been presented after external military defeat or enfeeblement of the state they oppose. Evidently he had no confidence that if Indonesia were to suffer this fate at British hands, and Sukarno were to be unseated, the PKI, despite its millions of members and extensive coverage of the country, would be able to seize power. He feared, and perhaps with justice, that the game would go to the army.

For the time being, however, events fulfilled Aidit's wishes. In January 1964 the United States attorney general, Robert Kennedy, attempted to settle the Malaysia dispute by visiting in turn Sukarno, Macapagal and the Tunku. He persuaded Sukarno to decree a ceasefire, though the latter affirmed that his policy was still to crush Malaysia. The foreign ministers of the three states met in Bangkok in February and agreed that Thailand would supervise the ceasefire. All this was to little avail for less than four weeks later overt fighting began again.

Hostilities were intensified in May 1964 when Nasution, despite his previous assertion that Malaysia was a *fait accompli,* announced that volunteers were being mobilised; Sukarno issued an 'Action Command', and a 'brigade' of these volunteers was declared proceeding to the border with Sarawak accompanied by regular troops prior to crossing over. Training centres were set up in various islands near Singapore, and Indonesian-trained communist Chinese from Singapore and the peninsula were sent back there for sabotage. A meeting in Tokyo in June between the Tunku and Sukarno achieved nothing and next month the then Russian deputy prime minister, Mr Anastas Mikoyan, in the course of a visit to Indonesia, reaffirmed his country's support for Indonesian hostilities. Indonesian guerrillas were landed by sea and air on the Malayan peninsula itself but were quickly killed or captured by the local population.

Now, however, the western world bestirred itself on Malaysia's behalf. Britain, Australia and New Zealand abandoned their one-sided courtship of Indonesia, gave specific promises to defend Malaysia against attack, and their troops assisted her forces in eliminating Indonesian troops who either infiltrated across the Malaysian border in Borneo or were landed in the peninsula; Australia adopted peacetime conscription for the first time in her history. Britain stopped Colombo Plan Aid to Indonesia; while the United States also suspended all assistance except for food. France announced that no more arms contracts would be signed with the country.

Sowing the Wind

This smouldering war was, of course, precisely what Aidit had wished, in order to take the pressure of the army off his party. It now turned to fish in the troubled waters of peasant discontent. Maladministration had left the rural areas open to a plague of rats, which had ruined the 1963 crop on Java. There was consequently much privation among the peasantry who of course accounted for four-fifths of the population. In February 1964 the PKI sent out 'research teams' to survey villages in West Java, with similar surveys of the other two provinces of the island, Central and East, in April and May. It had carried out earlier enquiries in 1959 but not on quite so large a scale. It is a revealing commentary on the Indonesian situation that the PKI was the only political organisation to carry out such an investigation in this overwhelmingly peasant country, while to this day reliable surveys from Indonesian academic sources are conspicuously rare.

The purpose of this 'research' soon became evident: the party resolved on a new form of peasant agitation, called the *Gerakan Aksi Sefihak,* meaning unilateral action movement, abbreviated to AKSEF. The object was to incite Javanese peasants to implement the 1960 Basic Agrarian Law and the Law on Crop-Sharing, 1960 (see pp. 199, 200), without waiting for official approval; in other words to take matters into their own hands. The party's agents in this activity were of course to be the officers of its peasant front, the BTI.

As implied above, the redistribution of land in Java is simply a way of increasing the number who cannot live off their holdings. Nevertheless, one can only deplore the unsurprising fact that four years after the regime enacted its laws of land reform, less than half the amount specified had changed hands—451,068 hectares against 966,150—thus handing the PKI and the BTI a ready-made cause for turmoil on a deceptively legitimate basis.

As the agitation developed, curiously it became concentrated on East Java. This is of some interest, since agrarian conditions over the whole island are not markedly different and could all have provided material for incitement, particularly of landless peasants. It cannot be explained by the relative strength of PKI followers, for in fact these were mainly in Central Java, not East. The suspicion emerges that the agitation was directed not at landholders as such but at those of them who belonged to or supported the Nahdatul Ulama Party, whose principal base was precisely in East Java. As we have seen, this was the last party which was both permitted to exist and had not succumbed to PKI infiltration. The other Muslim party, the Masjumi, not very strong in Java, had been proscribed; while the PNI had lost a substantial part of its strength to the PKI and in any case, being dependent on Sukarno, offered no obstacle to the PKI's pervasive strategy.

The Nahdatul Ulama, as an Islamic party, were not particularly endearing to the president, who had firmly nailed his colours to the mast of the secular state. So here too there may have been a collusion of interest between Sukarno and Aidit in whittling away the strength of the last political obstacle to their designs. Certainly while the agitation was in progress the PKI made great efforts to portray itself as the true executor of the presidential intentions, in particular at its forty-fourth anniversary celebrations on 23 May 1964, when incidentally it claimed some three million members (though the government estimated the figure at less than two million). Lukman expressed himself convinced of the 'ultimate victory' of communism in Indonesia, emphasised the PKI's growing participation in government, and castigated any who objected as not being true followers of Sukarno, not democratic, progressive or revolutionary. Three days later, Subandrio told the participants at the celebrations that the PKI was 'leftist, progressive, and revolutionary', and observed that the party had always interpreted Sukarno's teachings militantly. In other words, both speakers were asserting that the PKI's virtues lay in embodying the principles of which Sukarno stood, not in the aims which it may have claimed to pursue in its own right.

But the PKI found that portraying themselves as faithful presidential lieutenants did not diminish the resistance to their AKSEF. For the Nahdatul Ulama followers, while prepared to temporise with Sukarno's NASAKOM in pursuit of office in Djakarta, did not regard this as giving the BTI a licence to filch their land. When attacked, they defended themselves and an increasing number of incidents of violence were reported in the first half of 1964, especially from East Java. So on 15 June Johannes Leimena, the acting president (Sukarno was on another junket abroad) ordered the Department of Home Affairs to prevent by mutual consultation all 'unilateral actions'; in other words the police were to stop them. And here we observe one of the early signs that, once again, the tail was trying to wag the PKI dog. The BTI immediately announced that it was planning more intensified and consolidated actions against landlords. This was no idle threat; on 10 July a number of its members were put on trial at Klaten near Jogjakarta after clashes with the police as a consequence of their 'unilateral actions'.

Aidit himself came to the BTI's support at the PKI's national conference in Djakarta from 3 to 5 July 1964, criticised the delay in land redistribution, announced that his party would support 'unilateral actions', and demanded that land reform courts be set up with representatives of the BTI on them. He had also evidently realised that this method of weakening the Nahdatul Ulama was counter-productive, for another decision of the PKI conference was to study the development of religion in Indonesia 'as a basis for better NASAKOM cooperation'. Since the Nahdatul Ulama was the only party permitted to represent Indonesia's organised Muslims, this decision is perhaps best interpreted as expressing a desire to achieve a 'united front from below', i.e. to abduct NU followers into the PKI.

In August the party obtained another figurehead appointment: Nyoto was appointed minister attached to the praesidium or inner cabinet. This marked the furthest point Sukarno reached in moving towards the NASAKOM cabinet he had persistently demanded. But Nyoto was only attached to, he was not a member of the praesidium. It is fair to presume that while Sukarno proposed, the army, his partners in 'guided democracy', disposed, and would not permit a PKI functionary to hold one of the levers of power, while being perfectly willing to allow him to appear to share in the responsibility for cabinet decisions.

In his 1964 Independence Day speech, Sukarno made clear the identity of policy between himself and the PKI. On the one hand he declaimed 'to hell with all foreign aid that has strings attached to it . . .' ('strings' being his term for lack of belligerence), on the other he ordered the immediate completion of the Basic Agrarian Law of 1960 on Java, Madura and Bali. This was a prelude to a decision on 24 September by the cabinet praesidium to create a committee to expedite agrarian affairs, including Nyoto among its members, and also to establish land reform courts, on which all NASAKOM parties were represented.

Aidit was concerned as ever to proceed cautiously. To appease the poverty-stricken peasants he advised the national conference of the BTI on 10 September to eat rats, asserting that both he and the president had partaken with relish of this delicacy. On 27 September, speaking to the fourth national congress of SOBSI, he warned communists not to be anti-religious, in other words not to take on the Muslim landholders. He was probably only too well aware that in a fight between them and his followers the odds were on the former.

The militants in the BTI accordingly adopted another tactic, namely the demand that government-owned land be redistributed to the landless. In mid-October they led violent riots at Indramayu in West Java which involved some two thousand peasants, demanding that they be given state forest land. These disturbances were quickly and effectively quelled by the police.

Unfortunately, little was being done to implement the land reform laws, despite Sukarno's oratorical orders. The responsible committees included representatives of all interests, among them the landholders who belonged to the Nahdatul Ulama and nationalist parties. Not surprisingly, few decisions to redistribute land emerged. The PKI accordingly decided to bypass these committees and to encourage unilateral actions. But matters rapidly went out of control, to such an extent that the PKI found itself being isolated politically. In December the general chairman of the BTI chided its East Java branch for engaging in terrorism and even in murder, while Aidit told the BTI that it had been too precipitate. A conference at Bogor in West Java that same month resulted in a 'declaration' by the leaders of the PKI, NU, and PNI calling for negotiations and consultation to solve land problems and condemning violence and other forceful acts. It was clear that the principal object of this exercise was to pacify the Nahdatul Ulama, which had been dangerously aroused, and at the beginning of 1965 the first presidential decree made a further peace offering by reinforcing criminal charges for anti-religious behaviour.

Sukarno, meanwhile, found himself friendless on the world stage where he loved to parade. The UN security council meeting in September 1964 considered a Malaysian complaint against Indonesian aggression. Of the eleven members, nine voted in favour of a Norwegian motion deploring the Indonesian action. What was more galling than the size of the majority was the fact that among them were two Afro-Asians, the Ivory Coast and Morocco, members no doubt of the 'new emerging forces'. The motion went nowhere, however, as the Russians used their veto. This did not imply that they were totally committed to Indonesian policies. When Sukarno visited Moscow in October on his way to a non-aligned conference in Cairo, and asked for more arms, his hosts agreed only to a postponement of payment for those already delivered, despite the support for the hostilities expressed by Mr Mikoyan only three months previously.

Indonesia had the largest delegation at the conference, presumably in the belief that numbers would erase the humiliation of the security council vote. In the deliberations, Sukarno struck fanatic poses, calling for worldwide hostilities against 'neo-colonialism', by which he meant the formation of Malaysia. But most of the other delegates could not see his ghosts and the tone of the conference was moderate.

Disappointed by the Russians, disowned by the neutralists, Sukarno turned to China (he had exchanged visits with the Chinese head of state, Lin Shao-chi, in 1963). When on 16 October 1964 she detonated her first atomic bomb, a *rapprochement* between Indonesia and China was revealed, in terms of what Sukarno called a Peking-Pyongyang-Hanoi-Phnom-penh-Djakarta axis (a term which Peking, however, avoided for a long time).

The reasons for this departure are not difficult to deduce. In brief, Sukarno had closed all other options. Needing an external enemy to rally his divided countrymen behind him, he had chosen Malaysia. Thereby he had alienated not only the western powers but also the neutralist Afro-Asians. The Russians, while encouraging animosity to the new western-oriented state, evidently saw little value in continuing their material support; Indonesia's economy was too mismanaged to offer hope of any return on investment. That very reason, however, compelled Sukarno to seek assistance in reorganising the economy to provide the funds needed to keep the state in being and buttress his own position. The only major power to which he could turn was China. It should not be assumed that he did so reluctantly, whatever his feelings towards the Chinese (especially those in Indonesia) as an ethnic group. He had never believed in representative government, but rather in authoritarian rule, and had suffered the incipient democracy of 1945 to 1958 only because the political constellation at the time had left him no other choice. Once the levers of power were in his hands he had fashioned a form of corporate state, principally distinguished from totalitarianism by its greater inefficiency—not even its apologists could claim, as did those for Mussolini's Italy, that the trains ran on time. And it will be remembered that he had launched on his noxious endeavour immediately after his first visit to communist China in 1956 (where he had found an object of admiration in the ant-like activity of the people).

Having made clear where he stood abroad, Sukarno removed all possible doubts about his relationship with the PKI. That party's general advance, both in numbers and into the structure of state had alarmed many politicians. In September, Adam Malik, then minister of trade, and B. M. Diah, a newspaper editor, formed an organisation calling itself the *Badan Pendukung Sukarnoism,* or the Body Supporting Sukarnoism. Forty newspapers pledged their support, the army extended a welcome, and so did six of the ten legal political parties. But Sukarno saw it for what it was, a body of politicians determined with army support to oppose the PKI. This would not have suited his book—the PKI was a better servant and any weakening of it placed him in danger of the army. So, in December, he browbeat a majority of party representatives in the BPS into supporting his NASAKOM system, and on 17 December decreed the 'body' banned, temporarily suspending as a punishment twenty-one newspapers which had supported it. The president thus made perfectly clear that he would tolerate no organised opposition to the PKI, however loyal to him it might declare itself to be.

18

Killing
the
PKI

To Peking with Love

At the beginning of 1965 the central committee of the PKI asked its supporters to make that year the one in which they crushed the 'bureaucratic capitalists' i.e. the military administrators of state-controlled enterprises taken over from the British and Dutch. But the enmity of the PKI for the army was nothing new and this call should not be understood as a startling departure from Aidit's settled policy of permeation. The success of his strategy, at least in the numbers game, was beyond doubt. With less than eight thousand members in 1952, the PKI claimed over three million in 1964. In the same period SOBSI declared it had grown from one and a half million to over three and a half million; the BTI from eight hundred thousand in September 1953 to seven and a half million in April 1964. In addition, the Pemuda Rakyat asserted it had some two million members; the women's organisation, Gerwani, one and three-quarter million. All this had been achieved by fairly strict adherence to the letter of the law and support of Sukarno; there was no reason to think that the policy would not be crowned by further successes of the same kind. Indeed, at the time most observers, both Indonesian and foreign, were disposed to foresee not a violent revolution but a spreading oil stain which would inevitably cover all Indonesian political institutions.

And, in the conventional wisdom, the PKI's success would be assisted by the country's misery, which was experienced by all. The cost of living had now soared. From a base of 100 in 1957 it reached 36,000 in 1965. A litre of the people's staple foodstuff, rice, cost 41.25 rupiah in 1957 and 1,100 rupiah in September 1965. There was of course, no shortage of money—it rose from thirty thousand million rupiah to a million million over the same period. Only the rupiah was virtually without value—indeed it cost more to print than it was worth.

More important, both to the PKI and to the country, than the central committee's appeal was the further development of Sukarno's courtship of communist China. At the beginning of January, using as a pretext Malaysia's election to the security council (a matter decided a year earlier, without Indonesian objection), he withdrew Indonesia from the United Nations and several of its specialised agencies. (Indonesia however remained a member of the World Health Organisation. Speculation has it that this was not unconnected with the fact that Subandrio and his wife were medical practitioners.) On 23 January he sent Subandrio to Peking to negotiate an agreement which sealed the new alliance. A joint statement, published on 28 January, declared that there could be no peaceful coexistence between the 'old-established forces' and the 'new emerging forces', or (in case these terms were unclear) between imperialists and anti-imperialists. Of course, the statement denounced Malaysia and supported Indonesia's withdrawal from the UN (indeed, on 24 January the Chinese prime minister, Chou En-lai, had hinted that a 'revolutionary' United Nations might be set up). These acts of common faith, however, were the prelude to more substantial agreements on economic and technical cooperation; China extended credits to the value of thirty-five million pounds and it was agreed that trade and shipping would be increased between the two countries. But, perhaps most important, the parties also decided to extend their contacts in the field of defence and to exchange military as well as economic and other delegations.

Of major interest to our story, however, was the support by the Chinese on 25 January for the PKI proposal that Sukarno create a fifth force or militia, and an accompanying offer, alleged in later court trials, to equip it with one hundred thousand small arms. This appears to have been the sequel to a number of moves. We will remember that a similar proposal had been made in the early 1950s (see above, p. 170) by Sukarno's man in the then cabinet, Iwa Kusuma Sumantri, and scotched by the army. The same motives applied now as they did then—such a militia, under his control, however indirect, would significantly reduce Sukarno's dependence on the army, if not eliminate it altogether. In the 1950s the group to be armed would have been the PKI-controlled ex-servicemen's organisation, PERBEPSI. Also for the PKI now, as then, to have an armed body meant that they could agitate with a certain degree of immunity from the army's sanctions. So it was not surprising that on 14 January the PKI proposed the arming of five million workers and ten million peasants 'in reply to the large-scale military build-up of British imperialists in Malaya'. The PKI proposal received support from Sukarno's tame parliament and it was then that the Chinese made their offer. But it would be unwise to believe that this proposal had not been under discussion for some time and that their overt expression, whether by the PKI or the Chinese, was not carefully orchestrated by Sukarno himself. For it must be emphasised that Subandrio's mission to Peking was strictly on a governmental level; it included no element of a party-to-party link. But while the transfer of arms was to be from state to state it was to be kept out of the hands of the Indonesian army. The vehicle and

receptacle was to be the Indonesian air force, while Subandrio, who held the rank of air commodore, was to ensure
that the arms reached that body without interference by
the military.

Always small, and by comparison with the army somewhat neglected, the air force was imbued with envy for its
larger rival. Sukarno had duly exploited the situation; Omar
Dani, the air force commander, was his own appointee, and
in a very real sense that service was Sukarno's instrument.
It had accepted the PKI-declaimed ideas of a fifth force
and of 'NASAKOM advisory councils', a euphemism for political indoctrinators at all levels in the armed forces. This
had only further strengthened the army generals' conviction that the air force was communist infiltrated; they
themselves had rejected both demands.

Sukarno's Accolade

The president received the Chinese prime minister, Chou
En-lai, and Liu Shao-chi, now foreign minister, in April.
On the 19th of that month he laid the foundation stone
for the building of the Conference of the New Emerging
Forces (CONEFO), of which Djakarta was to be the centre.
(In a delusion of grandeur it was seriously suggested that
this conference would replace the United Nations.) At the
ceremony, Sukarno emphasised that Indonesia was now
firmly on the side of China and the other 'new emerging
forces', and against the 'old emerging forces'. This was, of
course, the Chinese attitude to the world and its utterance
now is perhaps best seen as part of Sukarno's serenade to
Peking. So also with his claim that Indonesia was now
entering the 'socialist stage', a phrase from the communist
lexicon referring to the period when a communist party
has taken over government and is implementing totalitarian
policies. Understandably the PKI, out of power, objected
to this infringement of their copyright and the president
finally admitted his error.

Between 10 and 13 May 1965 the PKI held its fourth

plenum. Despite Indonesia's 'confrontation' of Malaysia and Britain, it was the United States which was castigated as Enemy Number One, a further sign of the adoption of Chinese foreign policies. Aidit declared that Indonesia was now in a revolutionary situation and called for 'iron discipline', which may be read as a criticism of BTI terrorism, and underlined this by emphasising the necessity for 'research first before undertaking unilateral actions'. For evidently discipline among his front organisations, at least, was not all that could be desired. On 14 May, the day after the end of the plenum, a group of BTI squatters on a government plantation in East Sumatra, supported by Pemuda Rakyat, beat an army officer to death.

Later that same month, on 23 May, the PKI celebrated its forty-fifth birthday. More than a hundred thousand people attended this circus, held in the Senayan Sports Stadium in Djakarta. The air force dropped leaflets, some of which carried prizes, and entertainments were provided. Among them were speeches by both Sukarno and Aidit. Sukarno hugged Aidit with the declaration 'I embrace the PKI'. Aidit, true to form, reasserted the independence of Indonesian communism from external control. They thus made clear the bargain between them: Sukarno accepted the PKI as his loyal servant provided it owed no other allegiance.

It was in this month, and the two following, that rumours circulated which are said to have been of some importance in the cataclysm at the end of September. In May there began to be spread the story of a council of generals which intended to effect a *coup d'état*. Retrospective evidence suggests that these rumours were spread by PKI members and sympathisers; however that may have been, Sukarno called in General Yani, chief-of-staff of the army, and asked him what truth there was in them. Yani explained that in fact the only council of generals was one which considered promotons. Sukarno expressed himself reassured.

The next month Aidit admitted that members of the

Pemuda Rakyat were undergoing military training in the preparation of the fifth force he had asked be established. Yani unequivocally declared the fifth force to be no other than a fifth column. For though he may not have known in detail the plan for the movements of arms from communist China via the air force to arm the fifth force, he no doubt was well enough aware that the latter was part of the new alliance with China.

It was also rumoured that Sukarno's health had taken a turn for the worse—he was known to have weak kidneys. At the time, it was thought that his departure would be the signal for a trial of strength between the massed cohorts of the PKI and the army. Certainly, on 7 August, Aidit returned from a visit to China with a team of Chinese acupuncturists, apparently because Sukarno feared surgery. It was said that Sukarno suffered a collapse before his Independence Day speech on 17 August; nevertheless, he proceeded to make it. He described the Indonesian relationship to China as the beginning of an 'axis'. The vast majority of his countrymen, especially the Javanese, may have been bemused at this announcement of firm alliance with the home country of the minority they disliked. As if to provide visible symbol of the link, that same day Marshal Chen Yi, communist China's foreign minister, arrived in Djakarta at the head of an Independence Day delegation, remaining until the end of the month.

One of the most important, and revealing, parts of Sukarno's speech was his claim that the idea of the fifth force was his own. He told his audience that he would decide the matter later, but that 'we cannot maintain the sovereignty of our state without a people who, if necessary, are given arms. . .' . Equally significant, however, was his declaration that Indonesia's 'revolution' was 'still at the national democratic stage. . .' . This phrase indicates a period when communists and their allies fight against 'imperialism' and 'feudalism' and precedes the 'socialist' phase mentioned earlier. In other words, Sukarno was arguing that Indonesia was still at the stage where communist policies could not be put into effect; indeed, the PKI remained outside the inner cabinet.

The fifth force would have been composed largely of followers of the PKI. As if to express his complete confidence in the party, Sukarno now conferred on Aidit the state medal of 'Great Son' for service and loyalty to the republic. At the same time he ordered the total dissolution of the Murba party, whom we remember as followers of Tan Malaka. This was followed by another wave of political arrests. He thus unmistakably demonstrated that he considered the PKI to be Indonesian patriots and that the Murba, the only other contenders for the appellation of revolutionary nationalists, were expendable, apparently because of their opposition to communist China and their links with Russia. He had in this way pushed Tan Malaka's ghost off the pedestal of 'Father of the Country'. It was not Malaka and the Murba who were the revolutionary leaders of Indonesia but Sukarno and the PKI.

As a further expression of his new alliance, Sukarno now ordered the PNI to purge itself of all those who were inimical to the PKI. The former, hanging by its hair from Sukarno's favour and having little if any popular ground to stand on, did his bidding.

Though the Murba was dissolved, the Generation of 1945, which Sukarno had created as his personal political following, was still left in being. Aidit met Sukarno and the 'Generation' on 14 September and came out to declare that the time had come to 'operate on the cancer of society', namely the 'capitalist bureaucrats, economic adventurers, and corrupters'. It is reasonable to suppose that he was expressing the sentiments of Sukarno, for Subandrio on the same day declared that the 'time has now come to exterminate the capitalist bureaucrats', and Subandrio was never the PKI's mouthpiece but Sukarno's. He went on to contend that there were only two patriots, Sukarno and the workers and peasants; the army, who had borne the brunt of the fight for independence, of the claim for Western New Guinea, and were engaged on 'confrontation', were significantly omitted. The next few days saw the emergence of demands from the various PKI fronts that the corruptors be punished.

With September the pace of events began to increase. Subandrio had his own Central Intelligence Body; evidence at his trial alleged that this reported to him that the Pemuda Rakyat were being given their military training at Halim air base outside Djakarta. Subandrio ignored this report. Since he was both a minister and an air commodore, and could easily have taken steps to inquire into the matter and if necessary put an end to it, it seems reasonable to conclude that the training was proceeding with his knowledge and approval.

The courses at Halim were of course being given by instructors from the air force; and on 15 September Omar Dani secretly visited Peking to accelerate the shipments of arms promised in January. When we find Subandrio, Sukarno's confidant, and Dani, his appointee, both visiting Peking to obtain arms for the fifth force, we are encouraged to conclude that Sukarno was doing no more than tell the truth when he claimed the force as entirely his own idea.

Abortive Coup

Rumours were now to be heard in the capital that kidnappings were imminent. There was a certain historical plausibility about this; frequently during the struggle against the Dutch the various insurrectionary factions had seized each others' prominent men. Then, towards the end of September, the chairman of SOBSI renewed the demand for a fifth force, while another PKI front, the Estate Worker's Organisation (SARBUPRI), installed a brigade of 'volunteers', called 'Maruto Darusman', in Central Java. The next day, 28 September, Sukarno declared, in contrast with his Independence Day speech only five weeks earlier, that Indonesia was now about to enter the second stage of the 'revolution', namely the implementation of socialism.

We now engage ourselves in a consideration of the events surrounding what has become known as the '30th September Movement', or GESTAPU in its Indonesian acronym. We shall in the first place limit ourselves to facts which are generally agreed, leaving possible explanations to later discussion.

Dani declared at his later trial that he had informed Sukarno on 20 September that the men of a Brigadier-General Supardjo, who were discontented with the leadership of the army, could no longer be restrained and there was the possibility of conflict. This officer, it would appear, was the leader of a conspiratorial group from the Central Java Diponegoro division. As their agent, however, they chose a Lieutenant-Colonel Untung, mainly because he had just been transferred from the division to command a battalion of the 'Tjakrabirawa' regiment of the presidential guard, and in addition was given the responsibility for organising on armed forces day, 5 October, a parade in which each division would be represented by a battalion. He brought to Djakarta two battalions sympathetic to the plotters, one from his own division, and one from the Brawidjaya of East Java. They were to play critical parts in the events at the end of September.

The rumours about kidnappings were not unfounded. The force that was to commit them assembled at the Halim air base on 28 September. It included about a hundred members of the presidential guard but also several hundred communist cadres and auxiliaries from the Pemuda Rakyat and Gerwani.

Such a concentration could not be kept entirely secret and a couple of days later the head of the armed forces information centre warned Sukarno that the PKI had evil designs against the army. The president dismissed this as simple communist phobia. In his turn, Dani received information to the effect that Supardjo was about to take action on 1 October against the 'council of generals', supported by the commander of the guard at Halim, Air Force Major Suyono. The question was whether the conspirators were to be allowed to use air force facilities; Dani and his associates concluded 'that they could not be prevented'. There is little doubt that had Dani wished, he could have refused assistance and warned the army; he did nothing. The most plausible explanation is that either by choice or compulsion he was involved with the conspirators.

Sukarno, for his part, attended a technicians' rally and then returned to his palace, but not for long. He quickly went to the Hotel Indonesia and so to spend the night at the house of his Japanese wife, Ratna Sari Devi, in the suburb of Kebayoran.

Aidit arrived at Halim air base just before midnight. At about 3 am he was followed by Dani with Supardjo hard on his heels. The last immediately proceeded to the presidential palace where he placed on guard the two suborned battalions from the Javanese divisions.

Clearly the arrival of the latter two men at Halim was the signal for action to commence. For between 3 am and 7 am separate armed groups, with from twenty to a hundred army and Pemuda Rakyat men in each, went from the air base to the villas of seven army generals in Djakarta. The intention was to take them alive. But three resisted arrest and were killed; they included Yani, the army commander. Three were captured, but the most important target, Nasution, the minister of defence, escaped by leaping over the wall of his garden and taking cover in the grounds of the Iraqi embassy next door. The mutineers captured his ADC in mistake for him, and in the melée Nasution's young daughter received fatal wounds. The quick and the dead were then taken to Halim, where the former were despatched by the Gerwani to the accompaniment of torture and song. Meanwhile other groups, mainly from the Pemuda Rakyat, emerged from Halim and seized key points in the capital, such as the radio station, the telephone exchange and important crossroads.

In the meantime Sukarno, at Madame Devi's house, was told of the attack on Nasution and that the presidential palace was ringed by the two Javanese battalions, who had, however, not interfered with his guard. Shortly after, he heard it was unsafe to go to his palace and went to the home of another of his wives, Haryati. There he was given the full story of the night's events. Then, on the grounds that even this house was now considered unsafe, he made his way to Halim, where he arrived at 9.00 am. Dani, the next day, and Sukarno himself on 3 October, both declared that he had gone to Halim entirely of his own volition. He went on to argue that in the troubled state of Djakarta he felt the best place for him was near an aeroplane.

Once at Halim, Sukarno was given details of the night's events from the commander of the palace guard, General Sabur, as well as from Dani and Supardjo. The most important item was that Nasution had escaped his attackers. Sukarno's complacent comment was that such things were quite natural in a revolution and that Nasution's escape would have effects and consequences. He spoke, perhaps, more truly than he knew.

After the murders of the night there came the public relations exercise of the morning. Untung broadcast at 7 am declaring that the '30th September Movement' had affected a military takeover, directed against a council of generals which had planned to seize power. An Indonesian revolutionary council was to be established in the capital, with local councils throughout the country. They were to be composed of civilian and military personnel who fully supported the movement. Most revealing of the character of the movement, however, was the final announcement: all non-commissioned ranks were to be raised by one but no officer on the council was to hold a rank senior to Untung's of lieutenant-colonel!

It was time for Dani to show his hand, and he duly did so at about 9.30 am, issuing an Order of the Day to the air force in approval of the movement. Reports were now coming in to Halim that Major-General Suharto, commander of the army's strategic reserve, was successfully regrouping. Sukarno realised that the conspiracy had failed and at about midday ordered Supardjo to stop it on pain of death. Then, when Untung asked him to sign a decree establishing the Indonesian revolutionary council, and listing the initial membership of forty-five, he refused, thus depriving the movement of any shadow of legitimacy. After taking the precaution of having his children flown to safety at Bandung, at about 4.30 pm he asked his entourage for suggestions of who was to succeed Yani as army commander. He accepted Supardjo's suggestion of Major-General Pranoto Reksosamudro and issued an Order of the Day declaring that he had temporarily assumed command of the armed forces and had named Pranoto as interim head of the army.

However, when he sent an emissary to Suharto asking for Pranoto, the former refused, suspecting that a 'coup' was being attempted. For from the time when he had been woken by a neighbour at 5.30 am, Suharto had not been idle. Hastening to his strategic command headquarters he had quickly sized up the situation, obtained the support of the police and the navy (the air force had hedged), persuaded one of the two suborned battalions to return to allegiance (while the other abandoned its watch over the palace and went to Halim), compelled the rebel troops holding the radio station to vacate it under threat of force, disarmed a Pemuda Rakyat mob, and then formed an armoured regiment ready to take or destroy the air base. A second emissary from Sukarno arrived at this time and Suharto sent back a report on the situation and demanded that the president leave Halim. Sukarno complied, and by 10 pm had arrived at his summer palace in Bogor. Untung flew to Semarang, arriving at 1.30 am, and went into hiding. Aidit and Dani made for Jogjakarta, which they reached at about 2.30 am. By 6.10 am Halim was in Suharto's hands; there had been no casualties.

The quickly halted 'movement' proved to have roots, as one might expect, in the Diponegoro division. On 1 October mutineers seized its headquarters in Semarang, issued orders for the formation of revolutionary councils, received support from two of the division's battalions, and the garrison commander in Jogjakarta and his deputy were both murdered the next day. On 3 October, however, the divisional commander recaptured his headquarters, on the 4th the head of the 'revolutionary council' in Jogjakarta fled, and the mutiny there was at an end. The revolt took firmer hold in Surakarta, the other Central Javanese principality town. This was a stronghold of the PKI, and the revolutionary council was led by the mayor, himself a party member. It was not to be subdued for some three weeks.

After landing at Jogjakarta, Aidit had conferred with local PKI leaders in Central Java and then tried to fly to West Java or Bali. He failed to do so and went to ground on the slopes of Mount Merapi. Dani had toured a number of airfields before taking refuge with the president at Bogor.

Reaping the Whirlwind

Back in Djakarta, however, on 2 October Suharto's troops found the place of execution of the murdered officers. It was in a part of Halim used for training members of the Pemuda Rakyat and Gerwani. The bodies were exhumed on 4 October, when Suharto declared that in his mind there was no doubt that part of the air force, at least, was involved in the conspiracy.

The PKI's daily, *Harian Rakyat*, printed an editorial on 1 October, before the failure of the conspiracy was known, supporting Untung but describing the mutiny as 'an internal army affair'. This did not save the party. With the rebellion quelled, Suharto asserted that Untung and his associates were the main actors, Pemuda Rakyat and Gerwani members played the minor parts, while the PKI was the stage manager. Nasution expressed even more forcibly his conviction that the '30th September Movement' was another attempt, similar to the abortive rebellion of 1948, to seize power. With the two most senior officers in the Indonesian army thus declaring their belief in the guilt of the PKI, and with Sukarno compromised, the party's fate was sealed.

Nor did the activities of its supporters around Surakarta help exculpate the PKI. On 22 October gangs of Pemuda Rakyat attacked with primitive weapons the police station at Klaten and an army training unit at Bojolali, both small towns. They were repulsed with heavy casualties. Nevertheless, PKI adherents set up barricades round the towns and then at a given signal set houses on fire and kidnapped and killed their opponents, often in a particularly cruel fashion. But this was the end; the next day commando troops from Suharto's command subdued the military backbone of the 'revolutionary council', the Diponegoro mutineers in Surakarta, and accepted the surrender of the communist mayor.

The anti-communist tide was now in full flood. With the arrival of commando troops from Djakarta, seeking out members of the PKI, licence was given to the villagers to settle their old scores with supporters of the party and, of course, of Sukarno. The first to suffer were the unfortunate Chinese; racial hatred compounded political animosity. Then the PNI and Muslim (both Nahdatul Ulama and Masjumi) supporters took their revenge for the BTI's terrorism and murders. But only on the higher slopes of Mount Merapi, where Aidit and his colleagues had taken refuge, did the PKI make any real effort to defend the villages of its followers, though their arms were limited to bamboo spears and similar implements. Elsewhere, in Atjeh, in North Sumatra, in Central and East Java, in Bali, PKI supporters, overt and alleged, were massacred in large numbers, the most reasonable estimate being of the order of two hundred thousand. An equal number of suspects were placed in prison or in concentration camps. The killing was not limited to Islamic areas; it was quite as enthusiastic in the Protestant parts of North Sumatra and in Hinduistic Bali. Indeed, whereas in Javanese villages the arrival of soldiers precipitated the slaughter, they had to be sent to Bali to stop it.

Among those who lost their lives were the PKI leaders. Aidit was reported killed by the army in late November; his henchmen Usman and Sakirman met the same fate on 15 December. Lukman and Nyoto took refuge in the presidential palace at Bogor. This was no sanctuary; they were removed on 30 November and shot in the square of the naval academy there two days later. It was estimated that one-third of the leadership was killed or captured.

Effectively, this was the end of Aidit's PKI. Their enemies were now firmly in the saddle. Sukarno was forced to rescind his order appointing Pranoto as chief-of-staff and to confer the office on Suharto. Otherwise, however, he acted as if nothing had happened. He continued to voice his support for the PKI and to mouth the old slogans of NASAKOM and 'anti-NEKOLIM' (anti-neo-colonialist-imperialists). The establishment, including the army, seemed stricken with political paralysis and the younger generation took action. Grouping themselves into 'action fronts', of which the first and most important was KAMI, the Indonesian students' organisation, they demanded with demonstrations the dissolution of the PKI and more efficient government. Sukarno, far from bending to the wind, formed a new cabinet consisting largely of his old henchmen, many of whom supported the PKI, and excluding Nasution. He then banned KAMI and closed the University of Indonesia. These insensitive policies cost him his presidency, for they convinced certain army elements that action was now unavoidable. Troops advanced on his palace and he fled to Bogor, forty miles south of Djakarta. There, on 11 March 1966, three generals whose personal loyalty to him was unquestioned persuaded him to sign an order authorising Suharto to take all measures necessary to restore order. Sukarno's rule was over.

In power, the army rapidly propagated a formal ban on the PKI and the dissemination of Marxism and Leninism. Freedom was restored to the press and political prisoners were released. The cabinet was reshuffled and fifteen of Sukarno's ministers, including both Subandrio and Dani, were arrested. 'Re-tooling' of the PNI extirpated the PKI sympathisers; the MPRS was similarly purged and Nasution was made chairman; it set itself the task of dismantling Sukarnocracy. The president himself was ordered to account for his activities, particularly those on 1 October 1965. He made his report in January 1967; insulting in character, it gave ammunition to those who were demanding that he be put on trial. Suharto, however, counselled caution on such an explosive issue and the MPRS at its meeting in March 1967 contented itself with appointing him acting president, while leaving Sukarno with the powerless title. Even this he lost a year later, when Suharto was appointed president. Sukarno was condemned to a careful seclusion in Bogor; he died of natural causes in mid-1970 and was given a state funeral.

The remnants of the PKI grouped themselves into various undergrounds. One, led by Sudisman, was active in Djakarta in 1966. Its principal achievement was the publication of a 'self-criticism' which blamed the party's destruction on Aidit. Sudisman was caught and in 1967 brought before a military tribunal and sentenced to death.

Another group, reportedly led by B. O. Hutapea, who had been a member of the central committee, unlike Sudisman's urban underground attempted in 1967 to obtain support among the peasantry. In the first half of 1968 it tried to secure a 'liberated area' round the small town of Blitar in East Java. Members of Muslim organisations, especially the Nahdatul Ulama, were killed in reprisal for the murder of PKI followers after the failure of the coup. This uprising was soon repressed by the army.

Otherwise, communist activity has been of a shadowy kind, with underground groups being reported from various parts of the archipelago. An important source of trouble in the first two years after the coup was in West Kalimantan (Borneo), where the PGRS (see p. 233 above) was active, but now against the government. Joint operations by Malaysian and Indonesian forces rapidly decimated the guerrilla's strength. In brief, after 1965 the party was unable to form a central leadership; the PKI, as such, had ceased to exist.

19
Puppeteers
or
Puppets?

Pro and Con

The considerable obscurity that surrounds the unsuccessful coup has naturally given rise to a continuing controversy on the location of responsibility for it, in particular on the role of the PKI, despite the present Indonesian government's firm conviction, expressed by President Suharto, of the party's guilt. There is of course no denying the generally known facts that Aidit himself was at Halim air base during the crucial night of 30 September to 1 October, nor that members of the PKI fronts, the Pemuda Rakyat and the Gerwani, took an enthusiastic part in killing the generals and attempting to seize the capital, nor that the PKI newspaper gave its reserved support to the coup. What is questioned is that the party planned the conspiracy. On a subject as important as this it is perhaps useful to set out as fully as possible the arguments on both sides.

We may begin with the case for the prosecution against the PKI. Those putting it forward include not only official Indonesian opinion but also a number of American journalists and scholars. They point first to the public knowledge of the greatly increased militance of the PKI's activities from 1964, especially its *Gerakan Aksi Sepihak*. It is deduced (admittedly from hindsight) that these indicated that the party had decided that it would not be put off any longer and would now seize power. Support is drawn from the confession purportedly made by Aidit before he was shot and the proceedings of the trials of known conspirators and PKI leaders, who also declared that the party had been precipitated into action by rumours of Sukarno's illness, and had in any case already in late 1964 set up a Special Bureau which successfully suborned military men. The prosecution's case also draws colour from the fact that the PKI *émigrés* have admitted involvement of their party in the coup attempt, declaring that it was to be a preliminary to a 'People's Democracy'.

The case for the defence is made principally by, oddly enough, some anonymous American writers and a group of Dutch scholars. These argue that GESTAPU was an internal army affair. Some younger officers, disgusted with the corruption and venality of the army command, decided to remove them and so purify the army. They thus forestalled a coup by a 'generals' council'. In their support they enlisted elements of the Pemuda Rakyat and Gerwani, and the party's newspaper ill-advisedly gave a cautious welcome to GESTAPU. Aidit himself had been compelled or inveigled into going to Halim; in consequence the anti-communists in the army were able to throw the blame for the conspiracy entirely on the PKI.

In attempting to assess the strength of these rival cases certain considerations should perhaps be borne in mind. The first is the question of motivation. It is obvious that Aidit had no need for strong-arm measures to achieve power, if that indeed was his intention. At the time, September 1965, there was universal agreement, indeed apprehension, that the tide was flowing strongly in favour of the PKI. Not only was it widely expected that he would be swept to power on a surge of popular approval but also his party had considerable support among the military—Suharto later mentioned that some 40 per cent of the Diponegoro division was influenced by the PKI. At the very least, any attempt by the army to frustrate the popular will might well have met with resistance from within its ranks, not least because many officers still looked up to Sukarno as the father of the Indonesian nation, and he had left no doubt of his partiality for the PKI. And it seems better to rely on contemporary estimates of the party's strength and intentions, rather than now alter them to fit later unforeseen developments.

Secondly, there is no doubt that Aidit's staff work within the party left little to be desired. We have seen how he made his own position impregnable, providing himself with absolutely reliable lieutenants, and how he inexorably increased at least the nominal adherents of the PKI. It would therefore be reasonable to expect him to plan a *coup d'état* with at least the same thoroughness. In the event, at the time of GESTAPU his closest associates were nowhere near him. His first vice chairman and close friend of many years, Lukman, was in Semarang; Nyoto, the second deputy chairman, and colleague of as many years standing, was in Sumatra. One of the other members of the Politburo, Adjitorop, was in China (where he remained). Not only is this inconsistent with Aidit's manner of work but it would be an odd general indeed who went into action with his commanders scattered miles from the battlefield.

Then, we have seen how time and again Aidit was concerned about the training and discipline of party members. It would be reasonable to assume, therefore, that a conspiracy to seize power would have at least the cadres informed and prepared for the event. Only too obviously, they were not. Not only did they fail to rise in response to the appeal to form 'revolutionary councils', but none of SOBSI's many unions staged even a strike in support. Further, the party's supporters were completely unarmed. The air force equipped the Pemuda Rakyat they were training but not

PKI members in the base area of Central Java. These were left to face the army's guns with virtually stone age weapons.

Perhaps most important, such action was completely out of character for Aidit. We have seen how his policy was based entirely on support of Sukarno and, in general, avoidance of unconstitutional action. The one major exception to the latter rule, the Gerakan Aksi Sefihak, evidently had the president's blessing. It seems unlikely that Aidit would now adopt rash courses he foreswore when thirteen years younger.

There remains the question of the confessions in court, on which the prosecution lay such great stress. With the best will in the world one cannot accept as unimpeachable evidence statements made by people detained over long periods, which in total add up to a justification of the regime's theory of the events which brought it to power. One's suspicions of these testimonies is further strengthened by Sudisman's, who we remember was tried only in 1968. He declared that though no blame should fall on the PKI as a party, 'all actions were executed by individuals who happened to be members of the PKI'. Not only is this patently untrue, but since he was tried after the military ringleaders he must have known that it would be recognised as untrue. He may well have intended to show the absurdity of believing these confessions. (Apart from that, his statement is of incidental interest as reviving the argument put forward by Alimin in 1950 [see p. 143], distinguishing between individuals and the party to which they belonged.) Equally, an unreserved acceptance cannot be given to the 'confession' purportedly made by Aidit before he was shot. It is very curious that the army, with this priceless testimony in its hands, did not bring him back to Djakarta to bear witness.

Nor can one attach any weight to the assertions of the PKI émigrés. Since it is of the nature of communists to regard all statements as instrumental, their assertion could well represent a preference for the less humiliating alternative portraying themselves as knaves rather than fools.

However, if the case for the prosecution is not proven, neither is that for the defence watertight. Not only is there no evidence that the murdered officers were corrupt, but at least some of them were so short of money that, if bribed, they evidently were not charging the going Indonesian rate. In any case, Sukarnocracy had resulted in such maladministration that corruption was widespread; if the generals had been so affected, they would not have been more fit for censure than many other individuals. Equally, the theory that there was a 'council of generals' preparing a coup, which was pre-empted by GESTAPU, is highly dubious. Most of the sources for this rumour are apparently of PKI origin and therefore suspect: those that originate elsewhere are indeed reported as early as 1962, but rumours, like ghosts, do not acquire substance in ageing; if anything, they lose it. Indeed, so little were the generals plotting that they rejected pleas to strengthen the guard on their homes. Nor can one accept that Aidit and his henchmen were somehow inveigled into the conspiracy. After all, they were used to dealing with men at the highest level of state; it is not really plausible that they would support relatively junior officers (the most senior, it will be remembered, was Major-General Supardjo) in a military conspiracy where they played a minor role.

Presidential Plot?

It is therefore impossible to accept either of the alternative versions of culpability most discussed. But the reader of the arguments put forward by the respective sides cannot but be struck by an assumption they both make. It is that suddenly, towards the middle of 1965, Hamlet began to be acted without the Prince of Denmark; in other words that the contest was strictly between PKI and the army, and that the president's role can be ignored. Yet, until six months after the coup attempt, Sukarno continued to bestride the Indonesian political world like a colossus. The absence of his signature on the list of 'revolutionary council' members doomed the coup. Suharto's successful defence flowed from his being able to convince the suborned troops that Sukarno was not supporting the conspirators. The president was able, even after the coup's failure and when suspicions were being voiced about his own part in it, to reshuffle the cabinet and exclude Nasution, despite great military and popular sympathy with the latter's narrow escape from murder and for the killing of his daughter.

The account given above of the party's history from 1952 should have shown how completely Aidit had become Sukarno's client; he was only too well aware that only the president could protect him against the army. To believe that Aidit would have plotted a coup without first clearing it with the president is *prima facie* unlikely. In brief, it is inadmissible to assume that if there had been a PKI conspiracy Sukarno would have been unaware of it.

Equally, however, had there been an army conspiracy such as that of the 'council of generals', Sukarno would have known. Nasution was certainly no great friend of his, though obviously their interests had often found accommodation. But it would be wrong to assume that all of the general staff were opposed to him; Yani, the army chief-of-staff for example, was said to owe much to the president, as did many other senior officers. The web of intrigue which Sukarno had spun in the army would undoubtedly have alerted him to any conspiracy. Then, in addition to his direct links with both the PKI and the army, the president had, through his confidant Subandrio's Central Intelligence Body, a means of tapping every rumour of political activity. In brief, it is doubtful if any political movement in any quarter could have survived without his acquiescence. Though the *Badan Pendukung Sukarnoism* of 1964 was not a conspiratorial grouping, it may serve as an illustration. This, it will be remembered, enjoyed the support of not only politicians in good standing with the president but also of the army. However, one good wigging from Sukarno and the members of the body disbanded it, going home like schoolboys reprimanded by their headmaster.

One is therefore compelled to give credence to the suspicions voiced in Indonesia that Sukarno was more involved in GESTAPU than has so far appeared. There is certainly some circumstantial evidence in support. In the best tradition of who-done-its, one should first ask who stood to gain most by the success of GESTAPU? Generally, it has been assumed that since the objects of the conspiracy would have favoured the PKI it could not but have been involved. But this overlooks that the principal beneficiary would have been Sukarno. Unlike the great majority of attempts at *coups d'état* (a recent case in point is the 1971 abortive coup in the Sudan), GESTAPU was made not in opposition to, but in support of, the president of the country, a circumstance which has not excited as much attention as perhaps it deserves. It is surely surprising that a group of conspirators should undertake an enterprise of such unlimited risk for purely limited gains, namely that they obtain higher positions in the state, but subject always to an unpredictable president. For him, however, the gain would have been unlimited; the only threat to his position, represented by a recalcitrant army command, would have been removed, and the country's military force would have become as much his servant as the major political party already was.

Certainly, Sukarno never left any doubt of his support of GESTAPU. Even after its defeat he attempted to maintain as army chief-of-staff the conspirators' nominee, Pranoto. Only Suharto's refusal to surrender the powers he had assumed compelled Sukarno to retract. He pointedly absented himself from the funeral of the murdered generals; he could hardly have made clearer where his sympathies lay. And until his removal from office he continued to shelter the conspirators and support their objectives.

All the preceding would, of course, be consistent with the coup being a PKI plot which Sukarno had felt was worthy of his support. But certain other considerations shed

a different light. In the first place there is the motley nature
of the leading conspirators, which has often excited notice.
In addition to Aidit we have Untung, who presented himself as the leading man and went to his execution affirming
that he was no communist; Supardjo, admittedly sympathetic
to the PKI; and Dani, more Sukarno's man than anybody
else's. They would appear to have had only one thing in
common: they were all supporters, sometimes clients, of
Sukarno. Supardjo's own trial testimony made clear that at
Halim the president was not treated as a passive participant
but rather as a leader who had the right to order the movement to stop when its failure was evident. With regard to the
actual executants of the conspiracy, the loyalty to him of
the presidential guard was well known, as was that of the
Javanese divisions from which the two suborned battalions
were drawn. The Pemuda Rakyat and Gerwani involved
were, as mentioned, under training by Dani's air force; this
would seem to go far in accounting for their participation.

To the above one might add the fact that Untung's broadcast on the morning of 1 October, which expressed the
movement's purposes, identified it entirely with Sukarnoism,
while the bizarre collection of names on the list of members
of the 'revolutionary council' shared only one characteristic;
they were known supporters of Sukarno's then ideas.

In Indonesia, where personal loyalty counts for very much
more than ideological identification, it would be entirely
possible for the conspirators to be linked in their individual
capacities only by their allegiance to Sukarno, and were
his personal choice. But this carries the corollary that Aidit's
participation is no certain indication of his party's involvement, just as President Suharto admitted that Dani's presence among the conspirators did not necessarily implicate the
whole of the air force.

The core of the plot, as we have seen, was the removal of
senior officers by their juniors. As such, this was only an
extension of Sukarno's constant intrigues within the army;
we remember that in 1952 he instigated mutinies of pre-

cisely this character. We have also seen that thereafter he cultivated the PKI principally as a counterpoise to the army; it would seem not unnatural for him to use at least some of its supporters in an enterprise which promised to neutralise the military impediment to his designs.

We must therefore entertain the hypothesis that GESTAPU was of the president's own conception. This does not mean, of course, that he planned the details; he evidently was not aware of them all and an expression of his general intentions would have sufficed. A thirteenth-century English king's irritated cry, 'Who will rid me of this turbulent priest?', was sufficient to despatch the source of trouble; there were more than enough men devoted to Sukarno to perform a similar service. This is not to imply that he was party to the murder of the generals; imprisonment of his political rivals was much more in his style. Unfortunately, once again the tail wagged the dog and the thugs sent to capture the generals killed them instead.

Certainly the actions of the present Indonesian government give added colour to suspicions of Sukarno's leading role in the coup. It kept him in careful seclusion in Bogor from his deposition until his death in 1970. It was then announced that interrogation had revealed that 'he was involved', but that the findings would not be made public because his case had lapsed with his passing. This concealment is perhaps somewhat surprising. That he was implicated has long been widely believed in Indonesia. Charity being a stranger to politics, it would be unwise to assume that the interrogation has been suppressed in order to protect Sukarno's image. More likely, perhaps, evidence of his deep involvement might among his many supporters give GESTAPU a legitimacy it does not now have, with disruptive consequences for the army and the state. It is of interest that whereas the earlier arrests in connection with the coup were made on grounds of involvement with GESTAPU/PKI, as time has passed so the charges have changed to support for Sukarnoism.

Chinese Partners?

Determination of the authorship of the coup, however, would not by itself explain another puzzling aspect, namely the evidently hurried and inadequate nature of the preparations. Even granting that the conspirators did not have the benefit of Mr Luttwak's excellent instruction manual,[1] common prudence would have suggested a greater concentration of sympathetic forces, a better indoctrination of officers (the two critical battalions had been led to believe that they were guarding Sukarno), the preparation of rather more PKI supporters, so that they would know what to do when the signal was given, wider dissemination of arms, and recruitment of a group of men genuinely committed to the 'revolutionary council', instead of a list of names inserted apparently without their owners' consent.

Prima facie, there was no need for the coup to have been attempted on 30 September. It could equally well have been postponed for a few days to permit more adequate preparations (the Armed Forces Day parade was set for 5 October). Two suggestions have been made to account for the precipitate nature of the coup. One is the fear of Sukarno's approaching demise. This does not really bear examination. As mentioned above, whatever the nature of his ailment before his National Day speech on 17 August, it had not been grave enough to prevent him making it. And certainly he was as virile and active as ever thereafter. The other explanation advanced is the 'Generals' Plot' which the coup was designed to pre-empt; we have already discussed this as a PKI rumour.

The reason for haste must be sought elsewhere. If we assume, for purposes of argument, that Sukarno occupied a leading role in the plot, then his pronouncements and their timing have great relevance. As mentioned above, between 17 August and 28 September he suddenly moved from asserting that Indonesia was still a national democracy to

[1] Luttwak, 1969.

declaring that it was now time to move to stage two, socialism. Clearly, something occurred in the five weeks to change his mind. And we remember that the then communist Chinese foreign minister, Marshal Chen Yi, paid a state visit to Indonesia which covered the second half of August. As we have seen, Sukarno had become China's client; no other patron in the world would now help Indonesia. And there is strong evidence that the Chinese had inside knowledge of the coup. They were in possession of a list of the murdered generals, which included Nasution's name, five hours before the coup actually took place. A British historian who was one of the foreign guests invited to Peking for celebration of the National Day on 1 October has related that the only piece of news the visitors were ever told was of the attempted coup. It was apparently announced with an air of ponderous patronage, indicating some proprietary right in the event, and as a policy matter for the elite only, for news of it was never released to the Chinese public.[2] Soon after, Indonesian stamps reached Hong Kong from China overprinted 'People's Republic of Indonesia'.

It therefore seems reasonable to suppose that the Chinese were at least sleeping partners in the enterprise. They might well have intimated to Sukarno, through Chen Yi, that China's support of Indonesia, both politically and materially, depended on Indonesia's moving to a stage of 'socialism'. From their point of view this would have appeared as reasonable a demand as that of American senators who insist that recipients of United States aid develop private enterprise.

Sukarno, for his part, was hardly likely to object, if indeed the initiative did not come from him. He had already declared publicly that he had no objection to presiding over a communist state. A move to 'socialism' promised not only to remove his enemies in the army but also to enable him to play a greater role on the world stage as a partner in the Peking-Djakarta axis.

[2] Trevor-Roper, 1967.

It may therefore not be too extravagant to seek the reason for the coup being set for 30 September in the fact that the day following was 1 October, the Chinese National Day. Given the great, almost mystical importance attached to dates in Indonesia (it will be remembered that Tan Malaka set his Murba party's launching date to coincide with the anniversary of the Bolshevik revolution), it is entirely conceivable that the promoters of the coup wished to have Indonesia reborn as a socialist state on the day that China was similarly re-incarnated. China's National Day of the regime which overthrew the empire was 10 October; this was superseded by 1 October by the regime which brought in 'socialism'. So also in Indonesia the 17 August National Day which celebrated the end of colonialism was to be superseded by 1 October which not only ushered in 'socialism' but also indicated full partnership in the Djakarta-Peking axis. If this is considered fanciful, one can only remark that it is difficult to overestimate the importance of symbols in Indonesia. Whether Sukarno wished to ingratiate himself with his Chinese patrons in the manner suggested, or whether in fact he simply acceded to their wishes, regarding it as a fair exchange for the promise of world prominence, we shall probably never know.

What cannot be denied, however, is the use Sukarno made of external policies to entrench his position in the country. The campaign for Western New Guinea had brought about 'guided democracy'; the 'confrontation' with Malaysia had developed this further and created the 'national front' under his control; what more natural than that the alliance with Peking should give rise to a 'revolutionary council' all, of course, under his leadership.

It is unnecessary to emphasise that the foregoing is largely speculation. In trying to unravel the complicated web of intrigue represented by GESTAPU, however, guesswork is unavoidable.

20
The
Clay
Feet

Members

Whether or not the PKI was responsible for the attempted
coup, however, it remains surprising that, despite the very
large numbers of adherents the party claimed, they proved
completely inert and incapable of defending themselves.
For it must be remembered that the killing of PKI followers, or alleged followers, was mainly at the hands not of the
Army, but of fellow-villagers. It could be argued that BTI
village members were typically not well organised and so
could not defend themselves against fanatics. But this could
not be said of the myrmidons of SOBSI, far more numerous
than PKI members themselves. They made no protest, they
took no strike action, against the hounding of PKI members
or the proscription of the party and its satellites, including
their own organisation. This political giant did indeed
prove a broken reed.

In attempting to account for this surprising immobility it
may be useful to consider certain related topics. They are
first the character of the members of the PKI and its front

organisations; second the policy followed by the party's leaders; and last the nature of the leadership itself.

In recruiting members to the PKI, as we have seen, the emphasis was placed on quantity. Virtually from the beginning of Aidit's period of leadership he opted for vast increases in numbers. His success in this endeavour, as events were to show, was on the basis of a straightforward exchange. If the peasants and workers would give him their votes, he would provide them with material benefits. He faithfully followed the Leninist injunction to emphasise the 'minimum programme', that is to say he accepted the concerns of the peasants, he did not impose the communist 'maximum programme' on them. As he put it: 'Only by practical work among the peasants, only by leading the peasants in the struggle for their everyday demands . . . can party cadres and members have close relations with the peasants and receive their trust.' 'Passionate and leftist' measures would only put off the peasants. A PKI guide for its peasant cadres urged them to undertake activities of benefit to the peasants, such as cheap distribution of fertiliser, seedlings and tools, repair of water channels and fish ponds, distribution of fish eggs, etc.[1]

The various PKI fronts achieved success only when they adopted Aidit's policy. SOBSI obtained major victories in improving the conditions and pay of the workers while taking care, from 1952, not to antagonise either government or national employers. Though it included some 50 to 60 per cent of organised workers, it was unable to lead them in political strikes. Equally, the Pemuda Rakyat achieved mass membership only when it gave priority to social and economic activities. (Typically, it embraced the prejudices of the poorest, who were of course the most ignorant and traditional, and denounced films and modern dances which offended them.) The women's organisation, the Gerwani, similarly was principally attractive by reason of its social work, not its militance.

People recruited to an organisation on the basis of the

[1] Hindley, 1966: 174.

benefits it provides are hardly likely to be of revolutionary disposition; while the officials of such an organisation, concerned from day to day in organising welfare, are not really the stuff from which determined conspirators are made.

Indeed, one is entitled to doubt if Aidit ever had any 'maximum programme' in mind. For he never presented himself as a revolutionary leader. On the contrary, he had wanted the PKI to be respected as a party of responsibility and restraint and always emphasised that it would never, unless attacked, resort to violence. The mass organisations were specifically designed to mobilise sympathisers who were not prepared to support the party directly. Though led by open or covert party members, these bodies in the nature of the case could not be militant; they were neither recruited nor organised on that basis.

The striking exception to the general rule is, of course, the militance of the BTI, with Aidit's support, in 1964. But as we have argued above, this was an agitation more in support of, than against, the state as embodied in Sukarno. Certainly with his downfall the BTI were no more able to defend themselves than the members of any other PKI organisation.

The lack of ardour of PKI followers is perhaps best attested by their very great reluctance to pay their subscriptions, so that for its funds the organisation was mainly dependent on Chinese sources: either the Chinese communities in Indonesia, subject to 'squeeze' by both the Chinese embassy and sometimes the SOBSI unions, or the embassy itself. The money was used not only to provide inducements which would attract members but also to pay the large number of officials (cadres) the party employed. One writer[2] estimates that the PKI itself engaged between two thousand and five thousand full-time employees, including officials and typists. To these must be added several thousand full-time workers of the mass organisations (many of whom held full-time jobs simultaneously in the party). SOBSI, for example, was estimated to have three hundred full-time work-

[2] *Ibid.*: 115.

ers in Java alone, with a thousand in member unions. This body of well-paid and well-trained full-timers, who enjoyed reasonable career prospects, distinguished SOBSI from other union federations. But while well-established bureaucrats are essential to an efficient organisation they are hardly likely, as argued already, to be of revolutionary temperament.

Even less given to disruption were the ordinary members of the PKI and its satellites. The party had been able to attract very few members of the Indonesian political élite, or senior officers within the armed forces, or officials within the bureaucracy. In consequence it was compelled to seek support among the lowest social orders, peasants, workers, the petty bourgeoisie, conditioned over generations to obedience and compliance. So their large numbers did not weigh much. In the countryside, for instance, the BTI counted for less than the smaller Muslim STII or the PNI's *Petani*, mainly because membership of the latter included persons of influence and authority in the villages. For their part, SOBSI leaders complained of the great difficulty of finding workers who could be trained as cadres; in consequence officials and leaders in this, as in all other PKI organisations, were drawn from the urban clerical middle class, hardly a revolutionary group.

In brief, the party organisations worked principally among the poorest, exploiting their human needs and desires for improvement of their situation, using the funds obtained from the Chinese in order, in one way or another, to provide the poor with benefits in exchange for their electoral support. And it is important to note that the party's success was not due to great devotion or remarkable efficiency but principally because it was left a virtually open field. The other political parties took little or no interest in organisational work or even surveys among the masses but contented themselves with politicking in Djakarta. This was particularly the case with the PNI, whose support was steadily swallowed by the PKI; the Muslim parties' followers, as we have noted, remained unseduced. This only goes to show that the PKI's strength lay not in its 'ideology' but simply in the fact that it seemed to care for those whom the Muslim organisations ignored. (We remember that at the time of the founding of the Third International, Asians were attracted to it not by reason of its dogma but simply because it took an interest in the Asian colonies which the Second International had neglected.)

Policy

The very great increases of membership of the PKI only confirmed Aidit's genius in comprehending, in 1952, the lesson that his party should have learnt from its bitter experience since its foundation: either it operated with official approval or it would once again be destroyed. Hence his careful and successful development of the party in support of Sukarno, on the assumption that the road to success was to follow Indonesia's most eminent nationalist leader. But in the nature of the case, building a legitimate party of large numbers meant recruiting conformists. This was no Leninist grouping of determined revolutionaries but an organisation which would play according to the rules.

Indeed, one must doubt if, towards the end of the period, and particularly in the years of Sukarnocracy, Aidit deliberately sought to increase the size of the party in order peacefully to overwhelm any opposition, so much as to continue, through sheer force of inertia, on lines established in the period of parliamentary democracy. For it must not be forgotten that when Aidit launched his new-style party, with loyalty to Sukarno as its device, the country was ruled by a parliament which had the firm intention, duly fulfilled, of subjecting itself to elections. Under those conditions, increasing the size of the PKI made sense; it was a road to power by constitutional means, and made militance unnecessary. And as we have seen, the national elections of 1955 and 1956, and the local elections of 1957, crowned this strategy with a success far beyond anyone's expectations, including Aidit's.

However, the situation was radically changed when Sukarno abrogated the democratic constitution and instituted
his own autocratic rule in 1958. The vast numbers in the
PKI and its satellite organisations were suddenly made
irrelevant, since electoral strength was no longer a qualifica-
tion for government—indeed elections were continually
postponed and would have been of little significance if they
had been held. Power was now in the hands of Sukarno
and the army, not parliament. In this context, the large
numbers enrolled by the PKI were in effect hostages to fortune, since they were encumbrances to the party and ready
targets for its enemies; principally of use not to the PKI but
to Sukarno in his attempts to overawe the army. If, under
the parliamentary dispensation, the president had been dependent on the PKI for support, now under Sukarnocracy
they were at least as dependent on him for protection
against the army. It is surprising that despite the public
knowledge that Sukarno's 'guided democracy' had been at
least part-authored by General Nasution, who held no love
for the PKI, and despite the intensive military interrogation
of Aidit and the other members of the Politburo in 1960,
which should have impressed on them where the real power
lay, Aidit continued as if nothing had changed from 1952.

But with the inception of 'guided democracy' and the bellicose policies that were its obverse, power began moving
into the hands of the army. Ultimate administrative responsibility came to lie with it under the president, while its
representatives in the highest councils of state grew increasingly numerous; it obtained a firm foothold in the
economy through its administration of estates and firms
seized from their Dutch and British owners, and of course
its size increased considerably. It is ironic that the PKI en-
thusiastically supported precisely those aggressive activities
of Sukarno which by their nature were strengthening the
army and so, relatively, weakening him, their protector
against the military.

There is a temptation here to think that the PKI might
have been better advised to go underground, slimming its

ranks to only the most dedicated and militant. But there is nothing in the historical record to encourage the view that this would have been a successful policy. The events of 1925 and 1926 showed how difficult it was to maintain discipline in a relatively large party which had been proscribed; while Musso's 'illegal PKI' of the 1930s had little, if anything, to show for its efforts.

One error in policy is perhaps obvious, namely a failure to reach accommodation with the military. There seems no reason to assume that this was unattainable. We have already seen the Leninist lengths to which Aidit was prepared to go in order to ensure his party's (and his own) survival. He abandoned communist symbols in favour of nationalist ones, declared that his party, and no foreign leader, was the best judge of its own interests, accepted the Pantja Sila (and so rejected a basic tenet of Marxism, historical materialism), declared that the national interest came before class, opted for 'peaceful and democratic' methods of persuasion, provided the authorities with a list of his party members' names and addresses, and made his publications support Sukarnoism. Aidit clearly had supple knees; bending them in the direction of the army command, instead of Sukarno, might well have saved him and his party. Instead the infiltration into, for example, the Diponegoro division, or the occasional convert among senior officers, simply deepened the army command's suspicion of the PKI. One is tempted to believe that Aidit pursued his master Sukarno's interests better than his own. The president needed to balance the party against the army in order to ensure the continuance of his own power; Aidit dutifully indulged in rabble-rousing against them. He might have been better advised to heed Mao Tse-tung's advice on where power really began.

Leadership

Failure to change policy when the situation alters is only too common and only too human. Like most of us, Aidit was unable to dance to new music, even when played by a brass band, and carried on with the old steps. Industrial, commercial and political organisations frequently find themselves obliged to dismiss their directors when the situation, economic or political, alters radically. And perhaps at the core of the PKI's weakness lay the fact that the three key figures who came to power in 1952, Aidit, Lukman and Nyoto, remained in control until its demise. Whether because they were totally identified with the policy of peaceful, open, expansion, or because they knew only this one stratagem, they continued to pursue it even when it was a source of weakness rather than strength. They did not lack reminders that their policy should be changed; we have seen no less a person than Khruschev remind them that a communist party's success was not to be judged by the number of its customers; while the raps on the knuckles from the military authorities should have brought home to them the fact that their increasing numbers were in no way restraining the army, which is what mattered. They acted like ice-cream peddlars who do not want to know that winter has come.

Why, then, it may well be asked, were they not removed from office, particularly since the record shows that there was some disquiet in their own ranks? The answer perhaps lies in the system of 'democratic centralism' followed by communist parties the world over; by ensuring that the leader can eliminate opposition it also ensures that new men, more in tune with the times, are not allowed to rise except by the assertion of mortality (as with Stalin's successors) or by external convulsion (as in the recent case of Gierek in Poland). But otherwise the party chief can stay until he decides to go, as with Ulbricht in East Germany. In contrast, it requires an effort of memory to remember who were the leaders of the democratic parties of the west in the days when Aidit first assumed ascendancy over the PKI, so many changes have occurred since.

One hastens to add that this is perhaps a characteristic of totalitarianism generally rather than communism specifically. It is now known that Hitler was aware by 1942 that he had lost the second world war, but remained unwilling to alter his offensive strategy and armament to a defensive one, which might well have saved his country the wide-spread destruction it suffered; he too remained immovable.

This political thrombosis, as one may call it, may well have been responsible for a weakness in the structure of leadership in the party. The 'lumpen-intelligentsia', the urban clerical middle class, who provided the cadres of the party, were not of a sufficiently high intellectual calibre to supply the guidance that was required. And no leaders were recruited from Indonesia's many university students, of whom only a handful were drawn to the PKI and its student front, the CGMI. Explanations of this surprising fact can vary from the idealistic, namely that the students were too patriotic to support the PKI, to the callous, namely that they were too little concerned with the welfare of their less fortunate compatriots (which assumes that student recruits to communist parties in other countries are so motivated). Certainly, given the disfavour with which Sukarno and the army looked upon political parties in general (until the latter embraced the PKI in 1965), and the fact that a qualified graduate was most unlikely to be unemployed, there would have been little encouragement to join the PKI even if it had been attractive to them, while their absorption into employment was not likely to make it so. But whether because the fixity of the leadership discouraged the ambitious, or because it had lost touch with the aspirations of the students, it remains an astonishing fact that Aidit's PKI failed completely to enlist the sympathy of the younger generation who eventually, as we have seen, forced the hands of their elders into ejecting the party from Indonesian political life.

The Three PKIS

Aidit's party fared no better, eventually, than the two previous incarnations of the PKI (ignoring the ISDV as a European precursor); namely from 1920 to 1926 under various leaders, but especially Semaun, Tan Malaka, and Darsono, and in 1948 under Musso. Disaster struck all three parties, though they were each very different from the others.

The 1920–6 party was already taking shape before the Bolshevik revolution in Russia and never became of much interest to the Comintern. Its main concern was to seize control of the nationalist movement of the time, the Sarekat Islam, by putting itself forward as the determined opponent of 'capitalism', which had come to mean the colonial government. As we have seen, what success it had was achieved primarily by promising to put back the clock of change and by enlisting Muslim fanaticism in its service. In this it was of course faithfully following the Leninist injunction to emphasise the 'minimum programme', or desires of its audience. But though this was intended as a means of communist revolution, it became an end in itself; the PKI was soon being led by bandits and fanatics. Against the Russians' advice, a revolt was planned; it was then set off by these elements but was so feeble in character that it was suppressed by the civilian authorities.

Musso's PKI differed from its predecessor as well as its successor both in that it was a military conspiracy rather than a popular party and also in that it was a direct result of Russian ambitions in the area. He himself had been sent out from Moscow to make a revolution, precisely at the time when there was a power vacuum between the withdrawal of western dominion and the establishment of the new nation states in South-East Asia. If Semaun's party had attempted to ride to power on the back of the Sarekat Islam, Musso's sought to profit from the nationalist war against the Dutch by emphasising PKI connections with Russia, hoping that the Indonesian political public would accept the argument that the enemy of my enemy is my friend. He miscalculated both the nationalists' devotion to their leader, Sukarno, and the strength of the Leninist anti-Russian opposition represented by Tan Malaka and his followers. And while the 1926–7 party had been able to obtain the support of the Muslim fanatics in certain parts of the country, now the Islamic parties were solidly against the PKI. To compound matters further, the planned revolt was set off prematurely by some of the PKI's undisciplined supporters.

Aidit's party sought to be unambiguously Indonesian, though linked with parties of similar faith to itself. Here too, however, just as Semaun had tried to profit from the nationalism of his time, so Aidit planned to climb to power on the coat-tails of the most prominent Indonesian leader of his day. And in the course of doing so, as we have seen, he abandoned many standard Marxist concepts in favour of Sukarno. What emerged was a large, mass party, organised on centralised lines to be sure but with exactly the same aims as the establishment, over which it admittedly had no influence. In the event, here too the tactic of supporting Sukarno became an end in itself and the party found itself dragged to destruction with him. It was never able to follow the example of Semaun's PKI and become a 'bloc within' an Islamic party. On the contrary, eventually it was the organised Muslims who decimated the PKI.

The two PKI's which appear to have achieved a fair degree of public, as distinct from military, support are of course Semaun's and Aidit's. As has perhaps become clear, it was gained not on the basis of their Marxist aims but rather as a result of their promises and attempts to relieve the discomforts and suffering of their audiences. In this respect Aidit's policy, of what may broadly be termed social welfare work among the masses, was undoubtedly more constructive and more successful than Semaun's; where it met failure was precisely in the BTI policy of inciting the peasants against the authorities. Throughout, however, it remains true that the PKI and its satellites were the only organisations outside the Islamic fold attempting to cushion the shock of economic change, brought about either by agrarian deterioration or modernisation.

What of the decimated, headless PKI? One would not expect a sect, no matter what disaster it had suffered, to reject its sacred texts; it will usually aver that the high priest was incompetent. So it is with the PKI. Aidit's policy was one of open, legal expansion; predictably this has been rejected by the survivors of his party, who now seek to pursue an opposed course and incite a peasant uprising, with support from China (the Russians being too concerned to cultivate the Indonesian army).

Their hopes of revolt are centred on Java, and with good reason. It is highly probable that for some time to come rural society there will suffer continuing disintegration; as mentioned above, the island is too overcrowded for any agricultural reform to offer a solution to its problems and there is little sign of population control. We may therefore expect that an increasing proportion of Javanese will find themselves landless or almost so, with the subsequent disintegration of their traditional social world, while industrialisation, which is the only feasible method of relieving their poverty, is likely to be just as disruptive of their society. They will be attracted to any organization which promises them the social support they have lost. The Islamic bodies provide it for the faithful; the army of course does the same for its many recruits. But those outside these two enclosures also need to be grouped into social organisations of a modern type. Unless, therefore, the Indonesian authorities or non-communist private secular organisations embrace these uprooted individuals, they are likely to prove susceptible to totalitarian organisations, which may of course be either fascist, or Malakist, or communist in the usual sense, or even, now, Sukarnoist.

Whether such extremists will be able to recruit large numbers, and whether they will flourish further, is however quite a different matter. For we have seen that the Indonesian Communist Party achieved a degree of success only when it was tolerated either by the Netherlands Indies government or its republican successor. When the party was banned, either by the Dutch or the Japanese, its achievements were more of a nuisance than a threat (the 1926 revolt had much sound and fury but signified very little). It is no doubt the knowledge of this fact that accounts for, and to some extent excuses, the present Indonesian government's policy towards all activity which might be construed as either PKI- or Sukarno-oriented, namely one of outright repression. Yet both wisdom and charity would urge a more constructive policy of creating organisations to meet the social needs which the PKI exploited. This might well pay substantial dividends in terms of the political stability which Indonesia, like any other country, needs if she is to develop her potential.

Selective Bibliography

Communism — General

Almond, Gabriel A., *The Appeals of Communism*, Princeton (U.P.), 1954.

Hunt, R. N. Carew, *The Theory and Practice of Communism*, London (Bles), 1950.

——, *A Guide to Communist Jargon*, London (Bles), 1957.

Koestler, Arthur, *et al.*, *The God That Failed*, London (Hamish Hamilton), 1950.

Kolarz, W., *Books on Communism*, London (Ampersand), 1963.

Leites, Nathan, *A Study of Bolshevism*, Glencoe, Ill. (Free Press), 1953.

Lenin, V. I., *Selected Works*, London (Lawrence & Wishart), 1936–9.

Luttwak, E., *Coup d'État*, London (Allen Lane), 1968.

Monnerot, Jules, *Sociology of Communism*, London (Allen & Unwin), 1953.

Nollau, Gunther, *International Communism and the World Revolution*, London (Hollis & Carter), 1961.

Selznick, Philip, *The Organizational Weapon*, New York (McGraw-Hill), 1952.

Seton-Watson, Hugh, *The Pattern of Communist Revolution*, London (Methuen), 1953.

Ulam, Adam B., *Lenin and the Bolsheviks*, London (Fontana), 1969.

U. S. Senate Committee on Foreign Affairs, *The Strategy and Tactics of World Communism*, Washington (U. S. Govt. Printing Office), 1948.

Utechin, S. V. (*ed.*), *V. I. Lenin's What Is to Be Done?*, Oxford (Clarendon), 1963.

Indonesia — General

Anderson, B. R. O'G., *Some Aspects of Indonesian Politics Under the Japanese Occupation*, Ithaca, N.Y. (Cornell U. Modern Indonesia Project), 1961.

Benda, Harry J., and Castles, Lance, 'The Samin Movement', *Bijdragen Tot de Taal–Land–en Volkenkunde*, vol. 125, Part 2, 1969, pp. 207–40.

Feith, H., *The Decline of Constitutional Democracy in Indonesia*, Ithaca, N.Y. (Cornell U.P.), 1962.

Kahin, G. McT., *Nationalism and Revolution in Indonesia*, Ithaca, N.Y. (Cornell U.P.), 1952.

——, 'Indonesia', G. McT. Kahin (*ed.*), *Major Governments of Asia* (2nd ed.), Ithaca, N.Y. (Cornell U.P.), 1958.

McVey, Ruth (*ed.*), *Indonesia*, New Haven (HRAF Press), 1963.

Mangkupradja, *Raden* Gatot, 'The Peta and My Relations with the Japanese', *Indonesia*, no. 5, April 1968, pp. 105–34.

Mintz, Jeanne S., *Mohammed, Marx and Marhaen: The Roots of Indonesian Socialism*, London (Pall Mall), 1965.

Niel, Robert van, *The Emergence of the Modern Indonesian Elite*, The Hague & Bandung (Van Hoeve), 1960.

Reid, Anthony, 'Nineteenth Century Pan-Islam in Indonesia and Malaysia', *Journal of Asian Studies XXVI*, no. 2, February 1967, pp. 267–83.

Samson, Allan A., 'Islam in Indonesian Politics', *Asian Survey*, vol. 8, no. 12, 1968, pp. 1001–17.

Schrieke, B. (ed.), *The Effect of Western Influence on Native Civilization in the Malay Archipelago*, Batavia (Kolff), 1929.

Sitzen, Peter H. W., *The Industrial Development of the Netherlands Indies*, New York (I.P.R.), 1953.

Communism in South-East Asia

Benda, Harry J., 'Reflections on Asian Communism', *Yale Review*, vol. LVI, no. 1, October 1966.

Brimmell, J. H., *Communism in South East Asia*, London (Oxford U.P.), 1959.

d'Encausse, Hélène Carrère and Schram, Stuart R., *Marxism and Asia*, London (Allen Lane), 1969.

Kennedy, Malcolm, *A History of Communism in East Asia*, New York (Praeger), 1957.

Pye, Lucian W., *Guerrilla Communism in Malaya*, Princeton (U.P.), 1956.

Communism in Indonesia

GENERAL

Brackman, Arnold C., *Indonesian Communism*, New York (Praeger), 1963.

Darsono, 'The Indonesian Communist Party', *Eastern World*, 11 December 1957, pp. 21–3.

Kroef, Justus M. van der, *The Communist Party of Indonesia*, Vancouver (U. of British Columbia), 1965.

Mitchell, David, 'Communists, Mystics and Sukarnoism', *Dissent* (Melbourne), no. 22, 1968, pp. 28–32.

Mortimer, Rex, 'Class, Social Cleavage and Indonesian Communism', *Indonesia*, no. 8, October 1969, pp. 1–20.

UP TO THE 1926–7 REBELLION

Benda, Harry J., 'The Communist Rebellions of 1926–1927', *Pacific Historical Review*, vol. XXIV, no. 2, May 1955, pp. 139–52.

Benda, Harry J., and McVey, Ruth T., *The Communist Uprisings of 1926–1927 in Indonesia: Key Documents*, Ithaca, N.Y. (Cornell U. Modern Indonesia Project), 1960.

Blumberger, J. Th. Petrus, *De Communistische Beweging in Nederlandsch-Indie*, Haarlem (Tjeenk Willink), 1928.

Mansvelt, W. M. F., 'Onderwijs en Communisme', *Koloniale Studien XII*, pp. 203–25 (quoted in Niel 1960, pp. 233–6).

McVey, Ruth T., *The Rise of Indonesian Communism*, Ithaca, N.Y. (Cornell U.P.), 1965.

——, *The Calcutta Conference and the Southeast Asian Uprisings*, Ithaca, N.Y. (Cornell U. Modern Indonesia Project), 1958.

Schrieke, B., 'The Causes and Effects of Communism on the West Coast of Sumatra', *Indonesian Sociological Studies*, Part I, The Hague & Bandung (Van Hoeve), 1955, pp. 83–166.

Stromquist, Shelton, 'The Communist Uprisings of 1926–27 in Indonesia: A Reinterpretation', *Journal of South East Asian History*, vol. 8, no. 2, September 1967, pp. 189–200.

1949–65

Hindley, Donald, 'President Sukarno and the Communists: the Politics of Domestication', *American Political Science Review*, vol. LVI, 1962, pp. 915–26.

——, 'The Indonesian Communist Party and the Conflict in the International Communist Movement', *China Quarterly*, no. 19, July–September 1964, pp. 99–119.

——, *The Communist Party of Indonesia 1951–1963*, Berkeley & Los Angeles (U. of California Press), 1966.

Lubis, Mochtar, 'The Indonesian Communist Movement Today', *Far Eastern Survey*, vol. XXIII, no. 11, November 1954, pp. 161–4.

Lyon, Margo L., *Bases of Conflict in Rural Java*, Berkeley, Cal. Center for South and South-East Asia Studies (University of California), 1970.

McVey, Ruth T., 'Indonesian Communism and the Transition to Guided Democracy', Barnett, A. Doak (*ed.*), *Communist Strategies in Asia*, New York (Praeger), 1963, pp. 148–95.

Pauker, Guy J., 'Indonesia: The P.K.I.'s "Road to Power"', Scalapino, Robert A., *The Communist Revolution in Asia*, Englewood Cliffs, N.J. (Prentice-Hall), 1965.

Silverman, Jerry Mark, *Indonesianizing Marxism-Leninism: The Development and Consequences of Communist Polycentrism (1919–1965)* (unpublished Ph.D. Thesis, Claremont Graduate School and University Center), 1967.

Singh, Vishal, 'The Communist Party of Indonesia, 1949–58', *International Studies*, New Delhi, vol. I, no. 2, October 1959, pp. 117–36.

Wertheim, W. F., 'From *aliran* towards class struggle in the countryside of Java', *Pacific Viewpoint*, vol. 10, no. 2, September 1969, pp. 1–17.

THE ATTEMPTED COUP OF 30 DECEMBER 1965 AND ITS AFTERMATH

Bass, Jerome R., 'The P.K.I. and the Attempted Coup', *Journal of Southeast Asian Studies*, vol. I, no. 1, March 1970, pp. 96–105.

Brackman, Arnold C., *The Communist Collapse in Indonesia*, New York (W. W. Norton), 1969.

Dommen, Arthur J., 'The Attempted Coup in Indonesia', *China Quarterly*, no. 25, January–March 1966, pp. 144–70.

Hindley, Donald, 'Political Power and the October 1965 Coup in Indonesia', *Journal of Asian Studies*, vol. XXVI, no. 2, February 1967, pp. 237–49.

——, 'Indonesian Politics 1965–67, The September 30 Movement and the Fall of Sukarno', *The World Today*, August 1968, pp. 345–56.

——, 'Dilemmas of Consensus and Division: Indonesia's Search for a Political Format', *Government and Opposition*, vol. 4, no. 1, Winter 1969, pp. 70–99.

———, 'Alirans and the Fall of the Old Order', *Indonesia*, no. 9, April 1970, pp. 23–66.

Hughes, John, *The End of Sukarno*, London (Angus & Robertson), 1968.

Kahin, George McT., 'Comments', in *Tsou*, vol. 2, pp. 353–6.

Kroef, Justus M. van der, ' "Gestapu in Indonesia," ' *Orbis*, vol. X, no. 2, Summer 1966, pp. 458–87.

———, 'Indonesia's "Gestapu": The View from Moscow and Peking', *Australian Journal of Politics and History*, vol. XIV, no. 2, August 1968, pp. 163–76.

———, 'The Sino-Indonesian Rupture', *China Quarterly*, no. 33, January–March 1968, pp. 17–46.

———, 'Indonesian Communism since the 1965 Coup', *Pacific Affairs*, vol. XLIII, no. 1, Spring 1970, pp. 34–60.

———, 'Interpretations of the 1965 Indonesian Coup', *Pacific Affairs*, vol. XLIII, no. 4, Winter 1970–1, pp. 557–77.

Lev, Daniel S., 'Indonesia 1965: The Year of the Coup', *Asian Survey*, vol. VI, no. 2, February 1966, pp. 103–10.

McVey, Ruth T., 'Indonesian Communism and China', *Tsou*, vol. 2, pp. 357–94.

———, 'PKI Fortunes at Low Tide', *Problems of Communism*, vol. XX, January–April 1971, pp. 25–36.

Mortimer, Rex, 'Émigré Post-Mortems on the P.K.I.', *Australian Outlook*, vol. 22, no. 3, 1968, pp. 347–59.

Mozingo, David, 'China's Policy Toward Indonesia', *Tsou*, vol. 2, pp. 334–52.

Pauker, Guy J., 'Indonesia: The P.K.I.'s "Road to Power" ', in Scalapino, Robert A. (ed.), *The Communist Revolution in Asia*, Englewood Cliffs, N.J. (Prentice-Hall), 1965, pp. 256–89.

'Rey, Lucien', 'Holocaust in Indonesia', *New Left Review*, vol. 36, March–April 1966, pp. 26–40.

Sutter, John O., 'Two Faces of *Konfrontasi*: "Crush Malaysia" and the Gestapu', *Asian Survey*, vol. VI, no. 10, October 1966.

Trevor-Roper, H. R., 'Understanding Mao; or, Look Back to Stalin', *New York Times Magazine,* 12 February 1967, quoted in Brackman, 1969, pp. 149–50.

Tsou, Tang, *China in Crisis* (2 vols), Chicago (U.P.), 1968.

Usamah, 'War and Humanity: Notes on Personal Experience', *Indonesia,* no. 9, April 1970, pp. 89–99.

Wertheim, W. F., 'Indonesia before and after the Untung Coup', *Pacific Affairs,* vol. XXXIV, nos. 1 and 2, Spring and Summer 1966, pp. 115–27.

Index